Responsibility in world business

Responsibility in world business: Managing harmful side-effects of corporate activity

Edited by Lene Bomann-Larsen and Oddny Wiggen

**United Nations
University Press**

TOKYO · NEW YORK · PARIS

The views expressed in this publication are those of the authors and do not necessarily reflect the views of the United Nations University.

United Nations University Press
United Nations University, 53-70, Jingumae 5-chome,
Shibuya-ku, Tokyo 150-8925, Japan
Tel: +81-3-3499-2811   Fax: +81-3-3406-7345
E-mail: sales@hq.unu.edu   general enquiries: press@hq.unu.edu
http://www.unu.edu

United Nations University Office in North America
2 United Nations Plaza, Room DC2-2062, New York, NY 10017, USA
Tel: +1-212-963-6387   Fax: +1-212-371-9454
E-mail: unuona@ony.unu.edu

United Nations University Press is the publishing division of the United Nations University.

Cover design by Joyce C. Weston

Printed in the United States of America

UNUP-1103
ISBN 92-808-1103-7

Library of Congress Cataloging-in-Publication Data

Responsibility in world business: managing harmful side-effects of corporate activity / edited by Lene Bomann-Larsen and Oddny Wiggen.
    p. cm.
Includes bibliographical references and index.
ISBN 9280811037 (pbk.)
1. Social responsibility of business. 2. Business ethics. 3. International business enterprises—Management. 4. International business enterprises—Moral and ethical aspects. 5. International business enterprises—Environmental aspects. 6. International business enterprises—Social aspects. I. Bomann-Larsen, Lene. II. Wiggen, Oddny.
HD60.R473   2004
658.4′08—dc22   2004007656

Contents

Foreword

The UN Global Compact – Secretary-General Kofi Annan's initiative on responsible corporate citizenship – aims at "producing practical solutions", "sharing good practices", "rallying around universal principles", and "making the global economy more sustainable and inclusive". It is with great satisfaction that Global Compact acknowledges the publication of this book, which so admirably strives to contribute to the realization of these goals.

It is the Global Compact's firm belief that business has an important role to play in achieving peace and social development. Launched in Davos in 1999 by the Secretary-General, the Global Compact "seeks to advance corporate citizenship so that business can be part of the solution to the challenges of globalisation". Through its engagement, the Compact provides an international platform that facilitates mutual understanding and the development of practical solutions among business, labour, civil society organizations, government, UN agencies, and leading experts from the academic and public policy spheres.

Integrating corporate social responsibility into business behaviour can be achieved only by developing a much clearer understanding of the obligations underlying the term. This involves clearly distinguishing between what is absolutely required from companies and what society expects from them in addition. Through a Policy Dialogue on "Roles and Responsibilities of Societal Actors in a Global World", the Global Compact has been exploring these critical issues to help advance a shared understanding in this area. It is clear that the private sector must consider its overall impact on society, both locally and globally. Indeed, the focus on responsibility for one's operations found in this volume is a valuable contribution both to the work of the Global Compact and to the debate on corporate citizenship.

All jobs require the right tools. And, the more complicated the task, the more important it is to find the appropriate tools for getting the job done. The responsibility for unintended side-effects and the dangers of complicity are indeed among the most complex questions facing us within the field of corporate social responsibility. Finding better tools for handling such questions must be high on our agenda. The Global Compact "Business Guide on Conflict Impact Assessment and Risk Management" is an example of such a tool. It was developed by a multi-stakeholder group to provide a practical means for companies to develop strategies that minimize the negative effects and maximize the positive effects of investing in areas of potential conflict. In this volume, the authors have taken this work to a higher theoretical level.

In ethics, as in many other fields, philosophers, theologians, and social scientists have often addressed similar questions to the ones we are grappling with here. But are we resourceful enough in utilizing their ideas and their language? In this book, researchers from the International Peace Research Institute in Oslo (PRIO) and the United Nations University, together with top academics from several different fields and from all corners of the world, have taken the centuries-old tradition of "just war" (or, more broadly, the "ethics of war and peace") as their point of departure in addressing some important challenges in this area.

Even if all of the intended, direct effects of one's actions are legitimate (perhaps even morally laudable), side-effect harm may be of a kind that disallows one's actions from being performed. But what kinds of side-effect are relevant? How much must one do to find out about the possible side-effects of one's otherwise legitimate actions? If negative side-effects do come about, who is responsible? And, not least, who should be entrusted to make the final decisions in such complex cases?

It is our belief that this book – both its philosophical groundwork and the case-studies – will become an important tool in our continued work on corporate citizenship. It reminds us that the consequences of conducting business are manifold and complex. We at the Global Compact are grateful to the United Nations University, PRIO, and all the authors and institutions represented in this book for contributing to advancing our thinking in this important area

Georg Kell
Executive Head of the Global Compact Office
United Nations, New York

Acknowledgements

A number of individuals and organizations have provided invaluable assistance and support at various stages of this book project. First, we wish to thank the Norwegian Ministry of Foreign Affairs, the United Nations University, and the Karl Popper Foundation for co-funding the project. We would also like to thank Cecilia Arruda and the Fundação Getulio Vargas in São Paulo for hosting the project workshop. We are grateful to the European Business Ethics Network (EBEN), the International Society of Business, Economics, and Ethics (ISBEE), the Business Ethics Network, Africa (BEN-Africa), Amnesty International Norway, and the UN Development Programme's office in Oslo for giving us access to their networks. We also appreciate the valuable feedback on the project from Georg Kell, Denise O'Brien, and Ellen Kallinowsky at the UN Global Compact Office.

We deeply appreciate the logistical and administrative assistance provided by Yoshie Sawada of the Peace and Governance Programme of the United Nations University and the administration at the International Peace Research Institute, Oslo. We are grateful to Iselin Frydenlund for excellent editorial assistance in the preparation of the manuscript. We thank the United Nations University Press, particularly Gareth Johnston and Scott McQuade, for attentive work in the publication process, and Liz Paton, who copyedited the volume. We would also like to thank our anonymous peer reviewers for constructive comments.

We thank all of our contributors for sharing their insights, and in particular G. J. (Deon) Rossouw and Andrew Clapham, who provided invaluable input, especially in the early stages of the process.

Finally, we are especially grateful to Henrik Syse and Greg Reichberg for their original idea that business has something to learn from the just war tradition and for their collegial support, academic input, and editorial assistance.

Lene Bomann-Larsen and Oddny Wiggen
December 2003

Contributors

Robert E. Allinson, Professor, Department of Philosophy, The Chinese University of Hong Kong

Cecilia Arruda, Latin America Director, International Business Ethics Institute, and Associate Professor, Fundação Getulio Vargas, Brazil

Upendra Baxi, Professor of Law, University of Warwick

Lene Bomann-Larsen, Researcher, Ethics, Norms and Identities Programme, International Peace Research Institute, Oslo, and Research Fellow, Department of Philosophy, University of Oslo, Norway

Andrew Clapham, Professor, Graduate Institute of International Studies, Geneva, and Special Advisor to the UN High Commissioner on Human Rights on Corporate Social Responsibility

Heidi von Weltzien Høivik, Associate Professor, Norwegian School of Management BI, and President of the European Business Ethics Network

Ogbonna Ike, Partner in BP&C Associates, associate faculty member of the Lagos Business School of the Pan African University, and affiliated with the Business Ethics Network, Africa (BEN-Africa)

Chris Marsden, Chair of Amnesty International UK Business Group, Associate Professor at the University of Warwick

Florence J. A. Oloo, Director, Centre of Professional Ethics, Strathmore College, Kenya, and Regional Representative to the Business Ethics Network, Africa (BEN-Africa)

Gregory Reichberg, Senior Researcher, Ethics, Norms and

Identities Programme, International Peace Research Institute, Oslo

G. J. (Deon) Rossouw, Professor and Head of Philosophy Department, Rand Afrikaans University, South Africa, and President of the Business Ethics Network, Africa (BEN-Africa)

Julita Sokołowska, llecturer in economics, University of Cardinal Stefan Wyszynski, Warsaw

Henrik Syse, Senior Researcher, Ethics, Norms and Identities Programme, International Peace Research Institute, Oslo, and Post

Doctoral Research Fellow, Department of Philosophy, University of Oslo

Patricia Werhane, Ruffin Chair in Business Ethics and Senior Fellow, Olsson Center for Applied Ethics, Darden Graduate School of Business, University of Virginia, and founding editor of *Business Ethics Quarterly*

Oddny Wiggen, Academic Programme Associate, Peace and Governance Programme, United Nations University, Tokyo

Abbreviations

Abecitrus	Associação Brasileira dos Exportadores de Cítricos (Brazilian Association for Citrus Exporters)
Abrinq	Associação Brasileira dos Fabricantes de Brinquedos (Brazilian Association of Toy Manufacturers)
ACE	Advisory Council on the Environment [Hong Kong]
AIDS	Acquired Immuno Deficiency Syndrome
ATCA	Alien Tort Claims Act [USA]
CED	Cameroon Environmental Defence
CEO	chief executive officer
CNMS	Centro Nuovo Modello di Sviluppo [Italy]
CSR	corporate social responsibility
DMKL	Del Monte Kenya Limited
EIA	environmental impact assessment
EPD	Environmental Protection Department [Hong Kong]
FEPA	Federal Environmental Protection Agency [Nigeria]
Fundecitrus	Fundo de Defesa da Citricultura (Fund for Citrus Plant Protection) [Brazil]
HKBWS	Hong Kong Bird Watching Society
HKSAR	Hong Kong Special Administrative Region
IBGE	Instituto Brasileiro de Geografia e Estatística
ICC	International Criminal Court
ILC	International Law Commission
ILO	International Labour Organization

INDAL	Indian Aluminium Company
ISO	International Organization for Standardization
JWT	just war tradition
KCRC	Kowloon-Canton Railway Corporation
KHRC	Kenya Human Rights Commission
LS	Levi Strauss
MIC	methyl isocyanate gas
MNC	multinational company
MOSOP	Movement for the Survival of the Ogoni People
MP	state of Madhya Pradesh [India]
NGO	non-governmental organization
NNPC	Nigerian National Petroleum Corporation
OMPADEC	Oil Mineral Producing Areas Development Commission
PDE	principle of double effect
PIRC	Pensions & Investment Research Consultants
PRIO	International Peace Research Institute, Oslo
PSSP	Prakrutiko Sompodo Soroichya Porisodo (literally: The Organisation for the Protection of Gifts of Nature from Harm) [India]
RSISTF	Rivers State Internal Security Task Force [Nigeria]
SEC	Supplementary Education Center (Fundecitrus) [Brazil]
SGS	Société Générale de Surveillance
SP	São Paulo State [Brazil]
SPDC	Shell Petroleum Development Company
UAIL	Utkal Alumina International Limited
UCC	Union Carbide Corporation
UCIL	Union Carbide India Ltd
UNICEF	United Nations Children's Fund
UNU	United Nations University
UOI	Union of India
USC	United States Code

Part I

Introduction

1

Addressing side-effect harm in the business context: Conceptual and practical challenges

Oddny Wiggen and Lene Bomann-Larsen

In 2001, 51 of the 100 largest economies in the world were private companies, not states.[1] This makes the private sector a major actor on the global arena – an actor with considerable impact on the societies in which it operates. With such power comes responsibility.

Increased scrutiny of the actions of private companies has placed the responsibility of the private sector on the global agenda. Non-governmental organizations (NGOs), researchers, policy makers, media, consumers, and public opinion – and not least the United Nations, with its Global Compact initiative and Millennium Development Goals – all have a critical eye on corporate actors. To accommodate these increased expectations, the private sector itself has responded with corporate social responsibility (CSR) initiatives and programmes for promoting development, such as the World Business Council for Sustainable Development. New concepts such as corporate citizenship and corporate governance are on everyone's lips, and new and unexpected alliances pop up under headings such as "partnership for development".

The focus on the private sector and its social and environmental obligations increases awareness of social and environmental issues both externally and internally, and may lay the groundwork for a reinterpretation of the role of corporations, of their purpose and legitimacy beyond the profit margin. On the other hand, the many competing concepts and approaches, as well as a lack of coherence in expectations and responses, may not only lead to fatigue but also serve as a wordy cover-up for a

3

reality where not much is being done. When those corporations that speak the loudest about ethics, that are in partnerships with the most respected NGOs and that show up at all research conferences on corporate responsibility suddenly are exposed for violating labour rights, hollow slogans are revealed as just that.

With power comes responsibility. But what is the *content* of corporate social responsibility and its related concepts? The responsibility of the private sector needs to be given a concrete meaning, so as to avoid the honourable speeches and the misrepresentation they may entail. An important aspect is that a responsible company does not have an entire division writing up CSR slogans and nurturing relationships with NGOs while business goes on as usual in other departments. Instead, in all its activities, a responsible company is concerned with the questions: What is the potential impact of our operations on people and the environment? If some degree of harm is unavoidable, what measures can we take to minimize it?

Staying away from all difficult spots is hardly a solution for the private sector in the developing countries. Thus, in general, *responsible engagement* is better than *no* engagement. This book aims to clarify and delimit the responsibility of corporations in relation to specific contexts in which they operate. It is the editors' opinion that any actor – including a private company – must, first and foremost, take responsibility for its own actions and the impact of these on its multiple stakeholders.

The ethics of double effect

The key concept of this book is *double effect*. Double effect refers to the fact that actions often have more than one outcome, i.e. actions may produce side-effects. The phenomenon of double effect becomes a moral problem when the side-effects are not desirable, and especially when they are harmful for those affected. Actors are *responsible* for such side-effects when these are foreseeable and they still choose to proceed. Actors are *blameworthy* for harmful side-effects when they allow them to happen if they could have been prevented, or when they make no, or only an insignificant, attempt to minimize them.

The considerations on side-effects above are entailed in what is called the *principle of double effect*, also known as the *doctrine* of double effect. The doctrine of double effect is perhaps best known from the "just war" tradition, though it also plays an important role in many other fields of applied ethics. Owing to the inert connotations of the word "doctrine", this book will consistently refer to the "principle of double effect" (PDE).

The PDE is a moral principle for assessing actions that produce side-effect harm. In short, it states that, although actors are *responsible* for harmful side-effects that ensue from their actions, actions that produce harmful side-effects are nevertheless permissible provided that (1) the primary goal of the action is legitimate; (2) the side-effects are not part of the actor's intended goal; (3) the side-effects are not means to this goal. Further, the side-effects are permissible only if (4) the actor aims to prevent or minimize them and (5) no alternative courses of action could have been taken that would have led to fewer or no side-effects.

The main emphasis of this book is the PDE not as a principle of *permissibility* but as a device for ascribing *responsibility*. As such, the PDE can be used both as a tool for analysing actions that have already taken place, and as a prerequisite for moral judgement of these actions. More importantly, it can be used as a guide for action in obligating actors to consider in advance what side-effects might result from their actions and, if presumed harmful, how these effects can be prevented or minimized.

The PDE is well known yet not undisputed in academic circles. One major reason for the controversies is the principle's assumed heavy reliance on *intentions* – about whose importance ethicists emphatically disagree. However, the present book wants to emphasize the basic intuition that it *does* make a difference what one intends to do to others. If Peter attacks Mary in order to hurt her, and she falls and breaks her arm, we will judge him differently than if he aims to hug her, trips and falls on her with the same result. Not only will we, as spectators, judge him differently, but it will probably also make all the difference in the world to Mary, even though the broken arm hurts just the same. This is the very simple point that lies at the heart of the PDE; it *does* matter what one's project is. But the PDE is not merely about distinguishing actions from accidents in terms of blame. It is also about ascribing responsibility proper. Because even if Peter had the best intentions in trying to hug Mary, and is not blameworthy for hurting her, he is still to a certain extent responsible for her fall, and we would expect him to offer to help her toward a speedy recovery.

The example is presented to bring out shared intuitions about intentions. The gist of the PDE, however, is not that simple. It deals with actions where the side-effects are in some way chosen, i.e. where they are situated within the sphere of the voluntary because they are *allowed to happen*. This entails that, in order for side-effects to be truly subject to PDE assessment, they must be foreseeable and knowable to agents. This means either that agents foresee that the side-effects will occur, or that they *should* have foreseen them and that their ignorance is in itself culpable. Thus the PDE expands far beyond the Peter and Mary example above. Even with this expansion, however, the PDE lies well within the common-sensical. It seems intuitively apt to say that, although we do not blame anyone for any accidents they cause, we do blame them if the accidents are the result of recklessness or negligence, and we would expect them to have acted otherwise. The PDE is a principle of fairness: it blames actors only for those things that lie within their power to do something about.

The PDE, then, in spite of the controversies regarding the role of intentions in moral assessments, supports some common-sense intuitions. In addition, it has been developed and debated over a time-span almost as long as the life of philosophy itself, and it has survived and accommodated numerous attacks. It has been rephrased and reinterpreted, and through this we dare say it has been strengthened rather than weakened. It is, in spite of some disagreement about its validity, an ethically well-grounded principle.

The PDE employed in this book is an adaptation as well as a rephrasing. Adaptation was necessary in particular to accommodate the particularities of the business *actors*, but also to take seriously other aspects of the business context, such as the need for stakeholder dialogue. If the attempt has been successful, the PDE revised for the business context manages to combine the legitimacy of a moral principle with a long discursive history with the concrete reality of corporations in the world today.

The casuistic approach

The business context is a complex mixture of political, ethical, and judicial factors as well as empirical risks, uncertainties, and changing environments. Moreover, no two situations are identical. Doing business in a well-functioning democratic welfare state is quite different from doing business in a conflict- and corruption-ridden country or where a large part of the population is illiterate and poor and lacks social security systems. Not only is it different because of the risks to the company; it is also different because of the risks to the community. The potential for harm is greater in vulnerable societies – and, therefore, the responsibility to avoid or minimize it is also greater.

Although the obligation to "do no harm" applies equally to all settings, *how* the requirement should be met will depend on contextual factors. This is why an ethical framework addressing business challenges should be flexible and adaptive to the variety of difficulties that require a moral response from companies; in short, a context-sensitive approach is needed.

That an approach to ethics is context sensitive does not mean that it relativizes the ethical case that lies at the heart of the CSR discourse. Rather, it can be argued that the ethical case demands that particular features of each situation are taken into account when practical responses are being formed. For instance, doing business in the same manner in Nigeria as in Norway – that is, simply operating in the manner that domestic law requires – might cause tremendous harm in the former context owing to a legal framework that does not protect employees and the environment. The ethical bottom-line is simple: you are responsible for the actual harm you cause or contribute to, no matter where you operate.

A context-sensitive approach, which applies moral principles as guidelines while allowing the particularities of the situation to determine the practical conclusion of moral reasoning, is properly called *casuistic*. A casuistic approach stresses that moral rules must be applied with great care and skilful judgement. This entails exercising what Aristotle called *phronesis* (practical wisdom). Casuistry is further a method for dealing with moral *problems*, i.e. situations in which the answer to what one ought to do is not clear. As Toulmin and Jonsen point out in their *Abuse of casuistry*, "We understand general maxims, whether about lending or borrowing, cruelty to animals, avoiding violence, or the rights of innocent life because – and to the extent that – we are familiar with the central unambiguous kinds of cases (the 'paradigmatic' cases) that those maxims are commonly understood to cover."[2]

Translated to the business context, we can say that a business environment that functions to the best for all – in which everyone benefits from the business activity and no one is harmed, in which business can be left to "mind its own business" because there are democratic laws and institutions that safeguard both business and the public – constitutes the paradigmatic case: a "rule of the proper division of labour". Yet, as Toulmin and Jonsen emphasize, "it is just those situations that are not covered by appeal to any single simple rule that begin to be problematic; and in just those cases our concern to act rightly gives rise to genuinely moral 'questions' and 'issues'".[3]

In war, the *prima facie* rule "do not kill" becomes problematic. In business, so does the appeal to a proper division of labour between governments and corporations, when a government does not attend to the common good or represent the people as a whole. Here the private sector should not be left to "mind its own business", because doing so would cause unnecessary harm. Whereas a proper labour division between the private and public sector is a necessity in a country such as Norway in order to retain democratic control, the same ideal applies ambiguously in, for example, Angola, where oil companies and similar corporations may need to take on some public responsibility in order to rectify harm to the community, a harm to which the company contributes. In other words, whereas the Norwegian state ensures a redistribution of wealth through an open, transparent system, this is not the case in many developing countries such as Angola, where large amounts of revenues are unaccounted for and "disappear" – into the pockets of the government and into the military budget – or where the environment or human rights are not protected. Thus, there is a morally relevant difference between these two types of settings that necessitates a differentiation in the degree of corporate involvement and range of responses. The particularities of the situation thus determine the degree and direction of a proper response.

Narrowing the scope of corporate responsibility

There are many different approaches to the issue of corporate responsibility, and they vary in scope and content. Some approaches impose a broad range of expectations on private sector actors. One example is the concept of corporate citizenship, which regards the business company as a part of a community, somewhat analogous to other citizens, and with the duties incumbent on these. At the other end of the scale, narrow approaches claim that the company is responsible only for acting in accordance with the law of its host country.

As suggested above, the double effect approach outlined in this book is situated somewhere in between. Operating legally is no guarantee that the result will be acceptable. From an ethical point of view, considering the impact on affected parties – an inclusive stakeholder approach – is necessary to ensure acceptability. On the other hand, business is business, meaning that it should and must attend to those purposes for which it has been created and is established by law. All ethical demands must, in order to be reasonable, be balanced against the legitimate purposes and needs of business. After all, a well-functioning economy is to the benefit of all.

Two issues of legitimacy are worth noticing in this context. The first is the legitimacy of the private sector itself and of the goal of sustainable value creation. Any approach addressing the responsibilities of the sector must, so as not to undermine its own project, accept this goal. Judging business as such as immoral leads nowhere; the concern must be focused on the question of how business can be conducted in a morally legitimate manner. The second issue of legitimacy is political: How far should the private sector go in taking on governmental duties in societies where no one else takes on these tasks? One way to answer this would be to restrict the scope of legitimate involvement to the sphere of the company's own impact; another would be to redefine the company's purpose or form partnerships between company, government, and NGOs.

The political legitimacy challenge is important because it may prove perilous to communities if the private sector, with its legitimate self-interest, meddles in public affairs. Such involvement might prove harmful to democratic processes and the development of the public sector. On the other hand, reference to the legitimacy challenge is also commonly used by companies as an excuse to avoid social responsibility at all ("We are only here to do business"). It is necessary to find the proper balance between doing too much and doing too little for the community in which the company operates.

This book does not provide an answer to the challenge of legitimacy, but it does suggest a way to go: by outlining a principle for assessing de facto corporate impact, the PDE establishes a *minimal-requirement* norm. This entails that the reply "We are only here to do business" or claims of "constructive engagement" cannot be used to evade responsibility for the negative impact of corporate activity. Further, the responses to prevent or minimize harm that are required by the PDE may extend beyond what is commonly thought of as cleaning up after oneself. For example, if corruption is the problem, measures to rectify a situation in which the company becomes an indirect contributor to the wealth of a private government may entail giving something back to the community – be it in the form of direct social services or in the form of supporting NGOs' work against corruption. The options are many.

However, even though the PDE is a minimal-requirement norm – simply to take responsibility for the harm one causes to others – this does not mean that there is no room for negotiating corporate responsibilities beyond the PDE's scope. As mentioned above, a reconstruction of the very idea and purpose of the business corporation is not unthinkable, nor is a discussion about the corporation as citizen. However, it seems pressing first and foremost to establish a reasonable minimum moral standard that everyone arguably is obliged to follow, and then, when compliance to such a standard is ensured, we may start discussing broader responsibilities. There is no point in planting flowers in the neighbour's garden if poison is leaking out in your own backyard, polluting the soil. Acts beyond what the PDE requires may perhaps best be regarded as supererogatory acts: one is morally praiseworthy for performing them, but not blameworthy for not doing so.

Thus, the aim of this book is to lay down a minimal moral duty requirement in the form of the PDE, a principle that everyone, on the basis of reason and fairness, should be able to adhere to and, it is to be hoped, comply with. This aim, however, does not exclude other approaches that go beyond what is minimally required and into the broader debate on the role of corporations in society.

Complicity

One of the advantages of narrowing down the notion of corporate responsibility is that it helps us frame the problematic concept of corporate *complicity*. The issue of complicity – here understood as being implicated in human rights abuses in particular, but also in environmental degradation and violations of labour standards – is at the forefront of many CSR debates. Furthermore, the word is frequently used by company critics as a reproach. Acknowledging the importance of the concept, the UN Secretary-General launched as his second principle of the UN Global Compact that "Companies should make sure they are not complicit in human rights abuses".[4]

The problem is not, however, agreeing that complicity in human rights abuses is something that should be avoided; the problem is agreeing on the content of the term. When is a company complicit in the wrongdoing of other actors – be they other companies, national or local governments, security or police forces, or even armies? An International Peace Academy workshop report from 2001 notes: "Establishing the extent to which a corporation is complicit in conflict is central to the notion of responsibility, yet there is no consensus on what 'being complicit' means."[5] We could easily substitute "human rights violations" for "conflict", without getting closer to consensus. The IPA further notes: "The continued broadening of and vagueness of the notion of complicity has the effect of 'moving the goalposts', whereby corporations meet one set of standards only to find themselves under criticism for failing to address others."[6] It goes without saying that such a situation is not very constructive if the goal is to make companies more responsible. What is needed is a conceptual clarification of the term "complicity" – at least where the term is not precisely defined or covered by law – which might serve to *fix the goalposts*.

In addition to laying down the minimal requirements of corporate responsibility, the PDE can also help define a more precise content of the vague notion of complicity. When the criminal or immoral intent is not shared, complicity is located within the realm of side-effects: "in the case of complicity, the permitted side-effect is another person's immoral or criminal action."[7] The PDE, by emphasizing the company's responsibility for the side-effects that ensue from its own activity, thus tailors the proper area for criticism and blame to the (foreseeable) *impact* of the company on its surroundings, rather than (more broadly) to the company's sphere of influence. Thus the PDE will cover both contributing to and benefiting from the wrongdoings of others, including exploitation of an unjust or weak legal framework, as categories of complicity. However, it is not given under the PDE that merely *bystanding* wrongdoings (so-called silent complicity) should count as complicity on the part of a company (though it might do so on the part of individual persons). It may be added that, although "being there" as such does not constitute complicity, the PDE in its classical expressions does ascribe responsibility for the side-effects of *inaction* as well as of action, but in those cases it must be proven that the agent is guilty of omitting a positive duty.

Which duties a business corporation has beyond the duty to take responsibility for its own impact on human rights, the environment, and so forth is, as suggested in the previous paragraph, open for discussion. Although there is no consensus – even within this volume – on where to place the *second* goalpost of corporate complicity, it is the contention of the editors that the PDE framework fixes the *first* goalpost by providing a minimal-requirement norm – and that this is a significant step in the right direction.

Structure

This book proposes a normative framework to help companies address the harmful side-effects of their operations. It also reflects a dialogical process towards a best possible normative map to fit the landscape. The book consists of two main parts: (1) a theoretical part comprising philosophical and legal considerations on the principle of double effect (PDE) and the fruitfulness of adapting the principle from the just war tradition to the business context, and (2) a case-study part, applying the revised PDE to concrete cases where corporations have faced relevant dilemmas, and evaluating the usefulness and potential shortcomings of a revised PDE with regard to the specific cases.

In the theoretical part, the chapters reflect the development of the project from the first idea that some tenets from the just war tradition could perhaps be successfully adapted to the CSR/corporate citizenship discourse, generating a concept of "just business". Provided sufficient analogies can be proven between war and business, the criteria determining when war is considered "just" (i.e. morally warranted) can also determine when business is "just".

Methodologically, the casuistry of the just war tradition – i.e. applying general guidelines to specific cases and letting the particularities of the cases determine the deliberative outcome and judgement – seems intuitively apt for addressing the complexity of the business world. In essence, however, there are some disanalogies between war and business that may not warrant a direct transfer of the rules from one tradition to the other. The presumed analogies and disanalogies are discussed in the first two chapters of the theoretical part. In chapter 2, "The idea of double effect – in war and business", Gregory Reichberg and Henrik Syse provide an introduction to the just war tradition and the historical origins of the doctrine/principle of double effect embedded in this tradition. They argue that there are certain analogies between war and business, and that the terminology of the just war tradition can be suited to the purpose of awareness-raising and conceptual clarification in the CSR discourse. In chapter 3, "Business is not just war: Implications for applying the principle of double effect to business", G. J. (Deon) Rossouw reminds us that there are also *disanalogies* between war and business that require a rephrasing of the principles from the just war tradition if they are to be adaptable to the business context.

A legal perspective is given in chapter 4, "State responsibility, corporate responsibility, and complicity in human rights violations". Here, Andrew Clapham provides a judicial discussion of the legal framework that exists in the international arena for dealing with issues of corporate complicity.

The fifth chapter discusses the role of intentions in assessing corporate conduct and in relation to the PDE, and shows how the PDE may serve to delimit corporate responsibility and serve as a constructive tool for corporate decision-making. In "Reconstructing the principle of double effect: Towards fixing the goalposts of corporate responsibility" (chap. 6), Lene Bomann-Larsen argues why the PDE is relevant to an assessment of the side-effect harm of corporate activity, in terms of both enhancing and narrowing this responsibility.

On the basis of the discussion in these chapters, as well as roundtable discussions within the project group, the conclusion of the theoretical part presents an alternative PDE, revised and adapted to suit the specifics of the business context while still keeping the philosophical coherence it has gained through its 2,000-year-old discursive legacy.

In the second main part of the book, the case-studies provide tests of the PDE framework on concrete dilemmas faced by corporations, and offer evaluations on the applicability of the framework in these situations.

In chapter 7, "The principle of double effect and moral risk: Some case-studies of US transnational corporations", Patricia Werhane discusses double effect in relation to three American companies operating in China and Africa respectively. She also discusses the notions of *moral risk* and *moral imagination* as fruitful tools for ethical decision-making.

In chapter 8, "An object lesson in balancing business and nature in Hong Kong: Saving the birds of Long Valley", Robert E. Allinson examines a potential double effect in which the side-effect would have been a serious negative impact on the natural environment in Hong Kong.

Chapter 9, Ogbonna Ike's "Shell in Ogoniland", looks at Shell's activities in Ogoniland, Nigeria, from a double effect perspective. Florence J. A. Oloo's chapter, "Del Monte Kenya Limited" (chap. 10), discusses means and side-effects as regards the exploitation of workers at a pineapple plant in Kenya.

In chapter 11, "The 'just war' for profit and power? The Bhopal catastrophe and the principle of double effect", Upendra Baxi examines the Bhopal disaster and argues that the scale of the predicament represents a challenge for the PDE. In "Dealing with harmful side-effects: Opportunities and threats in the emerging Polish market" (chap. 12), Julita Sokołowska discusses unemployment as a side-effect of the transition from a planned to a market economy in Poland.

In chapter 13, "The Orissa case", Heidi von Weltzien Høivik examines the effects on indigenous people in Orissa, India, of a joint venture in which the Norwegian company Norsk Hydro was involved. Cecilia Arruda's "Child labour in the Brazilian citrus sector: The case of Cargill's double effect" (chap. 14) shows how multinational companies can deal with child labour as a side-effect in terms of the measures taken to minimize and eventually eliminate it.

Chapter 15, "A commentary on the principle of double effect", written by Chris Marsden of the Amnesty International UK Business Group, gives an NGO perspective on the principle of double effect as a tool for business enterprises.

Finally, on the basis of the case-studies and the theoretical discussions, the editors sketch out some guidelines for operationalizing the PDE in corporate decision-making in the conclusion, "Towards improved business practice: Implementing the principle of double effect".

Notes

1. Lene Bomann-Larsen (ed.), *Corporate social responsibility in the Norwegian petroleum sector* (Oslo: INTSOK, 2002), p. 7.
2. Stephen Toulmin and Albert R. Jonsen, *The abuse of casuistry. A history of moral reasoning* (Berkeley: University of California Press, 1998), p. 8.
3. Ibid., p. 7.
4. See http://www.unglobalcompact.org/Portal/ (accessed 13 August 2003).
5. International Peace Academy, *Private sector actors in zones of conflict: Research chal-*

lenges and policy responses (New York: International Peace Academy, workshop report, 2001), p. 4.

6. Ibid.

7. Gregory M. Reichberg, "The hard questions of international business: Some guidelines from the ethics of war", in Heidi von Weltzien Høivik (ed.), *Moral leadership in action. Building and sustaining moral competence in European organizations* (Cheltenham: Edward Elgar, 2002), p. 311.

Part II

Theoretical discussion

2

The idea of double effect –
in war and business

Gregory Reichberg and Henrik Syse

Introduction

Most of us have little difficulty acknowledging that some kinds of behaviour are inherently wrong – murder, torture, rape, and fraud readily
come to mind. Other actions seem to present us with borderline cases –
bribery or lying, for instance, which are ordinarily wrong but which nevertheless may be warranted in some narrowly specified contexts. Finally,
some deeds carry few or no negative moral connotations. Providing
medical care to the sick, teaching youngsters how to read, or trading in
needed commodities seem *prima facie* to be morally good. Yet even such
acts can produce harmful results, as when the manufacture of a morally
legitimate product results in serious pollution or upholds a repressive
political regime.

When morally legitimate acts have undesired effects, we enter the area
of "side-effect harm". To what degree should the ethical implications
of side-effect harm be factored into corporate decision-making? What
weight should be given to such harm in the deliberations of business
people – leaders or even rank-and-file employees – who are concerned
about "doing the right thing"? If moral accountability for corporate behaviour is not restricted solely to purposive actions by members of the
corporation – and indeed it is a central premise of this book that *unintended* consequences must also be taken into account – then we must

delineate more clearly the nature and limits of this extended concept of responsibility.

"Double effect" is the heading under which the ethical quandaries surrounding side-effect harm have traditionally been discussed in philosophy. This term is shorthand for the two different kinds of effect that can emerge from our actions. On the one hand, there is the very state of affairs that our actions are meant to produce; we succeed at achieving this goal more or less well, depending on our skill. On the other hand, there are the side-effects that result from this deliberate intervention in the world. The idea that we are answerable for these side-effects, yet in a manner that is *different from* the accountability that obtains vis-à-vis our intentional projects, has been dubbed the "principle of double effect" (PDE). Originally developed within the framework of Catholic moral philosophy, and subsequently applied to military and medical ethics, the PDE can serve as a valuable tool within the ethics of international business as well.

The aim of this chapter is first to give a historical and philosophical background to understanding the principle, and thereby also to indicate some of its possible applications; we then discuss the analogy to the just war tradition (JWT), a context in which double effect reasoning has often been used.

A historical note

In Western philosophy, the first formulation of the principle of double effect is ordinarily attributed to the medieval philosopher-theologian Thomas Aquinas (*ca.* 1224–1274). Discussing the moral problem of killing in self-defence, Aquinas observed that

nothing prevents there being two effects of a single act, of which only one is in accordance with the [agent's] intention, whereas the other is really beyond [that] intention. However, moral acts get their character in accordance with what the agent intends, but not from what is beside his intention, since [what is beyond the intention] is incidental [vis-à-vis that intention].... Therefore from the act of self-defense there can follow a double effect: one, [the effect of] saving one's life, the other, however, the killing of the attacker. Since saving one's own life is what is intended, such an act is not, therefore, impermissible.[1]

Significantly, in this seminal text, reference to unintentional side-effects[2] functions as a principle that exonerates from wrongdoing. A private individual who kills another human being while protecting himself from the other's attack may be excused from the guilt that would ordinarily attach to such an outcome. Aquinas's point is not that those who thus defend themselves have no accountability whatsoever in relation to the death of the assailant. This outcome may be foreseen by the defender, and she has a responsibility to take reasonable precautions against such an eventuality. Aquinas thus adds to the above passage that

> it is possible for an act that proceeds from a good intention [protecting oneself from unjust attack] to become impermissible, if it is not proportioned to its [intended] end. Thus, if one uses greater force than is necessary to defend one's own life, [the act] will be impermissible. If, however, one repels the force with true moderation, it will be a permissible defense; for according to law, it is permissible to repel force with a force under properly defensive control.[3]

The upshot of this last comment is that the PDE cannot validly function as a blanket excuse for the production of harmful side-effects, as though these effects were in no way imputable to the agent. Thus, if this principle is to absolve agents from guilt, at a minimum it must be applied according to the requirements of *right intention* and *proportionality* (see the section on just war analogies below). If the likelihood of adverse side-effects is discounted and minimizing precautions are not taken, the responsible agent may be found blameworthy in the court of conscience, or even in a court of law.

To underscore that the PDE is indeed a principle of accountability, Aquinas cites the example of drunkenness in order to distinguish between two quite different sorts of volition (willing).[4] This distinction dovetails with the contrast made above between, on the one hand, directly intending something and, on the other, the accountability that we bear for the production of undesirable side-effects. In the first place, the drunkard is said *to will* the direct object of his intention, namely the pleasure of drink and the inebriation that ensues. Yet, secondly, he is said to will the misdeeds that he performs while in this state of drunkenness, not, however, *in themselves* but solely insofar as these are contained in the decision to get drunk, as in their cause (*in causa*). Even though his inebriation may be so overwhelming that he no longer possesses the capacity to deliberate rationally about his drunken actions and hence to exercise free choice over them, he nevertheless is responsible for them to the degree that he in fact willed their cause (the excessive consumption of alcohol). Aquinas takes care to note, however, that this *causal* mode of responsibility varies from the *direct* mode of volition mentioned above, wherein an object is willed in and of itself (either as a means or as an end). This direct volition more fully engages our aims and desires, our moral identity, than what we will as an effect only in its cause (volition *in causa*). Still, by describing the agent's causation of side-effect harm in terms of *volition*, Aquinas thereby underscores how such harm does indeed fall within our voluntary control.

In the same passage, Aquinas puts a further useful twist on this point. After observing that people have sometimes committed crimes while under the influence of strong passion (rage, for instance), he asks whether they can rightly be found guilty of their wrongdoing, inasmuch as passion diminishes freedom of choice, the condition *sine qua non* for ascriptions of moral and criminal guilt. To this Aquinas replies that we often have a margin of control over powerful emotions such as anger. True, the emotion may indeed just come over us; hence with respect to its inception we often have little or no choice. Nevertheless, whether or not we allow this anger to grow into full-blown rage is, in ordinary circumstances, something we can choose to prevent. For instance, I can direct my attention away from the indignity I have suffered and begin thinking about something else (say by counting to 10), or I can ponder the deleterious consequences of letting my rage go unchecked. If I *omit* to take such steps and *allow* myself to become engulfed by rage, the violent actions that I subsequently perform cannot be considered purely and simply involuntary. Nor, for that matter, can they be deemed unqualifiedly voluntary, since at that point I no longer possess full rational control over myself. To get at the special status of such acts, Aquinas terms them "indirectly voluntary". Here "indirect" is meant to signify that the acts in question flow from an *omission*. I wilfully neglected to calm myself down and as a result I am (indirectly) responsible for the negative consequences.

Later authors took Aquinas's comments outside of the quite limited sphere of their original application (self-defence, drunkenness, and strong passion) and applied them more broadly to the general problematic of side-effect harm. What the original examples illustrate, quite effectively, is that the PDE carves out a distinctive sphere of accountability, which, depending on the case, can exonerate from wrongdoing (as in the self-defence example) or, on the contrary, be the basis for ascriptions of guilt and liability (the examples taken from drunkenness and passion). As indicated by the preceding discussion, accountability for side-effects can be of two basic kinds:

- accountability for the harmful consequences that are *produced* by our deliberate *actions* – agents are said to will these side-effects *in their cause* (*voluntarium in causa*);
- accountability for the harmful consequences of voluntary *omissions* – agents are said to will *indirectly* (*voluntarium indirecte*) the side-effects that flow from their *inaction*.

Double effect and the "permission of evil"

A final historical comment is in order. It may usefully be observed that the idea of double effect was originally framed in a theological setting – the debate about whether the occurrence of evil is compatible with belief in God's existence. Theologians, among them Thomas Aquinas, have long struggled with this problem. If God is both all-powerful and wholly good, how can we account for the presence of evils in the world? If we say that God in no way wills these evils (thus to preserve our belief in his perfect goodness), we thereby seem to impugn his omnipotence. If we assert, by contrast, that he intends these evils, his omnipotence emerges intact but our confidence in his goodness is compromised.

To resolve this dilemma, the medieval theologians distinguished what God *wills* from what God merely *permits*. By direct intention God *wills* only goodness in the universe. He nevertheless *allows* evil to affect certain goods because, if he were to prevent such evil, other goods, of even higher value, would perforce be eliminated. The stock example was human free will. Many evils could have been avoided had God not created human beings free, since it is by our free actions that we do much evil. Yet, all things being equal, it was better for the universe to contain free agents than for the universe to be wholly without evil. God, it was argued, does not positively intend that certain human beings act badly. This they do of their own initiative. And this, in fact, is unequivocally repugnant to God's will. Nevertheless, he allows this evil, as a necessary concomitant (side-effect) of the creation of beings endowed with the power of free choice.[5]

This style of argumentation is closely related to the PDE. Under the PDE, we are never justified in willing an evil consequence, whether as an end or as a means. There will be circumstances, however, in which we must *allow* something negative to happen. This is not to act wrongly, since (a) one aims at the good, and (b) one does not actually commit immoral acts but rather allows (does not prevent) something bad (or maybe even evil) from taking place. On this reasoning, one may allow evils to occur on condition that the *prevention* of such evils would *necessarily* imperil other, even more important, human goods. Thus, in the context of double effect, accountability for side-effect harm is not automatically to be equated with culpability. I can sometimes (certainly not always) have good reason for *permitting* some forms of malfeasance, if the actions I could take to prevent it would result (as a side-effect) in the occurrence of an even greater evil.

This brings to light a major difference between *willing* evil and *permitting* evil. In contrast to the exceptionless prohibition against the first, there are circumstances in which the latter *may* be justified, and even required. For example, if I refuse to do something that has direct, negative consequences, and someone else steps in and performs the very same act in my place, the other person's wrongdoing may thus be described as a side-effect of my stepping aside. Nevertheless, my indirect contribution to the other's wrongdoing seems allowable in the circumstances, since I did *not* directly and intentionally bring this wrongdoing about. Naturally, had there been a way to prevent the other person from stepping in and performing the act in question – for instance, by alerting the relevant authorities – I would have had a positive obligation to do so.

As a corollary, it may be noted that calculations of the "lesser evil" can be valid with respect to allowing side-effect harm committed by others. However, this sort of calculation ought never to serve as an excuse for one's own deliberate commission of wrongful acts.[6]

Distinguishing consequences that should be allowed from those that ought to be prevented is no easy task. History is littered with improper appeals to the principle of lesser evil: during the Second World War, representatives of the French Vichy regime made ample reference to this principle to justify their collaboration with Nazi rule. This alone does not show that the PDE is invalid; it does indicate, however, that moral insight – and courage – are needed to apply it correctly. Later, we will indicate how the just war criteria of right intention, proportionality, and discrimination can provide guidance in making moral judgements of this kind.

Defining key terms

Before continuing our discussion of the PDE, it is opportune to define some key terms that are widely used in the philosophical literature on double effect.[7]

"Consequences" and "effects" are (for our purposes) interchangeable terms. "*Intended* effects" signifies those results that one specifically aims to bring about (for example, construction of an offshore platform by an oil services firm). These effects include both the final state of affairs that one hopes to achieve (e.g. profit to the firm), as well as the various means that one uses to achieve that goal (selection of the offshore site, purchase of materials, the hiring of staff, etc.).

"*Unintended* effects", on the other hand, are not part of the agent's goal-directed behaviour. They flow from this behaviour yet without being formally included in it, and hence are termed *side*-effects. There is thus a key distinction to be drawn between *aiming at a result* and merely *knowingly producing a result*. "The difference is that action intentionally aimed at as a goal is guided by that goal. Whether the goal is an end in itself or only a means, action aimed at it must follow it and be prepared to adjust its pursuit if deflected by altered circumstances – whereas an act that merely produces an effect does not follow it, it is not *guided* by it, even if the effect is foreseen."[8]

Now, some side-effects will be beneficial (in the offshore example this could be increased employment in the neighbouring coastal area), whereas others will be harmful (damage to a nearby coral reef as a result of offshore activity). Moreover, such side-effects (positive and negative) will often be foreseen, yet not always (for example, damage to the breeding grounds of a hitherto unknown species).

For the purposes of our discussion, "immediate" will qualify consequences that follow very directly from the action itself, for example, a window broken by a mis-hit ball in a backyard baseball game. More remote effects, such as the man inside the house becoming so angry that he kills the perpetrator's cat, may be termed "mediate", in that they come about only through the intervention of someone else's agency. The cat's untimely demise is by no means an immediate, or even a likely, consequence of the ball that was thrown, but it is nevertheless related, albeit in an indirect manner. If the window had not been broken, the poor cat would probably still be alive. Whether immediate or mediate, each sort of consequence is nested within the broader category of *side-effect*. Hence, according to the PDE, both are integral to the agent's moral deliberation about what is to be done – although, in ordinary circumstances, we bear a greater burden of responsibility for the immediate effects, inasmuch as these are more fully "our own". However, those effects that simply *cannot* be foreseen – either because they are so remote, or because they are particularly unusual or unlikely – fall outside the scope of deliberation and moral responsibility. We shall come back to this below.

Finally, the PDE is not concerned solely with the unwanted consequences of our deliberately chosen *actions*. Also to be taken into account are the foreseeable side-effects of *inaction*. Agents can decide *not* to perform certain deeds and, for the unintended results of these omissions, they can be held morally accountable. This *indirect* (to use Aquinas's term) responsibility obtains most especially (though not exclusively) in cases where agents have an obligation, by virtue of their professional *role*, not to shrink from a particular range of actions.

Responsibility for foreseeable side-effects

As has already been indicated, unintended effects may be divided into two kinds: those that can be foreseen and those that cannot. It is important to note that this is not a division between consequences that actually are foreseen and those that are not. In many cases it is meaningful to say "You should have known"; in other words, the (undesired) effect was so likely to follow from one's action that one should not have overlooked it.

Based on what has been delineated so far, PDE asserts the following:
• one bears moral responsibility for the intended consequences of one's actions;
• one also bears moral responsibility for the unintended consequences of one's actions that were, or should have been, foreseen.

However, the latter kind of responsibility is quite different from the former. Whereas there can be *no* justification for deliberately harming another human being, except perhaps in self-defence, however much this might be seen to benefit oneself or others, the same strict prohibition does not apply to the unintended consequences (even those foreseen with certitude) of otherwise good actions. In other words, there is a fundamental asymmetry between *harming others intentionally* and *allowing them to be harmed* as the unwanted side-effect of one's deliberate actions (or inaction). The former is always bad, whereas the latter is not necessarily so.

During the Second World War, Norwegian resistance fighters at Rjukan sabotaged a ferry that was carrying their countrymen across a lake. Their goal was to sink the ship in order to prevent the occupying German force from transporting a cargo of heavy water from the Vemork plant to the railway lines on the other side of the lake. Heavy water was an ingredient believed vital to the construction of an atomic bomb. The resistance fighters knew in advance that many civilians on board would die (and there was no way to warn them, for to do so would have endangered the mission). This, however, was not about doing evil so that good might result. Rather, the death of these civilians was a foreseeable side-effect of a legitimate military action: stopping the production of an enormously potent new weapon.

As this example illustrates, if side-effect harm is to be deemed justifiable, the following preconditions must be met:
• the intended consequences are in themselves morally legitimate (such as, in the example just given, the destruction of an enemy military target);
• the unintended consequences (e.g. the death of civilians as a side-effect) are unavoidable if the desired (i.e. good) consequences are to come about; in other words, it is impossible to achieve the desired aim without, at the same time, producing the undesired side-effect;
• the negative, unintended consequences are not so grave that they are out of proportion to the good being achieved;

- all possible measures are being taken to minimize the negative consequences of one's action.

There are several open-ended formulations in this list, especially regarding proportionality. What does it mean that negative consequences are "out of proportion" to the good being achieved? No mathematical rule exists for deciding such a question, so prudence and careful moral examination are called for. This is indeed important: PDE provides no calculus, but rather a set of fundamental considerations for prudential moral reasoning.

It should be noted that the proportionality criterion expresses a consequentialist or, to be more exact, a utilitarian line of argument. The gist of the utilitarian brand of consequentialist ethics is that an action should ideally produce the greatest possible good for the greatest possible number; or, negatively, it should minimize negative effects for as many people as possible. However, the PDE does not represent a purely utilitarian ethics, since it allows (in contrast to the utilitarians) for the existence of evil actions that are evil per se, such actions being disallowed in all circumstances. Still, the duty to weigh consequences against each other, and to avoid those courses of action that produce negative consequences out of proportion to the good achieved, certainly introduces an element of utilitarian ethics into the PDE framework.[9]

We may say that the PDE reminds us of two key elements implicit in all ethical conduct:

- The importance of being *honest* in evaluating the consequences of our actions. Often we tend to ignore those consequences that are not immediately obvious – because, for instance, they are further away in time or because they affect people who are not present or known to us. PDE insists that such consequences – if foreseeable and direct enough to be relevantly attributed to one's own action – are part and parcel of any moral evaluation of action. This does not mean that no actions with negative side-effects may be performed, but it does mean that a number of preconditions have to be fulfilled first.
- PDE is inconsistent with the idea that ends justify means. We must accordingly beware of distorting the PDE so that means with undesirable connotations are surreptitiously redefined as "unintended side-effects". As a variant of the same problem, some means to achieving intended ends may seem so morally repellent (for example, falsifying accounts to improve the performance of one's firm) that we can be tempted into classifying these means as "unavoidable, unintended consequences" of doing the right thing. In either case, the means in question are just as intended as the ends for which they were chosen; and, like these ends, they most certainly have the character of "willed actions". Thus, one

cannot use the PDE to absolve oneself from the guilt of having chosen these wrongful means.

Agents, actions, and evaluations

We are now in a position to understand better the usefulness of this framework in the corporate context. A crucial feature of international corporate activity is indeed the rich array of agents involved – political, corporate, NGO related, and others. All have moral responsibility for their actions, and often they together contribute to good as well as to undesired consequences, for instance in developing countries.

This means in practice that every corporate actor must evaluate the likely outcome of its actions not in isolation but in concert with other actors. Hence, not only are serious and honest predictions called for, but also transparency and cooperation between the parties involved. *Partial* responsibility for bringing about an undesired side-effect is still responsibility and cannot be removed from the field of moral reasoning.

The fact that moral responsibility is often shared in the international, corporate context implies that a reasonable division of this responsibility will need to be worked out. For instance, the social welfare of a population falls primarily within the purview of the political authorities. Corporations are not obliged to create a fair distribution of goods within an entire society. Also, within a reasonably well-functioning state, one must assume that environmental standards are established by law; hence, setting maximum limits for pollution is not the primary responsibility of the corporate sector. On the other hand, corporations participate in societal life in a way that makes it infeasible to shed all moral responsibility for seemingly political matters. A company that employs child labour or pollutes drinking water in a context where the political authorities allow it can hardly use political laxity as an excuse for not performing differently. This also draws our attention to the fact that countries and regions with weak governments, civil war, and human rights abuses demand more of the corporate sector in terms of responsibility and conscientiousness.

The multiplicity of actors, as a general feature of international business, leads us to another often-mentioned problem in corporate ethics; namely, if *you* do not perform the actions that have negative consequences, others will. In other words, if you pull your corporation out of a country that (say) exploits child labour, others will come in and do the same. However, such a line of reasoning creates two serious problems. First, it seems to imply that doing the wrong thing is wrong only as long as your act cannot be substituted by another's similar act. This surely makes for an intolerably weak notion of moral wrongness. Second, it creates the impression that there are only two solutions: either you act wrongly, or someone else does. This eclipses the whole range of intermediary possibilities – for example, doing something positively to right the wrong, either by changing your own actions or by warning against and/or counterbalancing the actions of others.

Once again, we see how the interaction of several actors in the same arena calls for a particularly thorough evaluation of consequences. Equally importantly, we see in the kind of situation just mentioned that "moral imagination"[10] – a central virtue for any corporate decision maker – is necessary if one is to find workable solutions. There is, in most cases, a host of intermediary solutions, often linked to transparency, honesty, and serious discussion of alternative courses of action.

Double effect and the "golden mean"

This all leads us towards a crucial point for understanding the PDE. There are what we may call two extremes in the moral discourse about consequences: either no side-effects are relevant to moral rightness or wrongness, or all side-effects count equally. The first leads to moral laxity, the second to moral paralysis. A simple example will illustrate this.

Following the morally lax view on responsibility for consequences, a company that decides to engage itself in a war-torn country can simply make sure that its actions are not strictly speaking illegal according to the laws of the country in question, and that its products and the salaries it pays are all within broadly "moral parameters". The company that insists on paying attention only to the direct, intended, and immediate consequences of its actions will not be disturbed that it, for instance, directly or indirectly encourages child labour, contributes to prolonging an (unjust) civil war, upholds (albeit indirectly) illegal activities, or uses the services of a corrupt police force. On the other hand, an extremely scrupulous company may decide never to engage itself in developing countries because any engagement has side-effects such as, for instance, contributing revenue to a corrupt government, ensuring jobs for the well-to-do and not for the poor, or creating pollution. Under the latter perspective, all consequences, no matter how unavoidable, remote, or indirect, are seen as one's own direct responsibility, leading to inaction and disengagement.

PDE insists on taking a middle road between these extremes. On the one side, it shows how we are answerable even for the unintended consequences of our activity (including those that are indirect and mediated by the actions of others). On the other side, it makes clear that not all negative side-effects disallow action. By drawing up the rules and preconditions delineated above, it seeks to delimit the scope of moral responsibility in a way that allows for ethically conscious action without such a level of moral scruples that real action becomes impossible.

Just war and just business – parallel concerns?

As we have already mentioned, this book, by using the PDE as its point of departure, exploits an idea that is mainly known from the so-called "just war" tradition (JWT) of moral enquiry.[11]

Of course, we – and this whole project – might have left it at that: we could have mentioned in passing the double effect doctrine's just war pedigree, and then simply left JWT by the wayside. When we do not choose that path, and instead enquire how the just war framework may be of use to us in the current project, even beyond double effect, it is for the following reasons. First, there are striking similarities between the morality of war and the morality of business. Although some may claim that the *dis*analogies and *dis*similarities are even more apparent – and G. J. (Deon) Rossouw expertly treats these in chapter 3 – we believe there is a case to be made for drawing important parallels. Second, JWT offers a comprehensive vocabulary for discussing ethics in a cross-cultural, international context.

Let us start with the analogies. A moral cloud seems to hang over business as well as war. This is most obviously the case with warfare: any resort to armed force – even for a just cause – results in suffering, destruction, and death. Soldiers are indeed taught how to kill. Furthermore, seemingly limited conflicts all too often expand once military means are introduced, leaving moral restraint and right intention helpless victims of ambition and cruelty. How can such a pursuit ever be moral?

More subtly, many see a similar problem with business. Although justified by its bringing goods and services to people who need them, business itself is ruled by a logic of profit, leading all too easily to lies, manipulation, and cruel competition. Many recent cases can be cited as evidence that big business often entails big deception, and that greed is more often than not an integral part of business activity. In short, in both warfare and business there are temptations and pressures – sometimes very strong – to engage in wrongdoing.

When it comes to war, there are at least three main reactions to this challenging "moral cloud".[12] The first is pacifism, which holds that participation in war is inherently immoral. No *direct* parallel to pacifism exists in the business world, but widespread protests and boycotts against market liberalist systems, combined with attempts at creating alternative and more just forms of business enterprise, clearly invoke the same idea, namely, that one has to break radically with the current regime in order to lead a moral life.

The second obvious reaction to the charge that war is inevitably immoral is simply to say that morality has nothing to do with it. This is the "realist" response. War is primarily waged for self-interested reasons. If we want to reduce its destructive force, we first have to accept that fact. Believing that rationales for waging war can be discussed in moral terms is tantamount to self-deception. Likewise, the view that business has its own set of rules, different from those of everyday morality, is quite common. According to such a view, those who hold up high, altruistic standards for business activity are naïve, lacking a real understanding of what goes on in the often cruel world of business.

Between these two we find JWT. It holds that warfare is not always immoral and that, in this context, moral constraints are both relevant and necessary. JWT's main tenet is that wars can indeed be waged in a moral fashion. Thus, commanding troops or taking part in combat can in principle be done justly. At the same time, this tradition recognizes that the dangers of injustice and excess are lurking everywhere on the battlefield.

Here we indeed find a useful parallel to business. While acknowledging the temptations and dangers accompanying the business profession, an intermediate position along just war lines holds that conducting business can be a just and honourable profession. Engaging in business may awaken the appetite for gain, which, when sought for its own sake, leads ineluctably to avarice and greed. But there are real alternatives: business dealings can be performed honourably, when they are done within the limits of the law, with the right intention, by someone yielding legitimate corporate authority, and with due concern for the consequences of these actions.

The just war vocabulary

This leads us into the just war vocabulary. Developed over many centuries with a special eye to creating categories for moral discourse acceptable in an international setting, JWT has articulated a set of conditions for just warfare that may prove to have relevance far beyond the purely military setting. It offers useful criteria for assessing the parameters of morally legitimate action in situations where our everyday moral intuitions are subject to doubt. Here we move into unfamiliar territory, where the danger of doing unjustified harm to other human beings is indeed significant. This description surely fits not only war but also the kinds of situations that international corporations often face, not least in conflict settings and in regions where human rights are systematically violated.

Within JWT, the idea of double effect has famously been used to delineate unacceptable side-effect harm to civilians. However, several other ideas from JWT also have business-related relevance. Below we indicate how some of the just war criteria have been understood within the just war context, and how they may be applied within the context of international business. This takes us outside the PDE understood in a narrow sense. However, since JWT is the soil from which the PDE originally developed, these musings on the relevance of just war criteria for business are altogether relevant to this project.

As a prelude, we should mention a crucial distinction within JWT. As Michael Walzer puts it, wars are "judged twice", morally speaking[13] – first, whether one should engage in war at all, often called the question of *ius ad bellum*; and then how war should be conducted, *ius in bello*. Although this distinction plays an important role in just war theorizing, it cannot readily be transferred to the business framework. Mainly, the decision to conduct business dealings is quite different from the decision to employ armed force. One may, of course, say that a decision to engage in corporate activity in a particular trouble spot can have affinities to just war reasoning. But the parallel easily becomes strained, since *ius ad bellum* reasoning deals with wrongdoing that needs to be corrected or stopped, whereas business decisions very rarely do. Moreover, there is much controversy surrounding *ius ad bellum* in the current debate on international ethics. Is there *any* legal room for resort to armed force, outside of self-defence, in modern international law? International lawyers may indeed claim that the *ius ad bellum* has been so decisively reduced to self-defence since the Second World War as to be rendered obsolete. Although there is considerable disagreement about this claim, not least in the face of the Kosovo and Iraq interventions, the whole debate surrounding the *ad bellum* side of just war reasoning should make us even more careful in drawing direct lines from its considerations.

In bello considerations, on the other hand, are more easily applied to business settings. Indeed, the relevance of questions about side-effect harm, discrimination between different groups of people, and proportionality between goods achieved and harm done is strikingly similar in war and business.

Having said this, it must be added that many of the criteria normally listed as *ad bellum* concerns are useful even outside that setting (that is, even within a more *in bello*-related setting). In the following we will therefore employ several of these criteria, but without thereby implying that we are comparing decisions pertaining to business to the decision to go to war.

Competent authority

According to JWT, the use of lethal force is not a matter for private citizens; nor does it fall under the responsibility of just anyone walking the corridors of power. Only specially designated public officials, paying due attention to legal constraints, have the authority to engage the nation on a course of armed conflict.

Applied within the business setting, the criterion of competent authority can serve as a reminder that one of the central tasks of a corporate manager, the CEO in particular, is to oversee the social impacts of the enterprise, a task that should be carried out with due attention to national and international law. Peter Drucker puts this nicely: "Managing the enterprise's social impacts has importance because no organ can survive the body which it serves; and the enterprise is an organ of society and the community."[14] Managers have responsibility for identifying and anticipating the harmful side-effects of their firm's operations. Attention to these adverse side-effects should be equated not with philanthropy – helping society alleviate ills not of the firm's making – but with an obligation of strict justice.

When negative impacts are the result of an exercise of authority, even if purely incidental and unintended, those in positions of authority have a responsibility to take measures to eliminate or mitigate these impacts. This holds true, not least, for human rights abuses, which represent a particularly pernicious variety of side-effect. The "competent authority" criterion tells us that corporate decisions with a bearing on human rights should be made at the highest levels of the corporate hierarchy. Flat management structures are no excuse for ignoring the undesirable consequences of the organization's operations. Delegation of authority to local managers should not be used as a convenient strategy for turning a blind eye to human rights abuses. Firms need to establish definite procedures for handling these sorts of issues. Decisions involving direct investment in countries with widespread human rights violations should be made through the proper channels and at a level of high competence and authority – not merely on an ad hoc basis or by persons or offices with little overview and knowledge.

There are additional reasons why competent authority is important, normatively speaking. In cases of fateful decisions, touching the lives of many people, the channels for making such decisions must be clear and predictable. It must be possible, both during the decision-making process and after the fact, to see clearly who made what decision, whether decisions were made at the right level, and whether questions should (or indeed could) have been handled differently. Not least in situations where secrecy abounds – which happens regularly in both business and war –

procedural transparency is crucial, so that those affected by the decisions in question can have some trust that the right persons are making them; or, alternatively, that the actual decision-making process will be revealed at some later stage, making it open to criticism and assignment of responsibility.

Competent authority is also closely linked to the issue of trust. The more serious and difficult the situation, the more one needs to have trust in the persons and institutions making the key decisions on how that situation is to be handled, both within the organization and in the organization's relationship with the outside public.[15] Lack of clarity about who has been entrusted with making the most crucial decisions results in lack of trust, widespread suspicion about the legitimacy of the measures taken, and counterproductive rivalry between key actors.

Right intention

In just war parlance, the criterion of right intention signifies that war should never be undertaken out of revenge or a will to dominate another nation. Hence, those who make the decision to engage in military action should think hard about what they hope to accomplish once victory is achieved, as victory is never sufficient unto itself. The ultimate goal of waging war ought to be the restoration of a just peace. Have we thought sufficiently about the shape of the peace to come? Are our military efforts likely to bring it about? This criterion takes note of the fact that an agent may have a just cause but nevertheless act from a wrongful intention – for example, the intent to dominate the other party instead of striving to achieve conditions to promote an equitable peace.

Applied within the commercial setting, this criterion focuses attention on the *goals* or *aims* of business and the way in which those goals should influence the actions performed and strategies followed. Just as victory cannot rightly be taken as the ultimate goal of war, so profits cannot rightly be taken as the ultimate goal of business. This does not mean that achieving victory or making profits cannot form a *part* of one's intentional structure, and a highly legitimate one at that. Ethically speaking, however, profit should never be taken as the ultimate goal of business. If that were the case, the profit motive could trump important moral considerations such as a concern for basic human rights. To adopt that course of action would of course be untenable.

We often talk about moral action in terms of restraint, of not doing what is bad. Yet, in adopting the language of restraint, we too easily forget that only the attraction of some *good* motivates a person to action. It is the attainment (or preservation) of some hoped-for good that truly creates motivation.[16] This forms an important part of the "right intention" idea: it seeks to direct our attention to the actual *good* we seek to attain through our actions.

What, then, is the good for the sake of which right-minded business people avoid doing wrong? Often this is described in terms of narrow self-interest: we might get caught; or our reputations might be damaged, thus impairing our ability to maintain and augment our customer base. Yet, to construe motivation solely this way seems demeaning to business as a practice, as though it were directed uniquely to the narrow self-interest of its practitioners. We would be loath to describe the purpose of medicine in terms of what is good for the physician. Rather, we define it by reference to the good internal to the activity itself – the restoration of health in the patient. What is business for? What is the goal internal to this practice? Does it merely aim to bring benefit to its practitioners – or is it directed outside of this self-referential circle to something else, to the customer, and ultimately to the well-being of the community of which the customer is a member? Can the goal of business, the good positively aspired to, have something to do with love of the community, its well-being; in a word, *service* to the community? Is there a special nobility in the business profession insofar as it, like the military profession, is meant to serve the good of society, with each practice aiming, in its own way, to promote the common good?

This being said, we should beware of setting social responsibility and profits in opposition, as though what you give to one subtracts from the other. In reality, clever profit-making solutions often represent the optimal solution to social responsibility problems. The mistaken opposition between profits and service is but an application of a broader, more philosophical error: the oft-assumed dichotomy between self-interest and altruism, such that the most moral behaviour must needs be self-sacrificing.[17] Actually, attempts at harmonizing ethics and profits can prove a good strategy, morally speaking, challenging us to ponder how considerations of ethics can help create a more ethically minded workplace and business setting. Fostering an environment of honesty and integrity within a company certainly enhances both the efficiency and the overall reputation of that company. Furthermore, paying heed to the ethically oriented customer can prove an important way to generate trust and customer loyalty. Here, ethics and (long-term) profits may go hand in hand.

There are times, however, when ethics and profits do not coincide. Perhaps the customer does not care about the moral message; or dishonest methods within an organization seem to generate considerable revenue; or dealings in a country ridden with conflict are so popular on the home front, owing to their profitability, that the voice of those oppressed is simply not heard. In such cases, and especially when matters of human rights and dignity are at stake, responsibility to one's fellow human being must outweigh profit. We should beware of some contemporary strategies that *subordinate* ethics to profit: "act ethically because the customer wants it." Fine within its order, this nevertheless cannot be the chief reason for acting ethically; otherwise, ethics would be held hostage to the vacillating beliefs of the customer.

Like military operations, where many tactics are surely outlawed even if they might be efficacious in bringing about victory, business dealings are nested within a larger social and political context. In articulating our corporate objectives, have we reflected upon our moral obligation to contribute to the well-being of the local and national communities in which we operate? This is the challenge of the "right intention" criterion.

Open declaration

Before resorting to force, efforts should be expended on publicly airing one's grievances against the other side. Transposed to the business setting, "open declaration" signifies that companies wishing to do business in places where human rights are systematically violated should publicly announce their goals and strategies beforehand. This will afford all interested parties the opportunity to express their views on the likely impact of the proposed business operation. Since the legitimacy of the foreign regime is in question, corporate decision makers must take care to listen to opposition leaders, aid organizations, representatives of labour unions, local committees, and others with intimate knowledge of the country's political environment.

Reasonable hope of success

A nation should not go to war unless it thereby stands a realistic chance of achieving its goals. Similarly, transnational corporations that opt for constructive engagement with repressive regimes should do so only after having diligently investigated whether such action is likely to yield the intended result. The claim that political conditions will improve as a result of the constructive engagement will have moral worth only to the degree that it is backed up by an objective study of the facts of the situation. In business, as in war, good intentions alone are never enough. Have we taken the trouble to conduct a human rights impact assessment on our (proposed) activities in country x?

Discrimination

Attacks should target only the military capability of the enemy. It is *never* permissible intentionally to kill or maim non-combatants on the other side, even when highly expedient – say, to break down the enemy's morale. Thus, military operations with indiscriminate effects – such as carpet bombing or the use of cluster bombs in urban settings – should be avoided.

Likewise, in evaluating the probable impact of business strategies, careful thought must be given to the questions: Who will benefit? Who will suffer? Members of the ruling élite or ordinary people? Discrimination should be taken into account when evaluating methods of constructive engagement, as well as when opting for withdrawal, and in general when conducting social impact analyses of one's business dealings. This is closely related to the problems associated with double effect and side-effect harm. Serious analyses concerning corporate social responsibility must necessarily deal with side-effects as well as direct and immediate impacts.

Proportionality

The destructive impact of particular military operations must be proportional to the intended benefits. Causing great harm, including significant collateral damage, for the sake of a strategic goal of minor importance is unethical. The principle of double effect, the basic focal point of this entire project, must not be used to eschew responsibility for collateral harm done to non-combatants. Not only should non-combatants never be intentionally harmed (discrimination); they should be shielded, as far as possible, from the harmful side-effects of military action.[18] Even though these side-effects are conditions *in spite of which one acts*, they must be brought into the moral deliberation over the act in question. In applying the double effect principle, we must scrutinize what these effects are likely to be, take them into consideration as part of the description of our action, and then weigh them against the state of affairs we intend to bring about. This is, as we pointed out above, not about ends justifying means. The question is whether some unintended effects can be justified because the intended effect of an action is so important to our overall end – *peace*.

Similarly, in business, we must give hard thought to the connection between the end we are deliberately aiming at and the damaging side-effects that arise as a consequence of pursuing that end. Right intention is crucial here. If profit is seen as the self-enclosed end of business, then the adverse social side-effects will inevitably be viewed as an extraneous element in corporate decision-making, or they will be deemed relevant only to the degree that they impact on profits. It is sometimes claimed, for instance, that, because free trade is a good of such magnitude, firms should not be held accountable for the misuse of their products or services by unscrupulous state clients.

Let us instead apply the principle of proportionality as follows: "the more serious the likely resulting social harm, the greater the individual's moral responsibility to ensure that assistance in producing this harm is not rendered; further, a certain level of personal and commercial convenience is overborne by the larger social interest of preventing serious criminal behaviour."[19] Efforts to prevent the violation of fundamental human rights must outweigh profit concerns. The inherent goal of business requires this of its practitioners.

Conclusion

This summary of just war criteria reveals questions and concerns of obvious relevance to the business setting, not least when business is being conducted in zones of conflict or human rights abuse. In such settings, everyday moral intuitions become blurred, and concerns that are normally ignored suddenly become pressing. Alas, it turns out that many corporations have shown little regard for these sorts of issues. The impact of a firm's presence on the local populations and natural environment is customarily overlooked where real profits stand to be made. However, a significant change in attitude towards this problem has been observed over the past decade, with the Global Compact initiative expressing and formulating much of the concern over good corporate governance in the international sphere.

Our hope is that a better understanding of questions regarding double effect, proportionality, competent authority, right intention, and transparency in declaring one's aims – concepts taken from just war reasoning – will contribute towards framing the questions that most need to be asked. It may even help us in suggesting solutions.

This said, we hasten to add that the PDE can nevertheless be utilized and understood perfectly well without subscribing wholesale to its just war pedigree. Readers of this volume who find that the idea of just war is a somewhat contrived detour for discussing side-effect harm may certainly persist in their view. The striking similarities between moral judgements in war and in business have nevertheless given rise to this book project. Showcasing these similarities, and also explaining the historical and philosophical background to the PDE, have been the purpose of the reflections in this chapter. We have striven to show how just war principles in general, and the PDE in particular, can provide valuable guidance through one of the densest of all corporate jungles – an international sphere that is often marred by violent conflict and sometimes even vicious wrongdoing. This chapter thereby offers a preliminary ethical map that may assist the reader in navigating less dangerously through this jungle.

Notes

1. Thomas Aquinas, *Summa theologiae*, II-II, q. 64, a. 7; translation [slightly amended] in Gareth B. Matthews, "Saint Thomas and the principle of double effect", in Scott MacDonald and Eleonore Stump, *Aquinas's moral theory* (Ithaca and London: Cornell University Press, 1995), pp. 63–78, at p. 66.
2. There is a debate in the scholarly literature on whether or not Aquinas, in the text just quoted, meant to situate legitimate killing in self-defence wholly within the category of side-effect. Some argue (see Matthews, "Saint Thomas and the principle of double effect") that such killing can in fact be taken as a *means* to ward off an aggression; hence, when Aquinas spoke of defensive killing as "beyond the agent's intention", the point was merely to deny that this act could be taken as the agent's chief end or purpose (i.e. as a punishment for the aggression). On this interpretation, q. 64, a. 7, should not be read as a statement of the PDE. We cannot go into this debate here. Historically, however, it cannot be doubted that this text has served as the springboard for the elaboration of the PDE. And even should one agree with the position of those who deny that q. 64, a. 7, contains the PDE, it remains true that other texts in Aquinas's corpus do in fact articulate a version of the PDE (without of course expressly calling it that). In addition to the texts quoted below, see, in particular, *Summa theologiae*, II-II, q. 64, a. 8; I-II, q. 20, a. 5; and I-II, q. 73, a. 8.
3. Matthews, "Saint Thomas and the principle of double effect", p. 66 (from II-II, q. 64, a. 7, in *Summa theologiae*).
4. See Aquinas, *Summa theologiae*, I-II, q. 77, a. 7.
5. For more ample discussion of the theological problem of God and the permission of evil, see "Evil and suffering", chapter 5 of Brian Shanley, *The Thomist tradition* (Dordrecht: Kluwer Academic Publishers, 2002), pp. 92–127 (especially pp. 102–109).
6. On the utilitarian calculus of the "lesser evil", see Bernard Williams, "A critique of utilitarianism", in J. J. C. Smart and Bernard Williams, *Utilitarianism for and against* (Cambridge: Cambridge University Press, 1963), pp. 75–155. Williams's example of George, the young Ph.D. in chemistry who out of conviction refuses to take a job in a laboratory producing chemical and biological weapons, even though he knows that another chemist, with far fewer scruples, will undoubtedly accept the position, provides a vivid illustration (and trenchant analysis) of the moral difficulties inherent in the utilitarian appeal to the "lesser evil" (pp. 97–107).
7. A selection of some of the most influential articles on PDE (by *inter alia* Warren Quinn, Philippa Foot, and G. E. M. Anscombe) may be found in P. A. Woodward (ed.), *The doctrine of double effect: Philosophers debate a controversial moral principle* (Notre Dame, Ind.: University of Notre Dame Press, 2001).
8. Thomas Nagel, *The view from nowhere* (New York and Oxford: Oxford University Press, 1986), p. 181.
9. It can rightly be said that the ethical reasoning found in this chapter contains elements of both deontology (duty- and rights-based ethics) and utilitarianism, as well as virtue ethics. For a useful introduction to, and dialogue between, these ethical traditions, see Marcia W. Baron, Philip Pettit, and Michael Slote, *Three methods of ethics* (Malden/Oxford: Blackwell, 1997).

10. See Patricia Werhane's chapter in this volume.
11. An often cited example of the PDE used in a just war context can be found in G. E. M. Anscombe's essay "War and murder" (1961), reprinted in Woodward (ed.), *The doctrine of double effect*, pp. 247–260. Also famous is Michael Walzer's *Just and unjust wars*, 2nd edn. (New York: Basic Books, 1992), referred to below. For a recent treatment of this theme, see Whitley Kaufman, "What is the scope of civilian immunity in wartime?" *Journal of Military Ethics* 2(3), 2003, pp. 186–194.
12. Nicholas Fotion, "Reactions to war: Pacifism, realism, and just war theory", in Andrew Valls (ed.), *Ethics in international affairs* (Lanham, Md.: Rowman & Littlefield, 2000).
13. Walzer, *Just and unjust wars*, chap. 1.
14. Peter F. Drucker, *Management* (New York: Harper & Row, 1974), p. 43.
15. For an excellent discussion of the relation between authority and trust, with special reference to the military profession, see Asa Kasher, "Public trust in a military force", *Journal of Military Ethics* 2(1), 2003, pp. 20–45.
16. We do not mean hereby to sidestep the problem of *evil* motivations. Our point is simply that ethics should not merely employ a negative language of restraint and prohibition, but should also focus on the good that actions and practices aim at.
17. Robert C. Solomon, *Ethics and excellence* (Oxford: Oxford University Press, 1993), p. 106.
18. Walzer, *Just and unjust wars*, pp. 151–159.
19. K. J. M. Smith, *A modern treatise on the law of criminal complicity* (Oxford: Clarendon Press, 1991), p. 157.

3

Business is not Just War: Implications for applying the principle of double effect to business

G. J. (Deon) Rossouw

Introduction

It is not uncommon to find comparisons or analogies between business and war. In the field of business management, war paradigms are often utilized, especially in strategic planning and marketing management.[1] It is, for example, argued that competitive marketing resembles warfare and consequently a number of offensive and defensive marketing strategies are identified that can be used by business either to gain new market territory or to defend existing markets.

This project too assumes that there are sufficient analogies between business and war to warrant the transfer of some principles of double effect originally developed within the just war tradition to the context of international business. In an earlier publication, "Hard questions of international business: Some guidelines from the ethics of war", Gregory Reichberg referred to a number of such analogies between business and war.[2] These include the following:

- both war and business involve groups of people structured according to channels of authority;
- both war and business are conducted across national jurisdictions;
- in both war and business the pressure to engage in wrongdoing can be intense, to the extent that wrongdoing is frequently justified as being "part of the game";

- both just war and ethical business constitute a *via media* between extremes.

This project depends to a large extent on the question of whether the above or any further analogies warrant a comparison between war and business. If a case can be built for sufficient analogies between war and business, then the principle of double effect that was developed within the context of just war may justifiably be transferred to the context of business. If, on the other hand, it can be shown that there are aspects of business that differ substantially from just war, then the transfer to business of a principle developed within the context of war becomes more problematic.

To decide whether an analogy is sufficient to warrant transfer from one context to another one needs to determine whether there are, besides the perceived analogies, also significant disanalogies between the two phenomena that are being compared.[3] Should there be significant disanalogies, transfer from one phenomenon to the other should be done with great care or even abandoned in the case of substantial disanalogies.

The purpose of this chapter is to investigate the disanalogies between war and business, because it is my contention that the just war background of the principle of double effect had some bearing on both the content of the principle and its manner of application. Not all possible disanalogies will be discussed, only those that might have a bearing on the focus of this project – that is, only those disanalogies that might affect the question of whether the principle of double effect can be applied to moral decision-making on foreseeable negative side-effects in international business. The outcome of this investigation will determine the appropriateness of transferring the principle of double effect from its traditional context of the just war tradition to the context of international business.

Three such disanalogies will be discussed. The first focuses on the difference in purpose between war and business. The second revolves around the fact that moral deliberation in war is done unilaterally, whereas in business it can be done multilaterally. The final disanalogy points out that business is subject to the jurisdiction of host countries, whereas in war compliance with the jurisdiction of enemy countries is not required. Given these disanalogies, the implications for transferring the principle of double effect from war to business will be discussed in the concluding part of the chapter.

Disanalogy 1: Peace versus value creation

The purpose of war and the purpose of business are very different. In the just war tradition it is accepted that the only legitimate purpose of war is self-defence or lasting peace. Consequently, the overriding concern in all decisions on war is whether the war effort has the potential of creating conditions that will favour lasting peace and friendship amongst and within nations.[4]

The purpose of business on the other hand is value creation. By rendering a product or a service, the business creates value for its stakeholders. There is, however, an ongoing debate about who the stakeholders should be who benefit from this value creation. The view that the only purpose of a business is to make a profit does not reflect the final objective of business, but is merely one answer in the ongoing debate about which stakeholders should be the beneficiaries of the value created by business.[5] The emphasis on profit as the objective of business is related to the idea that a business should create value for its shareholders. By creating profits, the business is able to pay shareholders a return on their investment in the form of dividends. Profits also create opportunities for increasing the market valuation of the company, which in turn increases the value of shareholders' shares in the company.

The view that shareholders should be the only party to benefit from the value creation of business is, however, flawed. Unless a number of other stakeholders also benefit simultaneously from the process of value creation, the business will not be a viable or sustainable enterprise.[6] A first group of stakeholders who should benefit from the process of value creation comprises the consumers of the products or services that the business provides. Unless the products or services provide value to them, they are unlikely to keep on supporting the business. The employees of the business also need to benefit from the process of value creation. Unless they share in the value created by the business, they will not be willing to devote their productive capacity to the business. The extent to which they benefit from the value created through their productive efforts also will have an impact on their levels of motivation and commitment to the business. In a similar fashion, suppliers, creditors, and other stakeholders need to benefit from the process of value creation in order to remain committed to playing their respective roles. There is thus a host of at least contractual stakeholders who need to benefit from the value created by a business in order to ensure the sustainability of any business.

Besides these contractual stakeholders, there are also non-contractual stakeholders who need to derive benefit from the business, or who should at least not be harmed by the business. Should the business become a negative value or a liability to them, the viability of the business will be jeopardized and its ultimate sustainability compromised. Amongst these non-contractual stakeholders count local communities, special interest groups, the natural environment, and the state.

The notion that business should create value for a range of contractual and non-contractual stakeholders and not merely for one stakeholder group, namely shareholders, is reflected in a number of recent developments. The current emphasis on inclusive corporate governance models, triple bottom-line reporting, corporate citizenship, and corporate social responsibility testifies to the growing conviction that the objective of business is sustainable value creation for a wide range of stakeholders.

It is, however, important to emphasize that the value creation should be sustainable. The value that various stakeholders derive from the activities of the business should not be such that it undermines the ability of the business to keep on generating value. Unless the business remains profitable it cannot sustain its operations and consequently also not its creation of value for its stakeholders. Should it become unprofitable, it is no longer a value to its stakeholders but a liability, with adverse consequences for all its contractual stakeholder groups and for some of its non-contractual ones as well. In order to look after the interests of all stakeholders who stand to benefit from their relation with the business, the business must also care about its own interest.

The above discussion has made it clear that the purpose of a business is sustainable value creation. It has also made it clear that a business has a moral obligation to ensure that its stakeholders benefit from, or at least are not harmed by, its activities. It simultaneously has a moral obligation to itself to ensure that it remains a profitable and therefore sustainable value-creating enterprise.[7] This purpose of a business, with its ensuing moral obligations, has a direct bearing on how a business will deal with the foreseeable negative side-effects of its business activities. Given the stakeholder view of business discussed above, it is beyond dispute that a business has the moral obligation to minimize the negative side-effects that its activities might have on its contractual and non-contractual stakeholders. But, given its purpose of value creation, typical value creation considerations also have a role to play in the moral deliberations on minimizing negative side-effects. Since these value creation considerations are not part of typical just war deliberations on double effect, they mark a disanalogy that should be taken into account when transferring the principle of double effect from its just war context to the domain of international business.

Disanalogy 2: Unilateral versus multilateral engagement

The nature of war is such that decisions about military engagement and the moral implications thereof have to be made unilaterally. At the point when decisions on military operations have to be made, negotiations between the warring parties have already broken down. The party that is about to be attacked is thus excluded from the planning of the attack and also from the moral deliberations about the foreseeable consequences of the attack. In the case of allied operations, of course, the allied parties are engaged in these deliberations, but that does not change the fact that the party against whom the offensive is intended (the victim) is excluded.

This necessitates a moral decision-making strategy that is unilateral in nature. The party planning the offensive needs to decide on its own what the foreseeable consequences of the military operation could be and whether these consequences are morally justifiable. In such a situation, a casuistic approach works well because it structures and disciplines one's thinking. It is a useful mechanism for ensuring that one attends to the most pertinent moral concerns that are relevant to such situations. The principle of double effect is a good example of such a casuistic approach. The six principles that should guide moral decision-making in this unilateral process are the following:

1. the action is in itself legitimate;
2. the actor intends only positive effects;
3. the negative effects are not means to achieve the positive effects;
4. the good effects outweigh, or are proportionally greater than, the negative ones;
5. active measures are taken to prevent or minimize the negative side-effects; and
6. the negative effects are inescapable (there are no other ways of achieving the intended effects).

By applying these principles to the situation beforehand, the party planning the offensive can ensure that the intended operation complies with the moral norms of just war.

International business is in this respect very different from war. The disanalogy lies in the fact that business has the possibility of engaging with those who might be affected by the foreseeable negative consequences of its actions. This possibility has important implications for the moral decision-making process that should be followed. When the opportunity exists of engaging with those who might be harmed by one's actions, it is morally preferable, if not imperative, to involve them in the process of moral deliberation. Thus, in the case of international business, there is no need to engage in unilateral moral deliberation because the possibility for bilateral or even multilateral deliberation exists.

Philosophically, the need to engage the "other" in moral deliberation has been made convincingly by Dwight Furrow in his book *Against theory*.[8] Drawing on the work of Emmanuel Levinas and Jean-François Lyotard in particular, Furrow argues that ethical principles, despite their pretension to be objective, tend to be parochial and impose ethical preferences and ethical interpretations upon others. One's own ethical standards, although parochial and self-referential in nature, are inevitably universalized as norms for others. In this way, the other's ethical experience and understanding are excluded; the ethical voice of the other is silenced. Consequently, unilateral ethical deliberations, despite the best and noblest intentions, contribute to ethical blind spots and assume narcissistic proportions. To counter these, it is morally imperative to allow the face and the voice of the other in unilateral moral deliberation.

The need to include the other in moral deliberation also receives philosophical support from the discourse ethics tradition. Discourse ethics emphasize that we should not rely merely on abstract or universal ethical principles in processes of unilateral moral decision-making. Instead emphasis is placed on the dialogical process of moral deliberation. Jürgen Habermas's ideal speech situation is a prime example of an attempt to embed moral deliberation in a process of tolerant and open rational dialogue in which the voices of all participants can be heard despite inequalities in power.[9] By structuring moral dialogue in this way, it is hoped that participants will be able to establish discursive provisional moral norms that can guide responsible conduct.

These philosophical concerns about moral deliberation seem to have found their way into the mainstream of corporate discourse. The possibility of engaging the other – that is, those who are not party to one's actions but who are nevertheless affected by them – in moral deliberation has been significantly enhanced by the emergence of inclusive models of corporate governance. The *King report on corporate governance for South Africa 2002*[10] is a good example of such an inclusive corporate governance approach and is often hailed as a landmark in the development of such approaches.[11] The inclusive approach stands in direct opposition to exclusive corporate governance approaches, which are characterized by their insistence that corporations should be run with the sole intention of serving the interests of shareholders. The inclusive approach, in contrast, maintains that a wider range of stakeholder interests should be provided for. Although there is no doubt that corporations should look after the interests of their shareholders, they need to go beyond that and also attend to the interests of all their other stakeholders. Within this context, a stakeholder can be defined as any party that either affects the corporation or is affected by it.

Looking after the interests of stakeholders implies that corporations should actively determine the concerns and perceptions of their various stakeholder groups. Corporations therefore need to engage actively with them and allow their voices to be heard in the deliberations to determine what responsible corporate behaviour entails.

It is exactly this opportunity for stakeholder engagement that can disappear from the moral radar screen if due consideration is not given to the important disanalogy between war and business, namely that moral deliberation in war is by necessity unilateral, whereas in international business it need not be like that. Or, to be even more specific, corporations do not have to deliberate on their own about the possible foreseeable negative side-effects of their actions, but can engage directly with those they suspect might be affected negatively to find out how they perceive the corporation's intended action. In such proactive stakeholder engagement the corporation might learn of more side-effects – both positive and negative – that it had not initially foreseen given its lack of knowledge of host country realities.

The above disanalogy does not mean that the principle of double effect and the casuistic guidelines for dealing with it are irrelevant to international business. It does, however, have important implications for how the principle of double effect is to be used in the context of international business. I shall attend to those implications in the concluding part of this chapter.

Disanalogy 3: Home versus host jurisdiction

When a campaign of war waged by one party on the territory of another country is compared with international business, where a home country expands its business to a host country, a third disanalogy emerges. In the case of war, the home country is not subject to the jurisdiction of the enemy country on whose territory the war is waged. It is subject only to the jurisdiction of the home country and to international conventions on war. Consequently it does not have to factor compliance with the jurisdiction of the enemy country into its moral deliberations. Whether the jurisdiction of the enemy is contravened or not in the act of war is not a relevant factor.

In the case of international business the situation is very different. The international corporation that faces decisions about its moral obligations in a host country is not above the jurisdiction of the host country but subject to it. Thus compliance with the host country jurisdiction needs to be factored into the company's moral deliberations. This complicates the process of moral decision-making and justification because it adds a dimension that is not considered in the case of war. This complication becomes particularly severe where the host country jurisdiction constitutes violations of human rights or the condoning thereof.

It might be tempting to avoid this complication by insisting on the distinction between morality and legality. It is possible to argue that host country judicial requirements do not necessarily impose moral obligations of compliance on international companies. It might even be argued that compliance with host country requirements would constitute immoral conduct on the part of the international company doing business there. The discrimination allowed in the apartheid era in South Africa is a case in point. By emphasizing that legality can never be equated with morality, companies doing business in South Africa could have argued that the immoral nature of the apartheid jurisdiction absolved them from the obligation to comply with that jurisdiction. Although the moral argument might be sound, matters are more complicated than the moral argument might initially suggest.

Even if the host country jurisdiction is perceived to be immoral, this does not automatically lead to the conclusion that it may be disobeyed. Besides the practical problems that illegal conduct would cause the business, there also is a moral issue at stake. Does the fact that a legal requirement is perceived to be immoral provide moral grounds for not adhering to it? Disobedience of laws on moral grounds – or civil disobedience as it is better known – has a long intellectual legacy. Suffice it to say that civil disobedience is a morally complex matter and an option that is generally considered to be a last resort after all legitimate means of resistance to the perceived immoral jurisdiction have been exhausted. Deliberate illegal conduct is a grave matter that can contribute to a general spirit of lawlessness and ultimately to the collapse of the rule of law, with adverse moral consequences. Consequently it is a course of action that should be avoided as long as other options remain viable.

The situation that international companies with operations in South Africa had to face during the apartheid era illustrates this well. Even if they were able to find ways of not participating in discriminatory practices, and thus were not party to human rights abuses, they nevertheless were perceived through their mere presence in the country to be lending legitimacy to the apartheid regime. Also, by creating revenue, they were perceived as assisting the apartheid regime to survive the international economic sanctions campaign. By not disinvesting they were undermining an international initiative to end apartheid, and thus were party to prolonging the life of an illegitimate regime. This is a clear example of a foreseeable negative side-effect.

Let us suppose a company were able to meet all six casuistic requirements of the principle of double effect discussed earlier in this chapter. The company would then be able to claim that the positive effects of its decision not to disinvest proportionally outweigh the foreseeable negative side-effects. The possibility of reaching such a decision is recognized by Wiggen and Bomann-Larsen in chapter 1 of this volume, where they say that "staying away from all difficult spots is hardly a solution for the private sector in the developing countries". Nevertheless, operating within the jurisdiction of an oppressive regime would still remain an un-addressed ethical issue.

This problem was clearly recognized by the Rev. Leon Sullivan's principles. In his set of 10 guidelines for ethical corporate behaviour in South Africa, Sullivan encouraged corporations not to be party to discriminatory practices in their own operations. Simultaneously he also called upon them to exert reformatory pressure on the South African government to end the institutionalization of racial discrimination. It is clear from the ultimatum that Rev. Sullivan issued that this obligation to exert reformatory pressure on an immoral regime to improve its human rights record was part of the moral justification for a continued presence in South Africa. If companies were not successful in obtaining the required reform by a specified date, they were expected to close down their operations in South Africa unconditionally.[12]

Applied to the issue of foreseeable negative side-effects, the casuistic guidelines developed for dealing with double effect in war indicate the impact of this disanalogy. The clash between home and host country jurisdictions is not recognized as a significant moral issue and consequently is not being dealt with. In order to transfer the principle of double effect and its casuistic guidelines from its original just war context to the domain of international business, this disanalogy needs to be taken into consideration. I discuss the implications in the concluding section.

Conclusion

The purpose of discussing the disanalogies between war and business was to determine whether the disanalogies are sufficiently substantial to make transfer of the principle of double effect from the just war context to the context of international business problematic. My contention is that these disanalogies are indeed substantial enough to caution against a direct transfer of the casuistic rules developed within the just war context for dealing with negative side-effects. Although the analogies between war and business do provide grounds for comparing war to business, the disanalogies show that the principles for dealing with double effect need to be adapted to the context of international business. They cannot be transferred unaltered from war to business.

In my view, the disanalogies warrant changes to three aspects of the principle of double effect when transferred from war to business. The first change concerns the parameters within which moral deliberation on double effect takes place. The second change deals with the manner in which moral decisions on double effect are taken. And the third change relates to the content of the casuistic rules for dealing with double effect.

The disanalogy in purpose between war and business provides the grounds for introducing specific parameters within which moral deliberation on double effect within international business should take place. Because the purpose of business is value creation, deliberations about double effect should be conducted within the parameters of the value creation discourse. Although there is no doubt about the moral obligation of business to ameliorate the foreseeable negative side-effects of its activities, this obligation must be dealt with in a way that does not undermine the value-creating potential of the business. If the obligation to deal with double effect jeopardizes the sustainability of the business, some trade-off must be found between the obligation to deal with negative side-effects and the business's quest to remain a sustainably value-creating enterprise. A compromise of some sort is thus required whereby profitability might be impaired but not to the extent that it threatens the survival of the business. This does not preclude the possibility of either closing operations down or shifting them elsewhere in cases where business cannot find a sustainable way of ameliorating negative side-effects. Disinvestment should thus never be excluded as an option.

The disanalogy between unilateral moral deliberation in war and the possibility of multilateral deliberation in business provides the grounds for a change in the manner in which moral deliberation is conducted. Unlike parties at war, who do not have the option of engaging with those who will be affected by negative side-effects, business does have this option. Given the danger of moral blind spots that always accompanies unilateral decision-making, business should engage with the foreseeable others who might suffer the negative consequences of double effect and engage them in the corporation's process of moral deliberation. This disanalogy thus imposes a moral obligation on corporations to engage with their stakeholders in a dialogical process of moral deliberation.

The disanalogy that results from business being subject to the jurisdiction of host countries, whereas compliance with jurisdictions of enemy countries is not required in war, calls for an extra provision to be added to the existing six casuistic guidelines for dealing with negative side-effects. When negative side-effects are caused by a jurisdiction that violates human rights or condones the abuse thereof, then there is an added obligation on the corporation to exert pressure on the host country government to improve its human rights record. It is thus suggested that a seventh guideline for dealing with double effect in international business should be introduced. It is proposed that it reads as follows:

When negative side-effects are caused by jurisdictions that abuse human rights, companies doing business there must exert pressure on such jurisdictions to improve their human rights record.

These changes to the parameters, manner, and content of the guidelines for dealing with double effect could turn the principle of double effect inherited from the just war tradition into a useful instrument to assist international business in dealing with the negative side-effects that it inevitably has to face.

Notes

1. P. Kotler, G. Armstrong, J. Saunders and V. Wong, *Principles of marketing* (Essex: Prentice Hall, 2001), pp. 425–429; G. Luffman, E. Lea, S. Sanderson and B. Kenny, *Strategic management: An analytical introduction*, 3rd edn. (Oxford: Blackwell, 1996), pp. 49–52; A. A. Thompson and A. J. Strickland III, *Strategic management: Concepts and cases*, 9th edn. (Boston: Irwin McGraw-Hill, 1996), pp. 139–141.
2. Gregory M. Reichberg, "The hard questions of international business: Some guidelines from the ethics of war", in Heidi von Weltzien Høivik (ed.), *Moral leadership in action. Building and sustaining moral competence in European organizations* (Cheltenham: Edward Elgar, 2002), pp. 304–318.
3. P. Van Veuren, "Fallacious arguments", in D. Rossouw (ed.), *Intellectual tools: Skills for the human sciences* (Pretoria: Amabhuku, 2000), pp. 42–50.
4. See Reichberg and Syse, chapter 2 in this volume.
5. Milton Friedman, "The social responsibility of business is to increase its profits", *New York Times Magazine*, 13 September 1970, pp. 32–33, 122–126.
6. W. M. Evan and R. E. Freeman, "A stakeholder theory of the modern corporation: Kantian capitalism", in T. L. Beauchamp and N. E. Bowie (eds.), *Ethical theory and business* (Englewood Cliffs, N.J.: Prentice Hall, 1993), pp. 75–84; A. Etzioni, "A communitarian note on stakeholder theory", *Business Ethics Quarterly* 8(4), 1998, pp. 679–691.
7. D. Rossouw, *Business ethics in Africa* (Cape Town: Oxford University Press, 2002), p. 4.
8. Dwight Furrow, *Against theory: Continental and analytic challenges in moral philosophy* (London: Routledge, 1995).
9. Jürgen Habermas, *Justification and application: Remarks on discourse ethics* (Cambridge: Polity Press, 1993).
10. Institute of Directors, *King report on corporate governance for South Africa 2002* (Johannesburg: IOD, 2002).
11. KPMG, *Corporate governance 2001 in South Africa* (Johannesburg: KPMG, 2001).
12. N. E. Bowie, "Business ethics and cultural relativism", in P. Madsen and J. M. Shafritz (eds.), *Essentials of business ethics* (New York: Penguin Books, 1990), pp. 366–382.

4

State responsibility, corporate responsibility, and complicity in human rights violations

Andrew Clapham

Introduction

This chapter takes a legal approach to the question of corporate responsibility. The chapter is designed to complement the philosophical and historical approaches being developed in the chapters addressing the "harmful side-effects of corporate activity". Some of the same concepts that are central to the philosophical debate are examined in their legal context. For example, questions of complicity, participation, intention, foreseeability, necessity, and proportionality all arise in the context of international criminal law. It is not suggested that the legal framework is the only framework of relevance for an understanding of corporate responsibility; in many situations the ethical or moral arguments will be more persuasive for corporate actors. The international criminal law framework builds in significant guarantees for defendants to ensure that individuals are not deprived of their liberty in unfair or unjust ways. A criminal law approach may therefore sometimes protect an entity from punishment where a morally based framework might hold the same "accused" blameworthy. In determining how corporations should act, international criminal law may provide some clear indications as to when a corporation or its officers will be liable in law. On the other hand, international criminal law should not be seen as the only framework; companies may have moral, operational, and utilitarian reasons for promoting and respecting human rights.

We will focus in this chapter on the difficult area of corporate complicity in international crimes committed by others. But before tackling the emerging legal regimes that govern this area, we should consider simpler cases in order to distinguish them. We will therefore start with a quick overview of the corporation in the context of general public international law of state responsibility as applied between states. We will first consider two different situations: situations in which a state is responsible for the acts of a corporation, and situations in which the state has a responsibility to protect people from the acts of corporations. Having considered the role of the corporation in this context, we will then move on to the question of crimes under international law. We will suggest that some international crimes could give rise to direct responsibilities under international law for the corporations themselves. We only then turn to the trickier issue of corporate complicity in crimes committed by others. In particular, we shall have to see how much participation is required under international law for an international criminal court to find an accomplice guilty of a crime where the principal perpetrator was someone else. In addition, we shall have to confront the question of what sort of intention triggers responsibility in this context.

Corporations in international law

The question of whether corporations are subjects of international law has given rise to a lively academic debate.[1] In the field of human rights it is becoming clear that international human rights standards can be applied to the behaviour of corporations, even if some lawyers would prefer that, "[w]hen non-State actors do not comply with human rights norms, they should be criticized for 'abusing' the rights of individuals rather than committing 'violations'".[2] But the reasons for such a distinction are, at least according to Weissbrodt, seemingly tactical and political rather than imbued with legal meaning: "The term 'human rights violation' should be limited to misconduct by governments, so as to avoid giving greater recognition and undue status to non-State entities."[3] Of course, in legal terms the corporation is sometimes assimilated to other non-state entities such as rebel groups and terrorists, hence the nervousness about placing non-state actors on the same plane as nation-states.

The question is essentially one of doctrine and, as we shall see, doubts around the doctrinal issues have not prevented courts from applying international law to the behaviour of corporations. Suffice it to say here that it is now beyond doubt that individuals (natural persons) have duties under international law not to commit international crimes;[4] corporations (legal persons), at least according to the present author, may have similar duties under international criminal law. Whether or not we decide that corporations could be subjects of international law, it is clear that in certain contexts corporations can act on the international legal plane, by bringing complaints before the European Court of Human Rights, by submitting disputes to the International Centre for the Settlement of Investment Disputes at the World Bank, or by becoming parties to disputes before the Tribunal for the Law of the Sea. States have clearly foreseen that corporations may have enough legal capacity to enjoy rights and duties on the international stage.

It is also clear that in certain cases their illegal acts may be attributed to the state under the law of state responsibility; and in a later section we will consider the mirror situation: when can a corporation be held responsible for participating in the illegal acts of a state? The rules of attribution are not the same. Let us now first consider the rules of state responsibility for corporate acts.

The international law of state responsibility

The international law of state responsibility is developing to cover privatized state corporations that retain public or regulatory functions. In 2001, the articles on "Responsibility of States for internationally wrongful acts" were finally adopted by the International Law Commission and annexed to a General Assembly Resolution.[5] Already in the early days of the process of drafting these articles, around 1930, the German government suggested that the principles of state responsibility could apply exceptionally to situations in which the state authorizes private organizations to carry out certain sovereign rights. The example it gave at that time was of a private railway company being permitted to maintain a police force. The International Law Commission (ILC) cited this example in 1974, in the context of its own work on state responsibility. But today, in an age of privatized detention centres, prison transfers, airports, housing associations, and even water services, the image of private railway police is only a starting point. The final Commentary of the International Law Commission gives a wide scope to the sorts of entities that could fall within the scope of the relevant Article, Article 5 of the Articles on State Responsibility. This Article is aimed at attributing state responsibility for the activities of what the ILC labels "the increasingly common phenomenon of para-statal entities which exercise elements of governmental authority in place of State organs, as well as situations where former State corporations have been privatized but retain certain public or regulatory functions".[6] Article 5 reads: "The conduct of a person or entity which is not an organ of the State under article 4 but which is empowered by the law of that State to exercise elements of the governmental authority shall be considered an act of the State under international law, provided the person or entity is acting in that capacity in the particular instance." The Commentary explains the intended scope of this article:

(2) The generic term "entity" reflects the wide variety of bodies which, though not organs, may be empowered by the law of a State to exercise elements of governmental authority. They may include public corporations, semi-public entities, public agencies of various kinds and even, in special cases, private companies, provided that in each case the entity is empowered by the law of the State to exercise functions of a public character normally exercised by State organs, and the conduct of the entity relates to the exercise of the governmental authority concerned. For example in some countries private security firms may be contracted to act as prison guards and in that capacity may exercise public powers such as powers of detention and discipline pursuant to a judicial sentence or to prison regulations.

An examination of the comments received from governments, and of the statements made at the General Assembly during the debate on the Articles, gives no reason to doubt that states do not consider these formulations as reflecting the current approach of international law to this topic. The state will be responsible at the international level for the acts and omissions of these privatized entities where such behaviour constitutes an internationally wrongful act and the entity was "acting in that capacity in the particular instance". We have then two cumulative tests: first, the entity must be empowered under internal law, and, second, the conduct must have concerned "governmental activity and not other private or commercial activity in which the entity may engage".[7] The state will be responsible for the acts of these empowered non-state actors where they carry out governmental activity, but not commercial activity. The example given by the ILC is that the exercise of police powers granted to a railway company will be regarded as acts of state under international law, but activity unrelated to those powers, such as the sale of tickets, will not be attributable to the state.[8] The state is responsible for the acts of non-state actors only when they have been empowered to exercise governmental authority and are in fact acting in such a capacity.

The International Law Commission has avoided trying to list what constitutes fields of governmental authority. Instead, it simply states:

Beyond a certain limit, what is regarded as "governmental" depends on the particular society, its history and traditions. Of particular importance will be not just the content of the powers, but the way they are conferred on an entity, the purposes for which they are to be exercised and the extent to which the entity is accountable to government for their exercise. These are essentially questions of the application of a general standard to varied circumstances.[9]

Article 5 covers those entities that have been privatized or granted governmental powers by internal law. The Commentary concludes in this way: "The internal law in question must specifically authorize the conduct as involving the exercise of public authority; it is not enough that it permits activity as part of the general regulation of the affairs of the community. It is accordingly a narrow category."[10]

There is, however, another category of cases that is not so narrow. Where a state actually controls or directs a company to act in a certain way, then there will be state responsibility for the acts of the company if there is evidence that the corporation was exercising public powers or that the state was using its ownership interest in, or control of, a corporation specifically in order to achieve a particular result. This is the conclusion of the ILC in its commentary to Article 8: "The conduct of a person or group of persons shall be considered an act of a State under international law if the person or group of persons is in fact acting on the instructions of, or under the direction or control of, that State in carrying out the conduct."

In these different categories of cases the state may be responsible under international law. This is important because not only do all the rules regarding countermeasures by other states apply, meaning that states would be entitled to sanction the culpable state in ways that would otherwise be illegal, but it also means that, where human rights bodies exist, such as the seven UN human rights treaty bodies or the regional human rights Courts, then the state can be held accountable for the behaviour of the company. Although the possibilities for individual complaints vary under each treaty and according to the optional procedures accepted by various states, the principle remains that states are accountable for the acts of corporations that violate international law. So far the issue has been touched on only in the context of airport noise and corporal punishment in private schools before the European Court of Human Rights,[11] and with regard to private prison health and education services at the level of the UN human rights treaty bodies,[12] but it is likely to become a primary method of accountability as more and more services are either privatized or handed over to the private sector.

The positive obligations of the state under international human rights law

The different regional human rights bodies have developed a set of positive obligations that oblige states to act to protect individuals and groups from private actors including corporations. The extent to which human rights law should be seen as encompassing such obligations was discussed at the time of the drafting of treaties such as the International Covenant on Civil and Political Rights,[13] and it is now clear that state responsibility at the international level is engaged not only through acts but also through omissions, and that failure to act to prevent, investigate, or punish certain human rights abuses committed by private actors will result in a finding that the state has failed in its international human rights obligations. This sort of indirect accountability for corporations is often overlooked as one considers the ability of the human rights regime to deal with corporate accountability. Nevertheless, greater attention is now being paid to the potential for the UN treaty bodies and the mechanisms of the International Labour Organization (ILO) to address the issues of state responsibility for these governmental omissions and the consequent indirect accountability of the corporations themselves.[14] At the regional level there have been several interesting developments.

Let us first consider a decision of the African Commission on Human and Peoples' Rights in 2001. The African Commission was faced with a complaint focused on the behaviour of an oil consortium between the state oil company and Shell in Nigeria.[15] According to the summary (para. 2):

The Communication alleges that the oil consortium has exploited oil reserves in Ogoniland with no regard for the health or environment of the local communities, disposing toxic wastes into the environment and local waterways in violation of applicable international environmental standards. The consortium also neglected and/or failed to maintain its facilities causing numerous avoidable spills in the proximity of villages. The resulting contamination of water, soil and air has had serious short and long-term health impacts, including skin infections, gastrointestinal and respiratory ailments, and increased risk of cancers, and neurological and reproductive problems.

The Commission found violations of the African Charter of Human and Peoples' Rights in several respects, but, in particular, it referred to the obligations of states with regard to private actors in the context of the people's rights to natural resources and the right to food. With regard to the first set of obligations, the Commission stated (para. 58):

The Commission notes that in the present case, despite its obligation to protect persons against interferences in the enjoyment of their rights, the Government of Nigeria facilitated the destruction of the Ogoniland. Contrary to its Charter obligations and despite such internationally established principles, the Nigerian Government has given the green light to private actors, and the oil Companies in particular, to devastatingly affect the well-being of the Ogonis. By any measure of standards, its practice falls short of the minimum conduct expected of governments, and therefore, is in violation of Article 21 of the African Charter.

With regard to the right to food, the Commission found (para. 65):

The right to food is inseparably linked to the dignity of human beings and is therefore essential for the enjoyment and fulfilment of such other rights as health, education, work and political participation. The African Charter and international law require and bind Nigeria to protect and improve existing food sources and to ensure access to adequate food for all citizens. Without touching on the duty to improve food production and to guarantee access, the minimum core of the right to food requires that the Nigerian Government should not destroy or contaminate food sources. It should not allow private parties to destroy or contaminate food sources, and prevent peoples' efforts to feed themselves.

There are reasons to believe that the Commission will continue to develop its approach to these issues, demanding that human rights are protected not only from the state but also from the activities of corporations and other non-state actors in the private sphere.[16]

In Europe, the European Court of Human Rights has had occasion to address the positive obligations of states in a number of contexts.[17] We might just mention here that states have been found in violation of their obligations in the context of the right to enjoy private and family life. For example, the Spanish local authorities failed to regulate the operation of a waste treatment plant, resulting in interference with respect for the applicants' home, private, and family life.[18] Similarly, Italy was held to have violated the European Convention on Human Rights when it failed to provide effective protection for the applicants with regard to toxic substances released from a factory. The failure to provide relevant information about pollution from the plant to the applicants resulted in a violation of their rights to privacy.[19]

In another set of cases, the European Court of Human Rights has clearly stated that the rights in the Convention create obligations for states that involve "the adoption of measures designed to secure respect for private life *even in the sphere of the relations of individuals between themselves*".[20] This has also been affirmed by the Court in the context of the right to counter-demonstrate: "Like Article 8, Article 11 sometimes requires positive measures to be taken, even in the sphere of relations between individuals, if need be."[21] The statements by the Court that the Convention covers the sphere of relations between private individuals has had important consequences beyond the scope of state responsibility for positive obligations as determined in that international court. First, the extension into the private sphere implicitly demands that we consider the actual obligations of these private actors between themselves.[22] We can judge the failure of the state to intervene only if we know the sorts of obligation that are owed to individuals by other private actors. Second, the extension of the scope of human rights into the private sphere has meant that, when national courts have occasion to deal with a complaint against a private actor, they will consider that that actor has human rights obligations stemming from the European Convention. This is sometimes known as the horizontal, or *Drittwirkung*, effect of the Convention.[23]

International crimes

International law has for some time served to tackle individual criminal responsibility for certain acts committed by individuals: slavery, genocide, crimes against humanity, and torture. International law attaches to certain non-state actors irrespective of their links to the state. Article I of the Genocide Convention of 1948 confirms that "genocide, whether committed in time of peace or in time of war, is a crime under international law". Article IV reminds us that persons committing acts of genocide shall be punished "whether they are constitutionally responsible rulers, public officials or private individuals". In other words, international law can fix obligations on the individual, and the violation of these obligations will be punishable at the national and international level.

We have already suggested that international law does not confine its reach to states and individuals. The draft Statute for the International Criminal Court before the delegates at the start of the Rome Conference in 1998 actually included a paragraph in brackets that ensured the possibility of trying "legal persons, with the exception of States, when the crimes were committed on behalf of such legal persons or by their agents or representatives".[24] Although this paragraph did not survive,[25] there is no reason to believe that international law cannot attach to non-state actors in the form of legal persons. The point is that international law may be concerned with the duties of individuals in both their public and their private capacities, and that international law could easily extend this concern to transnational corporations. Although there are only rare instances of an international tribunal where a corporation could be the respondent in a dispute (such as a case before the Seabed Disputes Chamber of the Law of the Sea Tribunal[26]), corporations can still be the bearer of international duties outside the context of international courts and tribunals. Lack of international jurisdiction to try a corporation should not necessarily mean that the corporation is under no international legal obligation. Nor does it mean that we cannot speak about transnational corporations breaking international law. For present purposes, we shall concentrate on the rules which could be applicable to corporate violations of international criminal law and corporate complicity in others' violations of international criminal law.

The Alien Tort Claims Act in the United States

This vision that corporations can violate international law has led to an interesting string of cases before the US courts under a piece of US legislation known as the Alien Tort Claims Act 1789. The origins of this piece of legislation are misty and have been the subject of conjecture as legal scholars have applied their imagination to events over 200 years ago.[27] Nevertheless, the effects of the Act today are very real as corporations find themselves as defendants facing multi-million dollar suits. The Alien Tort Claims Act (ATCA) confers upon the Federal District Courts original jurisdiction over "any civil action by an alien for a tort only, committed in violation of the law of nations" (28 United States Code [USC] §1350). A number of claims are currently pending or on appeal in relation to various oil companies accused of, among other things, forced labour, torture, and rape.[28]

The application of this Statute to the activities of multinational corporations abroad is not without its critics;[29] indeed the United States and other governments have recently filed objections in the Federal Courts objecting to the exercise of such jurisdiction.[30] But the evolving law on the application of the Alien Tort Claims Act is affecting not only the cases before the courts but also the sense of the parameters of legal liability in this area. This in turn affects the way that corporations and non-governmental organizations determine the meanings to be given to promises and undertakings (such as those found in the UN Global Compact) to (1) respect and protect human rights, and (2) avoid complicity in human rights abuses. It would be wrong to see the development of the law as hinging solely on the evolving interpretation of the Alien Tort Claims Act. Other jurisdictional statutes include the Torture Victims Protection Act (28 USC §1350) and the Racketeer Influenced and Corrupt Organizations Act (18 USC §1961). Both these Acts are also being used in the US courts against multinationals accused of participating in human rights violations outside the United States.

In the simple situation where a corporation's activities actually constitute genocide or slavery, the issue is clear. The corporation will have violated international criminal law and can at present apparently be held accountable in the US courts under the Alien Tort Claims Act. The US courts have been gradually refining the list of violations of the "law of nations" that attach to non-state actors as such. Accordingly, recent rulings have determined that genocide, slave trading, slavery, forced labour, and war crimes are actionable even in the absence of any connection to state action.[31] In addition, according to the *Kadic* v. *Karadzic* judgment in the US courts, where rape, torture, and summary execution are committed in isolation these crimes "are actionable under the Alien Tort Act, without regard to state action, to the extent they were committed in pursuit of genocide or war crimes".[32] An alien can sue in tort before the US Federal Courts under the Alien Tort Claims Act with regard to any of these international crimes. In fact the list is not exclusive because international criminal law continues to evolve. For example, the assumption that the crime of torture is confined to state officials has been rebutted as the Appeal Chamber of the International Criminal Court for the Former Yugoslavia has recently confirmed that there is no need for a public official to be involved for a private individual to be responsible under international law for the international crime of torture.[33]

However, such simple cases of a corporation being sued under the ATCA in the US courts as the primary perpetrator of such international crimes are rare, and, in any event, would be likely to be settled out of court if the facts were clear. Most of the cases that have recently been contested before the United States' courts concern situations where corporations are alleged to have aided and abetted a state in governmental violations of international criminal law. In other words, the cases turn on accomplice liability, or complicity.

Complicity

The corporate complicity cases before the US courts have become central to an understanding of the scope of corporate responsibility and accountability. Although the scope of the legal liability under the Alien Tort Claims Act is not congruent with the expectations currently placed on corporations by the corporate responsibility movement, the evolving case law at least points to a minimum standard that companies transgress at their peril, as there may be a group of plaintiffs ready to sue in the US courts. In addition, the developing case law has been used to help sketch the contours of corporate human rights responsibilities.

To take just one example, the Danish Human Rights and Business Project report, *Defining the scope of business responsibility for human rights abroad*,[34] contains the following passage:

In the modern world, the decisions taken by a business can have major implications for lives and communities geographically and culturally remote, so businesses do have to be discerning in identifying their indirect connection to violations. For example, in the early 1990s several international oil companies undertook a joint venture with the Burmese government and the state oil company, Myanmar Oil and Gas Enterprise (MOGE). MOGE assumed responsibility for providing labour and security for the construction of a gas pipeline for the project. Allegations later emerged that forced labour and child labour were used to construct the pipeline, and that other violations, including torture, and forced relocation, occurred in MOGE's operations to clear the area and provide security. Although the main Western partner, Unocal, did not directly carry out these purported violations itself, because of its involvement in the project, its liability for acting in concert with the Burmese government and MOGE in breaching universally recognised human rights standards is now under consideration in the United States District Court of California [*Nat'l Coalition Gov't of the Union of Burma v. Unocal Inc.*, 176 F.R.D. 329 (N.D. Cal. 1997)]. Businesses must, therefore, be alert to the extent to which they can be indirectly complicit in human rights violations.[35]

We will examine the 2002 Appeal Court judgment in the *Unocal* case in some detail, because it contains the most developed judicial reasoning on the concept of corporate complicity in international crimes. Before we turn to examine this case, it should be borne in mind that similar legal arguments have formed the basis for a number of well-known settlements involving the Swiss banks and German industrialists, as well as litigation in the United States against Japanese companies in relation to issues of slave labour in the Second World War.[36] The German Slave Labour Fund, jointly established by Germany and the firms, currently stands at US\$5.2 billion. These claims, together with similar claims made against the Swiss banks in the Holocaust Victims Assets Litigation (which have resulted in a Swiss fund of US\$1.25 billion), are based on the law developed during the Nuremberg trials of the industrialists and its application in the US courts. In and around 1999, more than 30 cases were brought against US, German, and Swiss companies, alleging complicity in Nazi era crimes, based on the original trials of the industrialists in Nuremberg. The latest round of claims concerns Swiss and US banks with regard to profits from business in South Africa from 1948 to 1993. The reported demand is for US\$50 billion.[37]

Corporate complicity in the Unocal ruling

There are various cases and rulings regarding the litigation concerning Unocal and its activity in Myanmar. The most important for present purposes is the ruling of the US Court of Appeals for the Ninth Circuit filed 18 September 2002. The case will in fact be reheard by the Court of Appeals with an expanded bench, but even if the ruling no longer stands the reasoning is worth examining in the present context. In the 2002 Unocal ruling, the Court of Appeals elaborated important clarifications concerning the elements of corporate complicity for the purposes of a suit under the ATCA alleging corporate liability for violations of international law.

In this case the plaintiffs allege that the Myanmar Military subjected them to forced labour, murder, rape, and torture. There are factual disputes concerning: whether the oil and gas company Unocal knew that the Myanmar Military were providing security, the influence of Unocal over the Military, and whether Unocal knew that the Military were committing human rights violations in connection with the project. Regardless of the eventual factual findings in this case, the Court of Appeals has clarified a number of issues.

First, on the question of whether a private actor such as Unocal could be liable for the violations of international law at issue, the Court has clarified with authority some of the ambiguous issues discussed above.

Thus, under Kadic, even crimes like rape, torture, and summary execution, which by themselves require state action for ATCA liability to attach, do not require state action when committed in furtherance of other crimes like slave trading, genocide or war crimes, which by themselves do not require state action for ATCA liability to attach. We agree with this view and apply it below to Plaintiffs' various ATCA claims.

The Court then concludes that forced labour is a modern form of slavery. In this way, forced labour falls among the international crimes that give rise to responsibility under international law, even in the absence of state action.

Second, and these are the parts that are of major interest in the present context, there are the legal tests that the Court applied in order to determine whether Unocal may eventually be ordered to pay damages for corporate complicity in violations of international law by the Myanmar authorities. The ruling states:

We hold that the standard for aiding and abetting under the ATCA is, as discussed below, knowing practical assistance or encouragement that has a substantial effect on the perpetration of the crime. We further hold that a reasonable factfinder could find that Unocal's conduct met this standard.[38]

On this point they disagreed with the lower court, which had demanded a higher test, that of "active participation" in the forced labour. What makes the case particularly interesting from an international perspective is that the tests have mostly been derived from the prosecutions for international crimes that followed the Second World War and the more recent international prosecutions by the ad hoc International Tribunals, established by the UN Security Council, with responsibility for prosecuting crimes committed in the former Yugoslavia and Rwanda. Although doubts were expressed about the appropriateness of using the case law from these recent ad hoc tribunals, it is the international criminal law of accomplice liability that lies at the centre of this litigation and other recent litigation in the United States concerning the accountability of Swiss banks and European insurance companies for atrocities committed during the Second World War.[39]

The Unocal ruling and the application of international criminal law on aiding and abetting

Although the claim in the national legal system is a tort, or civil claim, rather than a criminal claim, the Court of Appeals found it appropriate to use international criminal law rather than the law of the state where the events took place. In the present case, the Court pointed out that with regard to certain serious (*jus cogens*) violations of international law "the law of any particular state is either identical to the *jus cogens* norms of international law, or it is invalid".[40] As the Court found that the complaints in this case concerned *jus cogens*, the role for national law is minimized.[41]

We might here open a parenthesis to simply refer to the elaboration of the catalogue of *jus cogens* norms by the UN's International Law Commission. According to the Commission's Commentary to their Articles on State Responsibility:

So far, relatively few peremptory norms have been recognized as such. But various tribunals, national and international, have affirmed the idea of peremptory norms in contexts not limited to the validity of treaties. Those peremptory norms that are clearly accepted and recognized include the prohibitions of aggression, genocide, slavery, racial discrimination, crimes against humanity and torture, and the right to self-determination.[42]

In a later passage the Commentary adds the *basic rules of international humanitarian law*.[43] Our immediate concern is the elements that were seen to make up the complicity test in international criminal law, because it was these tests that the US Court of Appeals said were to be applied with regard to Unocal's activity in Myanmar. This was not really because international law was to be preferred, rather because "the standard for aiding and abetting in international criminal law is similar to the standard for aiding and abetting in domestic tort law".[44]

After a review of cases from the Yugoslavia and Rwanda International Tribunals, the Court focused on the test used in the *Furundzija* case and concluded that, based on the facts, they did not need to determine the minimum involvement required for accomplice liability:

we may impose aiding and abetting liability for knowing practical assistance or encouragement which has a substantial effect on the perpetration of the crime, leaving the question whether such liability should also be imposed for moral support which has the required substantial effect to another day.[45]

The international case law does in fact show that complicity in international crimes does not require full participation in the execution of the crime. The assistance given need not be necessary for the crime; we do not have to show that *but for* the assistance the crime would not have taken place. However, the support should have a "substantial effect" on the crime.

The US Court of Appeals examined the sort of support that Unocal is alleged to have given the Myanmar authorities in the context of the forced labour claims. Let us consider this under the two traditional headings in criminal law. First the *actus reus* (material element) and then the *mens rea* (subjective element).

The actus reus of complicity in the Unocal case

The ruling gives an indication of the sort of *practical assistance* that will be evidence of the material element of the crime:

The evidence also supports the conclusion that Unocal gave practical assistance to the Myanmar Military in subjecting Plaintiffs to forced labor.[46] The practical assistance took the form of hiring the Myanmar Military to provide security and build infrastructure along the pipeline route in exchange for money or food. The practical assistance also took the form of using photos, surveys, and maps in daily meetings to show the Myanmar Military where to provide security and build infrastructure.[47]

The Court found that this assistance had a *substantial effect* on the perpetration of the forced labour, and that the forced labour would most probably not have occurred in the same way "without someone hiring the Myanmar Military to provide security, and without someone showing them where to do it".[48] The Court paid particular attention to evidence from a representative of Unocal:

This conclusion is supported by the admission of Unocal Representative Robinson that "[o]ur assertion that [the Myanmar Military] has not *expanded and amplified its usual methods* around the pipeline *on our behalf* may not withstand much scrutiny," and by the admission of Unocal President Imle that "[i]f forced labor goes hand and glove with the military yes there will be *more forced labor.*"[49]

The Court applied a variation on a causation test. The participation by the company need not actually cause the violation of international law, but the assistance or encouragement has to be such that, without such participation, the violations *most probably* would not have occurred *in the same way*.

The 1998 Rome Statute for an International Criminal Court (ICC) contains no requirement that the assistance be either direct or substantial. According to Article 25, ordering, soliciting, or inducing any crime within the statute, which occurs or is attempted, gives rise to responsibility. In addition, aiding, abetting, or otherwise assisting gives rise to responsibility where this is done for the purpose of facilitating such a crime. Providing the means for commission of the crime is sufficient to give rise to responsibility as an accomplice in this context. However, it has been stated by one experienced commentator that the assistance need not be tangible, nor need the assistance have a "causal effect on the crime".[50]

The apparent requirement that there be support with *substantial effect* is not found in the new Rome Statute.[51] Furthermore the Statute includes accomplice liability not only for those who aid and abet but also for those who "otherwise assist". Because the complicity concept in the Statute is designed to cover those who act "for the purpose of facilitating" crimes, rather than those who make a direct and essential contribution to the commission of crime, we can conclude that the assistance provided has to meet only a very low threshold for there to be the objective element for accomplice liability under the ICC Statute even if, as we shall see in the next section, the subjective element may be more than mere knowledge of the crime.[52]

The US Court of Appeals and the mens rea (subjective or mental element) required for complicity in the Unocal case

The US Court of Appeals examined the evidence and applied a reasonable knowledge test. The requisite mental element for corporate complicity in these circumstances seems to be that the company knew or should have known that its acts assisted in the crime. The fact that a company benefits from the principal perpetrator's human rights violations has been emphasized and creates an important nexus.

[A] reasonable factfinder could also conclude that Unocal's conduct met the *mens rea* requirement of aiding and abetting as we define it today, namely, actual or constructive (i.e., reasonable) knowledge that the accomplice's actions will assist the perpetrator in the commission of the crime. The District Court found that

"[t]he evidence does suggest that Unocal knew that forced labor was being utilized and that the Joint Venturers benefitted from the practice." Moreover,
Unocal knew or should reasonably have known that its conduct – including the
payments and the instructions where to provide security and build infrastructure
– would assist or encourage the Myanmar Military to subject Plaintiffs to forced
labor.[53]

Non-criminal violations of human rights law

Not every claim regarding corporate complicity in governmental violations of human rights will involve international crimes. In such cases it
seems inappropriate to use international criminal law or even national
criminal law principles. For example, if the corporation is accused of assisting a government in restricting freedom of expression, neither the violation by the government nor the aid given by the company is, on its
own, an international crime. International law has not yet criminalized
violations of freedom of expression. Such a violation is rather an international tort or delict. The issue of corporate breaches of other types of
international law cannot be excluded as a possibility.[54]

The scope and detail of those non-criminal obligations as they relate to
transnational companies and other business entities have been elaborated in a set of Norms recently adopted by the UN Sub-Commission on
the Protection and Promotion of Human Rights and transmitted to the
UN Commission on Human Rights for consideration.[55] Based on an
amalgamation of existing standards, the Norms provide guidance as to
what sorts of obligations arise for corporations in the human rights
sphere. This concept is underdeveloped, but the issues are not wholly
academic. In the *Wiwa* v *Shell* case, several of the complicity complaints
against Shell concern Shell's involvement in such international torts. It is
to this issue that we now turn.

Wiwa v Shell *and the issue of complicity in international torts*

In *Wiwa* v *Royal Dutch Petroleum (Shell)*,[56] the plaintiffs alleged violations of international law in connection with the Nigerian government's
activities in the Ogoni region of Nigeria. The complaint was brought
against the oil companies and a named managing director for directing
and aiding the Nigerian government in violating the human rights of the
complainants. The allegations focus on the suppression of the Movement
for the Survival of the Ogoni people (MOSOP). It is alleged that Shell,
operating through Shell Nigeria, recruited the Nigerian police and military to suppress MOSOP. The company is said to have:

provided logistical support, transportation, and weapons to Nigerian authorities to attack Ogoni villages and stifle opposition to Shell's oil-excavation activities. Ogoni residents, including plaintiffs, were beaten, raped, shot, and/or killed during these raids. Jane Doe was beaten and shot during one raid in 1993, and Owens Wiwa was illegally detained.

In 1995, Ken Saro-Wiwa and John Kpuinen were hanged after being convicted of murder by a special tribunal. Defendants bribed witnesses to testify falsely at the trial, conspired with Nigerian authorities in meetings in Nigeria and the Netherlands to orchestrate the trial, and offered to free Ken Saro-Wiwa in return for an end to MOSOP's international protests against defendants. During the trial, members of Ken Saro-Wiwa's family, including his elderly mother, were beaten.[57]

Although the claims include allegations that Shell's conduct violated international law, including the law on crimes against humanity and torture, part of the claims concern violations "of the right to life, liberty and security of the person and peaceful assembly and association".[58] To the extent that the complaint relies on the participation by Shell in such violations of customary international law by Nigeria, we should be aware that such violations of international law would not all be international crimes but might nevertheless be violations of international law by Nigeria. Assisting in such violations would not therefore be addressed by international criminal law, because no international crime has been committed. Nevertheless, the claims suggest that the corporate activity could involve individual or corporate "civil responsibility" under international law.[59]

Because international law has focused so far on individual criminal responsibility and state "civil" responsibility, guidance on the international rules regarding "civil" responsibility may have to be sought in the developing law of state complicity as elaborated in the ILC's Articles on State Responsibility.

State responsibility for state complicity

In the law of state responsibility, the UN International Law Commission has redefined the scope of complicity as it relates to assistance by one state in the violation of international law by another state. In the articles adopted by the ILC in 2001, the relevant article reads as follows:

Article 16
Aid or assistance in the commission of an internationally wrongful act
A State which aids or assists another State in the commission of an internationally wrongful act by the latter is internationally responsible for doing so if:
(a) That State does so with knowledge of the circumstances of the internationally wrongful act; and
(b) The act would be internationally wrongful if committed by that State.

The Special Rapporteur, Crawford, introduced his work on this article by stating that it deals with "what in national law would be termed 'complicity', i.e. where one State provides aid or assistance to another State, thereby facilitating the commission of a wrongful act by the latter".[60] The emphasis is on actual assistance rather than advice, encouragement or incitement. The question arises whether the assistance has to be essential or merely facilitate the wrongful act. The Rapporteur dismisses the idea of a requirement that "the aid should have been an indispensable pre-requisite to the wrongdoing". This would, he said, "invite speculation as to other contingencies, and might create loopholes to the application of the rule".[61] The required connection between the aid and the wrongful act is explained in the final Commentary on Article 16. The Commentary states that it will be sufficient for the purposes of this complicity article if the aid or assistance "contributed *significantly* to that act".[62]

We should also note that the article limits complicity to situations where the accomplice state is already under an international obligation not to commit the assisted act. The picture becomes more complex when we try to determine what is wrongful for the various participants. Assuming for a moment that one can apply the ILC's complicity rule by analogy to corporate (non-state actor) accomplices, an assisting state, individual, or company may not have the same international obligations as the assisted state. It would then, at first sight, seem inappropriate to burden a corporation or an individual with an expectation of knowledge of *all* the international law obligations of the relevant assisted state. But these difficulties evaporate when we return to the most serious violations of international law. In the Nuremberg trials the attempt to claim that international law was too complicated for industrialists to understand proved to be no defence to those charges.[63] Can we extend this assumption of international law beyond international crimes such as war crimes and crimes against humanity? Can it be extended to international delicts (or non-criminal violations of international law)? In other words, should companies be expected to know what are the international human rights obligations of the state they are assisting?

As soon as we admit that the violations of customary international law that we are discussing are violations of human rights law, and that the sorts of violations that are alleged represent actions that are clearly wrong, the defence of ignorance of the law seems less viable. The human rights abuses that companies are accused of facilitating all relate to the fundamental human rights principles contained in the Universal Declaration of Human Rights. In the context of corporate social responsibility, the case has been made that all actors have to respect the Universal Declaration of Human Rights.[64] The Universal Declaration of Human

Rights is now regularly referred to by companies as part of human rights policy statements. Chris Avery, who maintains a website on business and human rights, has collected the company human rights policy statements that include explicit reference to the Universal Declaration of Human Rights. As of 28 November 2002, he included: ABB, Ahold, Balfour Beatty, BG Group, The Body Shop, BP, BT Group, CGNU Group, Conoco, the Co-operative Bank, Diageo, Freport-McMoRan, Ikea, National Grid, Norsk Hydro, Novo Group, Premier Oil, Reebok, Rio Tinto, Shell, Skanska, Stora Enso, Storebrand Group, Talisman Energy, Total-FinaElf, and Unocal.[65]

In sum, returning to the three limits regarding state complicity, first, one does not have to show that the assisting state shared the intention of the assisted state. What is required is knowledge of the circumstances of the internationally wrongful act. If we apply this rule by analogy to companies, one would not have to prove the intent of a company (a difficult and perplexing task in national criminal law[66]); one need merely show that the company knows the circumstances of the wrongful act. Second, to invoke the complicity of states in the wrongful acts of other states, one has to show that the aid actually facilitated the wrongful act and was given with a view to that purpose. However, one does not need to show that the aid was an essential contribution to a wrongful act. By analogy, one does not have to show that *but for* the corporate contribution the wrongful act would not have been committed. The corporate contribution need only *actually facilitate the wrongful act*. And third, under the rules of state responsibility, the accomplice state must be bound by the same obligation to be held responsible in international law for state complicity. By analogy, we can, without difficulty, state that all companies have international law obligations not to commit international crimes. With regard to international torts or delicts, it seems fair to say that a significant group of large companies recognize that any obligation to promote and respect human rights refers primarily to the rights in the Universal Declaration of Human Rights of 1948. Suffice to say that Weissbrodt simply states that, "although it is not its principal thrust, it appears that non-State entities have human rights duties under the Universal Declaration".[67]

The issue of reparations for acts involving beneficial complicity in human rights violations

There is a second, and separate reason, why it may make sense to focus not only on criminal law but also on tort law. Complaints of corporate complicity are aimed at achieving compensation rather than retributive criminal justice. In order to apportion damages, it will be essential in some circumstances to consider tort responsibility principles. The ILC Commentary to Article 16 states that, "in cases where the internationally wrongful act would clearly have occurred in any event, the responsibility of the assisting State will not extend to compensating for the act itself".[68] The drive to hold corporations accountable for complicity in human rights abuses stems in part from the need to claim reparations from the accomplice company in situations where it is difficult, if not impossible, to claim reparations from the offending government. Should the victims be able to hold a corporation responsible for the acts of the offending state?

Although a state may be responsible for the acts of a company, a company will be responsible for the acts of a state only where the company controls the state actors, where they are joint actors, or where the state acts as the agent of the company. If the company has simply assisted a state, the company can hardly be held responsible for the full damages resulting from the state's action that goes beyond the action that was actually the result of the company's assistance. The company and the state are not interchangeable in this way.

In this zone, some commentators have developed the notion of beneficial corporate complicity.[69] The challenge has been to see where the line should be drawn with regard to such beneficial corporate complicity. The expectations on companies clearly change according to the size and operations of the company. Most commentators would suggest that there has to be a nexus between the human rights violations committed by the government and the sphere of activity and influence of the company. Anita Ramasastry has given some guidance on the scope of such beneficial complicity:

This article advocates extension of accomplice liability only when the MNC [multinational company] is actively investing in the host country and is providing assistance to the state through its investment activities. Both the intention and the action of an MNC must be viewed over time. The Second World War cases involved forced labor and other criminal activity that did stretch over several years. The end of the war, however, curtailed the durations.

Today, when assessing accomplice liability, it is important to assess the level of knowledge possessed by the MNC at the point of entry into a host state. MNCs should be encouraged to engage in human rights risk assessment prior to investing in a country where there is corruption or repression emanating from the state. It is relevant to any inquiry about accomplice liability to determine what knowledge existed at the beginning of a business relationship and then, what knowledge was acquired by the MNC over time....

Moreover, the definition of aiding and abetting under international law requires that the accomplice's act constitute "substantial assistance." "Substantial," at least with respect to an MNC, involves collaboration with the host government.

Factors that are important in assessing whether the assistance is substantial include duration of the investment activity, duration of knowledge of the human rights violations, nature of the assistance to the host state (such as financial assistance), contractual agreements, and collaboration in a business venture. Substantial assistance should involve not only individual actions that are large in magnitude or scope, but continuous actions or presence that become substantial by virtue of their duration....

This article advocates encompassing beneficiary complicity within the scope of accomplice liability for MNCs. This would mean that an MNC's knowledge of ongoing human rights violations, combined with acceptance of direct economic benefit arising from the violations and continued partnership with a host government could give rise to accomplice liability.[70]

Further contemporary conceptions of complicity, including the notion in the Global Compact

This brings us to a final round of questions. Do corporations have responsibilities with regard to human rights abuses that come to their attention but that occur outside their sphere of activity? The notion of complicity has indeed been used in this context. It is used to suggest that companies have obligations to intervene with governments, even when they are not directly involved with the government in the sector concerned.

This use of complicity to denote guilt through silence means that corporate complicity in human rights abuses can extend to failing to raise certain human rights issues with the host government. In advising companies to outline their commitments beyond profit and efficiency, Peter Willetts recommends the following chapter for inclusion in any public document prepared by the company:

Avoidance of complicity with violations of human rights: public protests must be made against all political executions, disappearances and use of torture; employees must be allowed to organize in trade unions of their choice; freedom of speech must be sustained; and the right to a fair trial must be defended.[71]

According to the handbook *Corporate citizenship: Successful strategies for responsible companies,*

It is not only governments that can stand accused of failing to uphold fundamental freedoms. Citizens, be they individuals or corporations, can also be complicit if they fail to acknowledge or take action on known violations...

If corporations are citizens, from which we derive the concept of corporate citizenship, then they bear witness just as individuals do. If it is wrong for a person to turn away in the face of injustice, it is wrong for a corporation to do so. If you see your neighbor beating up another neighbor, do you do nothing? If a company operates in a country where there are systematic human rights violations, should the company remain silent?[72]

The realization that companies cannot remain silent in certain circumstances has driven some companies to develop strategies for raising human rights issues with governments. These companies are reacting to public expectations and they state that, according to the circumstances, they engage in public advocacy or discreet private meetings.

The meaning of complicity in the context of corporate responsibility is being treated as wider than the strict legal tests that allow for international prosecutions of those accused of international crimes such as genocide and war crimes. The Global Compact, which is not an accountability mechanism, because it is not intended to be a forum for criminal prosecutions, has two principles concerning human rights, including a specific principle on complicity:[73]

Principle 1: Businesses should support and respect the protection of internationally proclaimed human rights within their sphere of influence; and
Principle 2: Businesses should make sure that they are not complicit in human rights abuses.

The United Nations High Commissioner for Human Rights, Mary Robinson, summarized three categories of corporate complicity in her 2001 Report to the UN General Assembly:

In order to help define the responsibilities of business, I have suggested there are different degrees or types of complicity in this context: direct, beneficial and silent complicity.

109. A corporation that knowingly assists a State in violating principles of international law contained in the Universal Declaration of Human Rights could be viewed as directly complicit in such a violation. For example, a company that promoted, or assisted with, the forced relocation of people in circumstances that would constitute a violation of international human rights could be considered directly complicit in the violation. The corporation could be responsible if it or its agents knew of the likely effects of their assistance.

110. The notion of corporate complicity in human rights abuses is not confined to direct involvement in the execution of illegal acts by other parties. The complicity concept has also been used to describe the corporate position vis-à-vis government or rebel violations when business benefits from human rights abuses committed by another entity. Violations committed by security forces, such as the suppression of peaceful protest against business activities or the use of repressive measures while guarding company facilities, are often cited as examples of cor-

porate complicity in human rights abuses. Where human rights violations occur in the context of a business operation, the business in question need not necessarily cause the violations for it to become implicated in the abuses.

111. The notion of silent complicity reflects the contemporary expectation that companies should raise systematic or continuous human rights abuses with the appropriate authorities. Indeed, it reflects the growing acceptance within companies that there is something culpable about failing to exercise influence in such circumstances. Whether or not such silent complicity would give rise to a finding of a breach of a strict legal obligation against a company in a court of law, it has become increasingly clear that the moral dimension of corporate action (or inaction) has taken on significant importance.[74]

This categorization of complicity is now summarized in various publications and on the Global Compact website,[75] and it may reflect the way corporate responsibility is developing through the manuals and commentary. Of course it goes beyond the rules for legal liability elaborated in the previous sections of this chapter, but the world of corporate responsibility actually extends way beyond what companies are obliged to do under international law. The Amnesty International "Human rights principles for companies" include a policy recommendation that companies should establish procedures to ensure that all operations are examined for their potential impact on human rights and safeguards to ensure that company staff are never complicit in human rights abuses.[76] Human Rights Watch, in its report *Tainted harvest: Child labour and obstacles to organizing on Ecuador's banana plantations*, concludes: "Human Rights Watch believes that when exporting corporations fail to use their financial influence to demand respect for labor rights on their supplier plantations, the exporting corporations benefit from, facilitate, and are therefore complicit in labor rights violations."[77]

The *Shell Management Business Primer* includes the following paragraphs:

The responsibilities of Shell companies, as articulated in the business principles, include the promotion of equal opportunity and non-discrimination in employment practices; ensuring that freedom of association and the right to organize are respected, guaranteeing that Shell companies do not use slave labour, forced labour or child labour; ensuring that healthy and safe working conditions are provided; that security of employment is created and that the rights of indigenous people and communities are respected.

The individual operating companies must, within their capacity to take action, ensure that these principles are implemented and respected. Within areas where it has control, such as on company sites or in defining employment conditions, the company has full responsibility for meeting human rights standards.[78]

This advice to managers reflects the legal obligations that exist for companies under national and international law. The obligations correspond to the first principle of the Global Compact and concern the obligation to respect. The primer continues:

In almost all circumstances the operating company will be able to respect and protect the human rights of its employees. When a third party takes an action which infringes on the human rights of a Shell employee, whether that action takes place on a company site or elsewhere, the operating company must take appropriate steps to remedy the situation.

Where the operating company does not have complete control, that is, when the issue relates to incidents which did not take place on their site or where the company has limited legal or actual influence, the capacity to influence events is clearly diminished. However that does not mean that the issue can be ignored.

In such cases, the company should tailor its approach according to its capacities and its view of how best to achieve policy aims. For example, the obligation to express support for fundamental human rights within the legitimate role of business does not necessarily mean public statements of support. It may be that expressions of view behind closed doors are more effective in achieving the desired goal. If, in the judgement of the responsible executives, that is the case, then that approach should be taken. The emphasis must be on achieving a result which upholds the human rights standards of the Group's business principles.

The Group's business principles include respect for the human rights of employees as well as promoting the application of such principles with regard to contractors and suppliers and in joint ventures. We can see here the reflection of the direct complicity category. The same management primer also includes the following paragraph:

A potentially serious problem exists when companies choose to operate in one of the few countries that do not allow independent human rights or humanitarian groups even to enter. In these cases there is no possibility of any legitimate monitoring, and as a result the public may suspect abusive practices. Corporations which choose to work in such countries will be scrutinized by human rights organizations in two main respects: that their presence is a measurable "force for the good" in terms of human rights, and that the company does not seek to *benefit* from poor human rights laws on, for example, employment and health and safety.[79]

We find here the reflection of the beneficial complicity category. With regard to the wider responsibilities, Shell includes in its business principles a recognition of responsibilities to society "to express support for fundamental human rights in line with the legitimate role of business".[80] These principles and directives have, more recently, led to actual projects that illustrate how a company such as Shell may feel obliged to take on human rights issues even where it could not necessarily be accused of complicity in a court of law.

The 1999 Shell report *People, planet and profits: An act of commitment* had a human rights section, which included an explanation of Shell's actions with regard to child labour in the sugar cane sector in Brazil. In the 1970s, alcohol regulations were introduced to reduce Brazil's dependence on oil: the fuel distributors are obliged to include a percentage of alcohol from sugar cane in their gasoline. The Shell report states: "Shell Brazil would like to see an end to the use of children in the sugar cane industry. In this instance, it is difficult for us to take action because we have no direct control of the farmers."[81] In the end, the Shell website reports that Shell Brazil worked with various partners, including the families and distillers, to establish a fund to educate the children who would otherwise have had to work to support their families. This example highlights the way in which the different Global Compact principles combine to reflect the sense that, where companies are connected to human rights abuses, even if they do not directly participate in them, they should do what they can in their sphere of influence to find a solution.

Several legal commentators, in developing the scope of the obligations of corporations, have highlighted the fact that the obligations vary according to the nexus[82] and the leverage[83] that companies have with regard to the abuse. Similarly, the obligations surrounding beneficial complicity and silent complicity can combine to create a sense of obligation to act and speak out where a company seems to benefit from human rights abuses.[84] Of course, these sorts of responsibilities will rarely give rise to a case determined before a judge – but the organizing and moral force of complicity allegations should not be underestimated.

Conclusion and summary concerning corporate complicity

Now that corporations have themselves accepted their responsibility not to be complicit in human rights obligations, and to take on human rights responsibilities, we can expect to see continuing extra-judicial allegations of complicity based on the expectations of those making the allegations. It seems to be correct to conclude that, in a globalized world, expectations are high that companies have human rights responsibilities that go beyond the strictly defined liabilities one might find enforceable in national law. In many situations, corporations have promised that they will promote human rights and be advocates for human rights wherever they operate. Failure to play such a role may result in a broken promise and, in some circumstances, such behaviour could result in accountability before the courts. In this way, complaints of complicity respond to promises of ethical behaviour, an increased sense of solidarity with the victims of human rights abuses in other countries, and finally a sense that the complainer cannot stand to be associated with these acts as either shareholder, investor, purchaser, employee, citizen, or informed individual.

We can summarize the conclusions concerning complicity in the following way:

- Where a corporation assists another entity, whether it be a state, a rebel group, another company, or a private individual, to commit an international crime, the rules for determining responsibility under international law will be the rules developed in international criminal law. The corporation will be responsible as an accomplice, whether or not it intended for a crime to be committed, if it can be shown that (a) the corporation carried out acts specifically directed to assist, encourage, or lend moral support to the perpetration of a certain specific international crime and this support had a substantial effect upon the perpetration of the crime; and (b) the corporation had the knowledge that its acts would assist the commission of a specific crime by the principal.

- Where a corporation is alleged to have assisted a government in violating customary international law rights in circumstances that do not amount to international crimes, but rather are international delicts or torts, the international rules for responsibility suggest that (a) the corporation must be aware of the circumstances making the activity of the assisted state a violation of international human rights law; (b) the assistance must be given with a view to facilitating the commission of such a violation and actually contribute significantly to the violation; (c) the company itself should have an obligation not to violate the right in question, such obligations stemming for example from the principles in the Universal Declaration of Human Rights.

- Where a company assists a government through its presence and investment and it benefits from certain human rights abuses committed by the state or others, there is a growing expectation that liability will attach to the corporation if the corporation fails to use its influence to end the violations. The greater the knowledge of the corporation and the longer the duration of the human rights abuses, the more likely it is that this sort of beneficial corporate complicity will give rise to liability in a court of law. In any event, corporate compliance with human rights norms in this context is expected from civil society and from international organizations such as the United Nations.[85]

Notes

1. W. J. M. Van Genugten, "The status of transnational corporations in international public law: With special reference to the case of Shell", in A. Eide, H. O. Bergesen and

P. R. Goyer (eds.), *Human rights and the oil industry* (Antwerp: Intersentia, 2000), p. 80; P. Malanczuk, "Multinational enterprises and treaty-making – A contribution to the discussion on non-state actors and the 'subjects of international law'", in V. Gowlland-Debbas (ed.), *Multilateral treaty-making* (The Hague: Martinus Nijhoff, 2000), pp. 45–72; A. Clapham, "The question of jurisdiction under international criminal law over legal persons: Lessons from the Rome Conference on an International Criminal Court", in M. Kamminga and S. Zia-Zarifi (eds.), *Liability of multinational corporations under international law* (The Hague: Kluwer, 2000), p. 189.

2. D. Weissbrodt, "Non-state entities and human rights within the context of the nation-state in the 21st century", in M. Castermans, F. van Hoof and J. Smith (eds.), *The role of the nation-state in the 21st century* (Dordrecht: Kluwer, 1998), p. 194.

3. Ibid., p. 195.

4. The well-known sentences from the Judgment of the International Military Tribunal in Nuremberg may be recalled in this context: "Many other authorities could be cited, but enough has been said to show that individuals can be punished for violations of international law. Crimes against international law are committed by men, not by abstract entities, and only by punishing individuals who commit such crimes can the provisions of international law be enforced." *Trial of German major war criminals (Goering et al),* International Military Tribunal (Nuremberg) Judgment and Sentence 30 September and 1 October 1946 (London: HMSO), Cmd 6964 at 41; the judgment is also reproduced in *American Journal of International Law* 41, 1947, pp. 172–333.

5. A/Res/56/83, adopted 12 December 2001.

6. Report of the International Law Commission (ILC), adopted at its 53rd session, 2001, Commentary to the Draft Articles, UN Document, GAOR Supp. No. 10 A/56/10, Commentary to Article 5, para. 1, p. 92.

7. Ibid., Commentary to Article 5, para. 5.

8. Ibid., Commentary to Article 5.

9. Ibid., Commentary to Article 5, para. 6, p. 94.

10. Ibid., Commentary to Article 5, para. 6, p. 94; para. 7.

11. See A. Clapham, *Human rights in the private sphere* (Oxford: Oxford University Press, 1993).

12. The Office of the High Commissioner for Human Rights paper "The private sector as service provider and its role in implementing child rights" lists examples from New Zealand, the Netherlands, Mongolia, Ukraine, Finland, Croatia, Algeria, Venezuela, Spain, Mozambique, and Bulgaria. Submitted to the UN Committee on the Rights of the Child day of discussion, 20 September 2002.

13. See A. Clapham, "Revisiting *Human rights in the private sphere*: Using the European Convention on Human Rights to protect the right of access to the civil courts", in C. Scott (ed.), *Torture as tort: Comparative perspectives on the development of transnational human rights litigation* (Oxford: Hart Publishing, 2001), pp. 513–535.

14. For a carefully considered overview of the various bodies and their work in this area, see C. Scott, "Multinational enterprises and emergent jurisprudence on violations of economic, social and cultural rights", in A. Eide, C. Krause and A. Rosas (eds.), *Economic, social and cultural rights: A textbook*, 2nd edn. (Dordrecht: Nijhoff, 2001), pp. 563–595.

15. The Social and Economic Rights Action Center and the Center for Economic and Social Rights/Nigeria, 20th Session (13–27 October 2001), 155/96.

16. See R. Murray, *The African Commission on Human and Peoples' Rights and International Law* (Oxford: Hart, 2000).

17. K. Starmer, "Positive obligations under the Convention", in J. Jowell and J. Cooper (eds.), *Understanding human rights principles* (Oxford: Hart, 2001), pp. 139–159.

18. *Lopez Ostra* v *Spain*, 9 December 1994.

19. *Guerra* v *Italy*, 19 February 1998, para. 60.
20. *Case of X and Y* v. *The Netherlands*, Series A 91 (1985), para. 23; emphasis added.
21. *Case of Plattform "Ärzte für das Leben"*, Series A 139 (1988), para. 32.
22. S. R. Ratner, "Corporations and human rights: A theory of legal responsibility", *Yale Law Journal* 111, 2001, p. 465.
23. See A. Clapham, "The 'Drittwirkung' of the European Convention", in R. St J. Macdonald, F. Matscher and H. Petzold (eds.), *The European system for the protection of human rights* (Dordrecht: Nijhoff, 1993), pp. 163–206.
24. Article 23(5), UN Doc. A/CONF.183/2/Add.1, 14 April 1998. The background and fate of this proposal are discussed in detail in Clapham, "The question of jurisdiction under international criminal law over legal persons", p. 189.
25. See P. Saland, "International criminal law principles", in R. S. Lee (ed.), *The International Criminal Court. The making of the Rome Statute* (The Hague: Kluwer, 1999), p. 199.
26. See Articles 187 and 291(2) of the Law of the Sea Convention of 1982.
27. A.-M. Burley, "The Alien Tort Statute and the Judiciary Act of 1789: A badge of honor", *American Journal of International Law* 83(3), 1989, pp. 461–493.
28. S. Zia-Zarifi, "Suing multinational corporations in the U.S. for violating international law", *University of California Los Angeles Journal of International Law & Foreign Affairs* 4, 1999, pp. 81–147.
29. P. Z. Thadani, "Regulating corporate human rights abuses: Is *UNOCAL* the answer?", *William and Mary Law Review* 42(2), 2002, pp. 619–646.
30. The complaint filed against Exxon Mobil regarding activity in Aceh, Indonesia, in the US District Court for the District of Columbia on 11 June 2001 asks the court to enjoin "Defendants from further engaging in human rights abuses against Plaintiffs and their fellow villagers in complicity with the Indonesian Government and military." For full text of the complaint, see http://www.laborrights.org (last updated 31 August 2001). The US State Department argued that the case should not proceed because anti-terrorist efforts in Indonesia might be "imperiled in numerous ways if Indonesia and its officials curtailed cooperation in response to perceived disrespect for its sovereign interests". "State Dept. opposes suit against Exxon over Indonesian venture", *International Herald Tribune [IHT]*, 8 August 2002, p. 4. See also "Human rights and terror", *IHT*, 14 August 2002, p. 4, and K. Roth, "U.S. hypocrisy in Indonesia", *IHT*, 14 August 2002. See also R. Verkaik, "Ministers attempt to halt US human rights cases against British firms", *The Independent*, 11 February 2004, p. 2, regarding a case concerning human rights abuses in Mexico where the governments of the United Kingdom, Australia and Switzerland are said to have filed an *amicus* brief complaining that the Statute interferes with state sovereignty.
31. *Wiwa* v *Royal Dutch Shell Petroleum (Shell)*, US District Court for the Southern District of New York (28 February 2002), p. 39. See also *Doe I* v *Unocal Corporation* (18 September 2002), paras. 3 ff.
32. *Kadic* v *Karadzic*, 70 F. 3d 232 (2d Cir., 1995), pp. 243–244, cited with approval in *Doe* v *Unocal* (2002), para. 3.
33. "The Trial Chamber in the present case was therefore right in taking the position that the public official requirement is not a requirement under customary international law in relation to the criminal responsibility of an individual for torture outside of the framework of the Torture Convention." *Kunarac et al* case (12 June 2002), Appeals Chamber, International Criminal Tribunal for the Former Yugoslavia, para. 148.
34. See Human Rights and Business Project, *Defining the scope of business responsibility for human rights abroad*, available at http://www.humanrights.dk/humanrightsbusiness/index.html (last visited 31 August 2001).
35. Ibid., at 13.

36. M. J. Bazyler, "Nuremberg in America: Litigating the Holocaust in United States courts", *University of Richmond Law Review* 34, 2000, pp. 1–283, and A. Ramasastry, "Corporate complicity: From Nuremberg to Rangoon. An examination of forced labor cases and their impact on the liability of multinational corporations", *Berkeley Journal of International Law* 20, 2002, pp. 91–159.

37. "Banks sued for financing S. Africa's apartheid regime", *Financial Times*, 18 June 2002, p. 8.

38. US Court of Appeals for the Ninth Circuit, filed 18 September 2002, para. 4.

39. A. Ramasastry, "Secrets and lies? Swiss banks and international human rights", *Vanderbilt Journal of Transnational Law* 31, 1998, pp. 325–456; Ramasastry, "Corporate complicity"; Bazyler, "Nuremberg in America".

40. US Court of Appeals for the Ninth Circuit, filed 18 September 2002, para. 5.

41. "Regarding the first factor – international consensus – we have recognized that murder, torture, and slavery are *jus cogens* violations, i.e., violations of norms that are binding on nations even if they do not agree to them. See *Matta-Ballesteros*, 71 F.3d at 764 n. 5; *Siderman*, 965 F.2d at 714–15. As discussed *supra* in section II.A.1., rape can be a form of torture and thus also a *jus cogens* violation. Similarly, as discussed *supra* in section II.A.2.a, forced labor is a modern form of slavery and thus likewise a *jus cogens* violation. Accordingly, all torts alleged in the present case are *jus cogens* violations. Because *jus cogens* violations are, by definition, internationally denounced, there is a high degree of international consensus against them, which severely undermines Unocal's argument that the alleged acts by the Myanmar Military and Myanmar Oil should be treated as acts of state." Ibid., p. 14233.

42. Report of the ILC, Commentary to Article 26, para. 5, p. 208 (footnotes omitted).

43. Ibid.; and Commentary to Article 40, para. 5, p. 284.

44. Ibid., Commentary to Article 26, para. 7, p. 208 (footnotes omitted).

45. Ibid., Commentary to Article 26, para. 8.

46. Footnote 29 in the original reads: "The evidence further supports the conclusion that Unocal gave 'encouragement' to the Myanmar Military in subjecting Plaintiffs to forced labor. The daily meetings with the Myanmar Military to show it where to provide security and build infrastructure, despite Unocal's knowledge that the Myanmar Military would probably use forced labor to provide these services, may have encouraged the Myanmar Military to actually use forced labor for the benefit of the Project. Similarly, the payments to the Myanmar Military for providing these services, despite Unocal's knowledge that the Myanmar Military had actually used forced labor to provide them, may have encouraged the Myanmar Military to continue to use forced labor in connection with the Project."

47. US Court of Appeals for the Ninth Circuit, filed 18 September 2002, para. 11.

48. Ibid., para. 12.

49. Ibid., para. 12; emphasis added in the Court's ruling.

50. K. Kittichaisaree, *International criminal law* (Oxford: Oxford University Press, 2001), p. 243.

51. The relevant paragraphs are as follows:

25(3). In accordance with this Statute, a person shall be criminally responsible and liable for punishment for a crime within the jurisdiction of the Court if that person:
(a) Commits such a crime, whether as an individual, jointly with another or through another person, regardless of whether that other person is criminally responsible;
(b) Orders, solicits or induces the commission of such a crime which in fact occurs or is attempted;
(c) For the purpose of facilitating the commission of such a crime, aids, abets or other-

wise assists in its commission or its attempted commission, including providing the means for its commission;

(d) In any other way contributes to the commission or attempted commission of such a crime by a group of persons acting with a common purpose. Such contribution shall be intentional and shall either:

   (i) Be made with the aim of furthering the criminal activity or criminal purpose of the group, where such activity or purpose involves the commission of a crime within the jurisdiction of the Court; or

   (ii) Be made in the knowledge of the intention of the group to commit the crime;

(e) In respect of the crime of genocide, directly and publicly incites others to commit genocide;

(f) Attempts to commit such a crime by taking action that commences its execution by means of a substantial step, but the crime does not occur because of circumstances independent of the person's intentions. However, a person who abandons the effort to commit the crime or otherwise prevents the completion of the crime shall not be liable for punishment under this Statute for the attempt to commit that crime if that person completely and voluntarily gave up the criminal purpose.

52. K. Ambos, "Article 25", in O. Triffterer (ed.), *Commentary on the Rome Statute of the International Criminal Court* (Baden-Baden: Nomos, 1999), pp. 474–493; W. A. Schabas, *An introduction to the International Criminal Court* (Cambridge: Cambridge University Press, 2001), p. 448.

53. US Court of Appeals for the Ninth Circuit, filed 18 September 2002, para. 13.

54. The issue of whether an individual could ever have international civil responsibility for a violation of international law was left open by the International Law Commission in its Article 58 of the Articles on State Responsibility.

55. *Norms on the responsibilities of transnational corporations and other business enterprises with regard to human rights*, UN Doc. E/CN.4/Sub.2/2003/12/Rev.2, adopted by Resolution 2003/16 without a vote on 13 August 2003.

56. US District Court for the Southern District of New York, decided 22 February 2002, filed 28 February 2002.

57. From the ruling at Part I.B; available at http://www.derechos.org/nizkor/econ/shell28feb02.html.

58. At I.C.2 of the ruling; for the actual claims, see paras. 121–126 of the Statement of Claim, available at http://www.ccr-ny.org.

59. The Commentary to Article 58 of the ILC's Articles on State Responsibility deliberately leaves open the possibility that international law, having developed to encompass individual responsibility in the context of the Nuremberg and subsequent international criminal trials, might similarly develop in the field of "individual civil responsibility". "So far this principle has operated in the field of criminal responsibility, but it is not excluded that developments may occur in the field of individual civil responsibility. As a saving clause article 58 is not intended to exclude that possibility; hence the use of the general term 'individual responsibility'" (Commentary to Article 58, para. 2). Article 58 reads: "These articles are without prejudice to any question of the individual responsibility under international law of any person acting on behalf of a State." Because the articles concern state responsibility, the focus is on individuals acting on behalf of the state; however, the Commentary is quite clear that all individuals may incur individual responsibility under international law. See paras. 2 and 4 of the Commentary to Article 58, which refer to the principle that individual persons "including State officials" may be responsible under international law for conduct such as genocide, war crimes, and crimes against humanity.

60. J. Crawford, *Second report on state responsibility*, International Law Commission, UN Doc. A/CN.4/498/Add.1, 1 April 1999, para. 159.
61. Ibid., para. 180.
62. Report of the ILC, Commentary to Article 16, para. 5; emphasis added.
63. See A. Clapham, "Issues of complexity, complicity and complementarity: From the Nuremberg trials to the dawn of the new International Criminal Court", in P. Sands (ed.), *From Nuremberg to the Hague: The future of international justice* (Cambridge: Cambridge University Press, 2003), p. 39.
64. M. Robinson, "Visions of ethical business", *Financial Times Management* (London: Financial Times Management, 1998/99), p. 14.
65. See http://business-humanrights.org/Company-policies-Examples.htm (last visited 28 November 2002). Now available at http://www.business-humanrights.org/Categories/Companies/Policies/Companieswithhumanrightspolicies/Companyhumanrightspolicies-referringtoUniversalDeclarationofHumanRights.
66. C. Forcese, "Deterring 'militarized commerce': The prospect of liability for 'privatized' human rights abuses", *Ottawa Law Review* 31 (1999), pp. 171–221.
67. Weissbrodt, "Non-state entities and human rights", p. 180.
68. Report of the ILC, Commentary to Article 16, para. 1.
69. Ramasastry, "Corporate complicity", p. 130.
70. Ibid., p. 150.
71. P. Willetts, "Political globalization and the impact of NGOs upon transnational companies", in J. Mitchell (ed.), *Companies in a world of conflict* (London: Royal Institute of International Affairs, 1998), p. 221.
72. M. McIntosh, D. Leipziger, K. Jones and G. Coleman, *Corporate citizenship: Successful strategies for responsible companies* (London: Financial Times Pitman Publishing, 1998), p. 114.
73. See the Global Compact website: http://www.unglobalcompact.org/Portal/?NavigationTarget=/roles/portal_user/aboutTheGC/nf/nf/theNinePrinciples.
74. Report of the United Nations High Commissioner for Human Rights to the 56th Session of the General Assembly, UN Doc. A/56/36, 2001.
75. See http://www.unglobalcompact.org.80/Portal/; and McIntosh et al., *Corporate citizenship*, p. 143.
76. Amnesty International, "Human rights principles for companies", AI Index 70/01/98 (1998).
77. Human Rights Watch, *Tainted harvest: Child labour and obstacles to organizing on Ecuador's banana plantations* (2002), p. 5.
78. *Shell Management Business Primer* (1998), p. 22.
79. Ibid., para. 3.9; emphasis added.
80. Shell, *Statement of General Business Principles* (1997), p. 2(e).
81. Shell report, *People, planet and profits: An act of commitment* (1999), p. 28.
82. Ratner, "Corporations and human rights", p. 465.
83. N. Jägers, *Corporate human rights obligations: In search of accountability* (Antwerp: Intersentia, 2002).
84. See Human Rights Watch, *Tainted harvest*, p. 5.
85. The UN Global Compact includes as its second principle: *2. The Secretary-General asked world business to make sure they are not complicit in human rights abuses.* The Global Compact website explains principle 2: "An effective human rights policy will help companies avoid being implicated in human rights violations . . . Relationships with Governments: Of course, if a corporation directly engages in acts of discrimination or undermines the political or judicial system through bribery or intimidation, the conclusion is clear. Should a corporation *benefit* from violations by the authorities, or entice,

encourage or support them in violating human rights, corporate complicity would be evident" (emphasis added). See also Report of the UN High Commissioner for Human Rights, A/56/36, 2001, para. 110. For reports on Sudan alleging corporate complicity by certain oil companies, see J. Harker, *Human security in Sudan: The report of a Canadian assessment mission* (Canadian Department of Foreign Affairs and International Trade, January 2000); Amnesty International, *Business and human rights in a time of change*, February 2000; Christian Aid, *The scorched earth: Oil and war in Sudan*, 14 March 2001, http://www.christian-aid.org.uk/indepth/0103suda/sudanoi2.html.

5

Reconstructing the principle of double effect: Towards fixing the goalposts of corporate responsibility

Lene Bomann-Larsen

This chapter discusses the advantages of relating the company's scope of responsibility to its *sphere of activity*. I will attempt to demonstrate how the principle of double effect (PDE) serves both to demarcate and to amplify corporate ethical responsibility,[1] including complicity as co-responsibility. The PDE augments responsibility when opposed to too narrow a view of responsibility (promoted primarily by companies) that denies responsibility for side-effect harm on stakeholders. Simultaneously, the PDE restricts responsibility when compared with too broad and encompassing a notion of responsibility that causes a "moving of goalposts", is unfair to companies and may undermine incentives to improve performance/investment in developing countries (promoted by many non-governmental organizations). This entails discussing how the PDE can help clarify the issue of complicity as well as what may be the reasonable content of "corporate citizenship". I contend that the PDE may serve to "fix the goalposts" of corporate ethical responsibility and complicity and create a solid base for addressing critical issues.

Corporations and intentions

Though the reconstructed principle of double effect (which is introduced in the next chapter of this book) avoids explicit use of intentional language, a distinction between the intended and the unintended is still implied by the very notion of *double effect*. The notion of double effect is based on the recognition that actions almost always have more than one effect – not just the outcome aimed at, but also by-products that may be good, bad, or indifferent. We are concerned here only with *harmful* side-effects, though we should bear in mind that, when companies speak of "constructive engagement", they are referring to the *positive* spin-offs of their investments.

Thus a distinction between intended and unintended effects – i.e. results aimed at and results not aimed at – lies at the crux of the idea of double effect. This gives rise to two crucial questions in our context: why do intentions matter at all, and how do we ascribe them to corporations? Unlike a utilitarian calculus, which focuses solely on the *actual* results of an action, the PDE allows for a distinction between what the agent wants to bring about and what he does not, thus permitting side-effect harm provided that certain criteria are met, yet also ascribing responsibility for these. However, like a utilitarian calculus, the PDE does also ascribe responsibility for regrettable unintended harms, because these follow from the initial, intended action – i.e. from the means deliberately chosen to a specific end. So what is to be gained from emphasizing the distinction?

A lesson from war

The importance of intentions to moral judgements can be argued if we look at a central distinction in war, namely that between strategic bombing (of military targets) and terror bombing (of civilian targets). According to the Geneva Conventions, targeting civilians in war is absolutely outlawed as a war crime. Yet it is not a war crime if civilian deaths come about as collateral damage from legitimate military activity; the Convention clearly states that it is *wilful* killing that is outlawed.[2] The operation against the transportation of heavy water by the Germans at Rjukan, Norway, during the Second World War is an infamous illustration of double effect at play (the case is referred to in full in chapter 2 in this volume): 18 people were killed during the sabotage of the ferry, most of them Norwegian civilians. Although the non-intended effect was foreseeable and foreseen, and the civilian deaths were inescapable, the importance of the military target was believed to outweigh the side-effects. It must also be added that trying to prevent or minimize the side-effects was considered impossible; warning people not to board the ferry would have made the Germans suspicious and thus jeopardized the whole operation.

It is important to note that the civilian deaths were not *means* to the intended end – the raid itself did not benefit from these deaths. A quite different case is the bombing of German cities late in the same war, at a time when many believed the war to be won in reality. The sole aim was to kill large numbers of civilians and destroy civilian property in order to break down German morale and force Hitler to surrender. Even though the allied war against Nazi Germany can be depicted as a "just war", the bombing of Berlin and Dresden in February 1945 is ruled out by the PDE as a violation of *in bello* rules.

The difference, which is useful to us in this project, is that we draw a line between a case where civilians deaths are part of the military strategy – i.e. part of the agent's project – and a case where they are incidental to the agent's project. This line distinguishes terror bombing from strategic bombing. To the dead civilians, this distinction might not matter. Nonetheless, not knowing who was to die and with stakes as high as in the Rjukan case, they would probably have agreed that the cause justified (or at least provided strong reasons for permitting) the number of deaths. Deliberately using civilians as means to a military end, on the other hand, is not acceptable to most people. Thus, by *side-effect harm* we mean *harm that falls outside of the agent's project*, that is not part of the objective or the means chosen to achieve this objective. If we disregard intentions as irrelevant and look simply to the consequences – counting our dead – the Rjukan case would still hold and the bombings of Dresden and Berlin in 1945 would still probably be ruled out, but we would lose the option of passing different judgements on the act of directly targeting a number of civilians to break down morale and win the war, and letting an equal number of civilians die as a consequence of a legitimate military operation necessary to win the war. We would lose the possibility of distinguishing between terror bombing and strategic bombing. But, most importantly, we would lose the incentive to attempt to protect civilians in war when something of great importance may be gained from killing them.

Does it matter if the cat is black or white – as long as it catches mice?

Many business professionals argue that what is important is doing the right thing, not doing it for the right reasons. Thus, whereas non-governmental organizations (NGOs) and researchers prefer to speak of the *moral case* for corporate social responsibility (CSR), business professionals often speak of the *business case* for CSR. In the contemporary business climate, many business professionals believe that there are profits to be gained from ethical performance because it attracts consumers, investors, and employees, and because it helps avoid expensive accidents that can be costly to wallet and reputation in the long run. In the business case for

CSR, the ethical prerogatives are subordinated to the higher goal of profit. The question is whether it matters if a company has a CSR policy merely for business reasons ("ethics pays") or for moral reasons – is not the point to get the job done?

It may matter. The business case is, at least to an extent, opportunistic. It is based on an assumption that ethics pays, which may not be correct or at least may not be correct at all times. The business case makes CSR incentives highly vulnerable to changes in public opinion, let alone to research that may prove the credo "ethics pays" to be untrue. A more solid ground for CSR is required if there is to be long-term commitment and permanently improved performance. However, the most accurate answer to the question of what motivates business to a commitment to CSR is probably that there is a mix of motives. The separation of the business case from the moral case creates a false picture that it must be one or the other. The conclusion, still, is probably that performance is more important than motives, though motives play a part as long-term incentives for performance. So why bother with intentions? The answer is short and simple: intentions may be equivalent to motives, but the term "intention" can also mean something other than motive. And it is in this other sense that I use the term here.

Peter A. French states that, "[i]n considering responsibility, few things are considered more important than to establish whether a man ... did A intentionally".[3] But what does it mean to do something intentionally? The classic notion of "*intentio*" is defined as "an act of the will in regard to an end". "Act of the will" implies that there is a decision behind the action; it is not a mere event, like a spasm or an accident. Thus, we can construe "intention" as an answer to the question: To what *end* do you/ did you do *x*? What are/were you aiming at? "Intention" may thus be equivalent to the objective sought (the desired object) through *x*, rather than the underlying reasons for desiring *x* (the motive). Of course, even means are deliberately chosen. Guided by the end pursued, we choose (it is hoped) the most efficient means to reach our goal. Thus we include means in our assessment of an intentional act. We are interested in what is decided upon – the deliberate *for what* and *how* (which we call the agent's project) – rather than the *why*. For example, profit maximization is a business objective and means are decided upon to this end (through the decision-making processes of a company) – companies have mission statements and they have strategies. As far as "intentions" are used in the sense of "deliberately sought objective by deliberate means", there is nothing mystical about speaking of intentions with regard to a business corporation. Yet the interchangeability of intentions and motives, yielding another sense of the notion of "intention", urges us to use the word carefully. We have therefore decided to evade intentional language by speaking of legitimate objectives and legitimate means in our revised PDE, presented in the next chapter.

Corporations don't have minds!

The issue of corporate personhood and agency is not to be settled once and for all. But, insofar as a company (or its board of directors) deliberates and decides upon company policy and company strategy and acts in the name of the company, and insofar as a corporation is a legal entity that can be held liable as such, there is absolutely no reason that it cannot be held morally responsible for its "actions" as well.

In an argument for corporations as moral persons, French suggests that the mind of a corporation is located in its corporate internal decision (CID) structure.[4] The CID structure constitutes corporate personhood. French claims that it is the decisions arrived at within the CID structure that form corporate intention, and the function of the structure generates reasons for acting that are not equivalent to the reasons of the human individuals within the structure. A corporation may act for corporate reasons, which are not reducible to the individuals' reasons or the sum total of the individuals' reasons. Although French's approach is interesting and points out something important, namely that a corporate body is not equivalent to the sum of its constituents, I do not think we need to establish metaphysical personhood in order to speak of corporations as moral actors. Moreover, I do not believe it is wise to do so, nor do I believe that his personhood thesis is correct. Corporations are not persons analogous to human persons. As DeGeorge points out, there are "fundamental ways in which corporations differ from human beings ... Human beings are not created by law."[5] The reason French misses this point is that he focuses too heavily on intentions and decision-making. Yet "corporations and other artificial entities are human creations. As such they are simply means for achieving human ends ... [C]orporations are not ends in themselves."[6]

DeGeorge, then, denies that corporations are moral persons. But he also denies that they need to be moral persons in order to be moral actors. "Being a moral actor is a status that corporations share not only with human persons but with all other human groups or collectives." As examples, DeGeorge mentions mobs, families, faculties, partnerships, countries – and armies. An army, to be sure, is also a collective actor. We pass judgements on the US army in Iraq, not on – or not only on – individual soldiers and officers. We want the army as a whole to behave properly, according to the conventions of war. In fact, we are often ready to excuse the soldier in the heat of battle, whereas we are not willing to excuse an entire army for violation of the rules of war. "To the extent that corporations or other collective entities act, their actions can be morally evaluated," DeGeorge preliminarily concludes. But then again, this kind of evaluation is passed from the outside. What we are interested in here is what happens on the inside – in the decision-making processes, where the (quasi-)intentions of corporations are formed. And in this instance, the internal decision-making structure and the command lines entailed in the structure will be relevant for ascribing responsibility. The fact that corporate decisions are being made that are not reducible to the decisions of individual constituents "responsibilizes" the corporation as such. Now, the important aspect is not *why* these decisions are being made but how they are carried out and to what ends – and who they affect.

Means and ends mala in se

Certain actions are plainly wrong, and some of these have already been mentioned: criminal acts; direct violation of people's rights; wilful participation in such acts when committed by others. Actions such as these are wrong for all companies and all lines of business. However, the PDE framework can also be used to evaluate lines of business that have a morally dubious image: the tobacco industry, the pharmaceutical industry, the arms industry, and the energy sector, to mention just a few.

The arms industry provides an interesting example. Can we condemn the arms industry *as such* from a moral point of view? From a just war perspective this is difficult, because weapons can be used for legitimate purposes, for example in self-defence or for humanitarian purposes. But we can still point to negative side-effects and to the responsibilities they entail. Misuse of weapons for crimes, terrorism, and aggression towards countries or groups of people are foreseeable side-effects of arms production, for which the arms industry must take its responsibility. Hence, the industry should be the first to embrace restrictions on who can buy and use their products as a way to minimize the harmful side-effects for which the industry itself is responsible. Unfortunately, the industry is not too keen on such restrictions, because they would probably impair profit to some extent.

But are there products that, considered in themselves, are so bad that their production should be completely abandoned in moral terms? I will propose here that there do exist commodities that are *intrinsically* "evil" (*mala in se*). In this category we find (1) products that can *only* be produced by morally illicit means (i.e. to which immoral means are a necessary condition) and (2) products that can *only* be used for immoral purposes. Commodities that fulfil either of these conditions are intrinsically evil and thus are not subject to assessment in terms of the PDE, because they are ruled out by the first criterion; namely that, in order for side-effect harm to be permissible, the agent must pursue legitimate objectives by legitimate means.

Child pornography is a prime example of the first type of intrinsically evil product. Abuse of children is its necessary condition, and it is thus intrinsically evil. An example of the second type is weapons that by their very nature kill indiscriminately, such as those that cannot be aimed only at legitimate targets in war or that are disproportionate and hence in violation of the rules of war.[7] Consequently, these weapons are deemed intrinsically "evil", and producing them can never be morally permissible. It is now widely agreed that this applies to anti-personnel landmines and biological or chemical weapons,[8] as well as to certain kinds of weapons constructed so as to inflict unnecessary (excessive) damage (e.g. dumdum bullets) and that are therefore prohibited from use in war.

Corporate decisions must be made for legitimate business objectives (i.e. sustainable value creation), and these objectives include the commodities that are produced (they are part of the value created). Further, the means decided upon to carry out the objectives must be legitimate; that is, they must comply with the law and with norms for acceptable business behaviour, and not violate people's dignity and rights. Not until these premises are firmly in place can we start to evaluate the permissibility of harmful side-effects.

Responsibility for side-effects

As stated above, side-effects are outcomes of an action that are *outside of* the agent's project. Yet both intended effects and side-effects are subject to moral evaluation, meaning that, in principle, one is morally responsible (accountable) for both. As Reichberg notes in a different volume: "Even if I in no way wished it to come about, I nevertheless can be said to will the negative side-effect indirectly, insofar as I allow or permit it to happen."[9] Reichberg's point is that, if the side-effects are foreseeable and I choose to act anyway, I am responsible for all the outcomes because I allow the side-effect to occur. The PDE is not an "ends sanctify means" doctrine, no matter how desirable the ends may be.

Critics of the PDE argue that it may serve as a blanket justification for bad effects. Michael Walzer has taken this criticism of the PDE quite seriously, and a fifth criterion has been introduced by him to deal with the risk that the PDE might become a slippery slope towards permissibility of wrongful acts. "Subject only to the proportionality rule – a weak constraint – double effect provides a blanket justification."[10] Therefore, "[t]he principle of double effect is defensible ... only when the two outcomes [i.e. the desired outcome and the side-effect] are the product of a *double intention*: first, that the good be achieved; second that the foreseeable evil be reduced as far as possible."[11]

Interestingly, this modification not only works as a moral constraint, it actually serves to verify the initial intention of the agent. In practical judgements, the notion of "intentions" is complicated because it is so hard to establish what someone's real intentions are. We can infer only from the observable action that is the expression of the intention. The intention is reflected in the action, but in the case of double effect it is hard to prove what the initial intention was. Only by aiming to minimize harmful side-effects (and accepting the costs involved) can agents prove that they have the best intentions, i.e. that harmful side-effects are not intended or means to the intended result. In short, *the effort to minimize side-effect harm must be included in the agent's project, in the decision-making procedures, and in corporate strategy.*

Foreseeability

Foreseeability is crucial to ascribing responsibility for side-effects. Within the realm of side-effects there are several distinctions. Some side-effects are good, some are neutral, and some are harmful. We focus, naturally, on the harmful ones, because they are the ones that pose a moral problem. Harmful side-effects can in turn be divided into two categories: foreseeable and unforeseeable. Both categories may be morally relevant, but I shall focus here primarily on *foreseeable* effects, because these are the only ones that can be involved in deliberations and taken into account in the planning of an action. When ascribing responsibility, it is sufficient that the effects be foreseeable, i.e. that they could *in principle* be known by an agent. However, the agent is also under an epistemic duty to put in the necessary effort to access knowledge; hence the foreseeable effects should also be *actually foreseen* by the agent.

There are undoubtedly grey areas between the foreseeable and the unforeseeable. That accidents may happen is as such foreseeable, at least in the business context, and some companies have policies to compensate those affected – should an accident occur – even though the accident was not caused by any recklessness or negligence on the part of the company. But a demand that all eventualities be predicted in advance should not be pushed too far. Suppose a plane crashes into a plant and kills people and pollutes the area. It might be that, given the situation *ex post facto*, the company ought to respond by taking measures to minimize the damage by, for example, paying compensation, but it would be unreasonable to demand that all such possible accidents should be taken into account in advance and given the same weight as other foreseeable results of the corporate activity such as pollution or relocation of populations. Good governance entails being prepared for eventualities, but it would be unreasonable to expect preparedness for absolutely every incident that might occur. Hence, when speaking of foreseeability, I restrict the term to denote the *reasonably foreseeable.*[12]

Reasonably foreseeable side-effects can in turn be divided into two categories: those that result from action and those that result from inaction. Neither of these is necessarily *blameworthy*. In this respect there is an asymmetry between intentional wrongful action on the one hand and the allowing of side-effect harm on the other. On moral grounds the former is always to be excluded, whereas this need not be the case with the latter.

Why permit side-effect harm at all?

Allowing a harmful side-effect to occur is thus not necessarily blameworthy, whereas intending harm is always blameworthy (again, consequentialists will disagree). To be accountable for side-effect harm does not necessarily mean that one is culpable in the legal or moral sense. Some side-effect harm may even be justifiable, if there are good reasons for permitting it.

As has already been suggested, preventing any side-effect harm from coming about would often render action in pursuit of a legitimate objective impossible, and acting itself would run the risk of becoming an immoral enterprise. Most would also agree that one should get credit for trying; in the corporate context it is particularly important that we applaud companies that do make CSR commitments and do not subject them to the same criticism that we direct against the "bad guys". Many companies are afraid of making CSR commitments because this makes them easy targets for NGOs and the media whenever they fail to live up to their own standards, whereas the ones that have no standards go free. This is not to say that a company should not be expected to comply with its own values, but it is an important incentive towards CSR that we discriminate between "good" companies and "bad" ones. Thus we need – for practical reasons as well as for reasons of fairness – to allow some side-effect harm to occur. On the other hand, accepting side-effect harm is not something to be taken lightly. An actor is responsible for the foreseeable side-effects that the initial action brings about, no matter how desirable the initial action may have been. The risk of side-effect harm can be called a *moral risk*, and must be dealt with through careful risk assessment and risk management.

Finally, it is not the primary concern of this project to create a tool for *allowing* the harmful side-effects of corporate activities. Our main concern is to *emphasize responsibility*. Thus we focus very strongly on the obligation to prevent or minimize side-effect harm. Once responsibility for side-effect harm has been established, this responsibility must be *taken on* by the agent: "I caused this to happen; it is my job to something about it." Ideally, of course, agents will deliberate on likely side-effects *in advance* and take active steps *before the fact* to prevent the harm from occurring but, if prevention turns out to be impossible (if the side-effects are inescapable), at least measures must be taken to minimize the harm caused.

Delimiting moral responsibility/complicity

The PDE promises to provide a normative framework for assessing the moral responsibility of corporations. This entails delimiting such responsibility by attaching it closely to the sphere of the company's activities by establishing a substantial link between its operations and the social impact for which it can reasonably be held accountable. In this section I shall focus on side-effects when they entail participation in the wrongdoing of others, because this is perhaps the most complicated grey area of side-effect harm. As is pointed out in chapter 1 of this volume, there are several problems regarding the vagueness of the concept of complicity and related concepts linked with expectations of business companies. As the International Peace Academy (IPA) notes: "The continued broadening of and vagueness of the concept of complicity has the effect of 'moving the goal posts', whereby corporations meet one set of standards only to find themselves under criticism for failing to address others. This is both unconstructive and unfair to private sector actors."[13]

I shall try to demonstrate how the PDE may help overcome this challenge of unfairness and unconstructiveness. Although, as we shall see, it does not address all concerns regarding CSR, it may at least demarcate the scope of a company's *mandatory duties*; i.e. those for which it can be subject to moral blame and due criticism.

Narrowing down "complicity"

It is easy to embrace the second principle of the UN Global Compact – that corporations should ensure they do not become complicit in human rights abuses. But what does it mean? In the absence of a clear legal framework regarding complicity, there is room for discussion about where to draw the line. And where we draw the line must be grounded in sound ethical principles.

As the IPA notes, "Some have defined complicity broadly to include all corporate involvement in countries in which wide-spread abuse of human rights take place. For many analysts, this definition is too encompassing to be conceptually or practically meaningful."[14] The PDE for its part may help narrow the concept of complicity when this can be regarded as a side-effect (for example, when a company, by operating in a particular country, becomes substantially involved in a negative framework, albeit unwillingly, by benefiting from or contributing to other actors' wrongdoing), in the same way as it works to determine responsibility for negative side-effects when no other perpetrators are involved. Thus, the PDE may help us avoid the danger of demotivating socially oriented companies, which not only harms the case for improved performance but in turn might harm investment in developing countries, thus hindering their prospects for development.

Complicity in conflict and human rights abuse

A company operating in a conflict zone may benefit with regard to security for employees and assets from the services of a police force that, while protecting the plant, acts more brutally against protestors than it ought to. This renders the company complicit in the human rights violations of the force. The link is that the side-effect harm ensuing from the need to protect the plant (a legitimate means because the company has a primary responsibility to protect its staff) also functions as a means to protect the plant, to the benefit of the company. However, it may be that the company has no choice but to protect itself; thus the side-effect harm is inescapable. It is not inescapable in the same sense as pollution is an inescapable side-effect harm of oil production, but it is inescapable given the framework in which the company operates. There are then two options open to the company: put pressure on the authorities to make the behaviour of the police more sensitive to human rights, or withdraw.

In some cases where the company risks becoming complicit in the wrongdoing of a third party, the PDE requirement to minimize and prevent side-effect harm may reduce the risk to a justifiable extent. Measures include entering into multiparty partnerships to improve human rights conditions and implementing company policy on human rights compliance. In other cases, such responses may be insufficient to rectify the harm caused.

In extreme cases, such as Burma, the burden of complicity becomes so heavy that withdrawal or staying out seems to be the only justifiable option. It is impossible for a company sufficiently to prevent or minimize side-effect complicity in the abuses of the Burmese military junta. (Another aspect to this is the duty to listen to affected parties, which is entailed in the requirement to consult. Nobel Peace Prize laureate and opposition leader Aung San Suu Kyi in Burma is very clear that a boycott is necessary to improve conditions in Burma.)

Side-effect complicity also takes the form of involuntarily yet foreseeably aiding and abetting wrongdoing. As an example, criticism of oil companies operating in war-torn Angola has been directed to such aid; the civil war was considered to be fuelled by revenues from the oil industry. Many business professionals have evaded the issue of complicity by refusing to pass judgement on the government and taking a stance on the conflict. In 2001, a Norwegian oil company presently engaged in Angola expressed its views on the matter as follows: "In the legitimate election of 1992, the MPLA won power. The UNITA subsequently armed itself, while the MPLA feels that the international community is not helping them implement the 1992 election results. A central question in this situation regards as well who is in fact telling the true story of Angola."[15] Passing judgement on a conflict is not a simple task. Is contributing to a conflict as such always wrong? One could easily find a counter-example, such as Norwegian companies supporting the resistance to Nazi Germany during the Second World War. And yet we must remember that, no matter who is at fault, the true story of any armed conflict is that it causes human suffering.

It is not always war itself that represents the biggest *direct* problem for stakeholders (although long-term war and civil strife of course tend to wear out a country, drain the economy, and increase social problems). Corruption and personal government may be just as daunting for the population as the effects of war. This is confirmed by Le Billon at the Overseas Development Institute in London, who, in an assessment of Angola, contends that: "While the war has a dramatic impact on many people, it is worth noting that the vast majority of the population is sheltered from its direct effects. Most of their suffering arises out of economic mismanagement and lack of public services."[16] In other words, anyone who thinks that Angola's problems were solved with the 2002 peace accord must think again.

Hence, we need not take a moral stand on the conflict itself in order to take a stand on the human suffering or human rights abuses that follow in its path. To the extent that companies become complicit in human suffering or human rights abuses caused by either party in a conflict or by corruption to which the company is linked via revenue creation or large signatory fees, the PDE imposes a duty on these companies to minimize this harm. This entails not only taking CSR measures to alleviate the suffering, but also working actively for long-term improvement. Encouraging transparency is one way of doing this, and is perhaps most effective in collaboration with other companies (both foreign and domestic) operating in the same country. If the situation is totally deadlocked, there is – once more – the option of withdrawal.

Thus the PDE does cover issues of complicity with regard to benefiting from and contributing to the wrongful acts of others. It covers cases where side-effect complicity is inescapable, at the same time urging the company to take measures to counteract or rectify the situation. Further, it covers other harmful side-effects that do not involve other perpetrators, such as environmental damage caused by the company's own operations, displacement of populations, and harmful impacts on local culture. The PDE demands corporate responsibility for such effects, requiring efforts to be made to foresee the foreseeable and measures taken to prevent and minimize it.

The PDE and corporate citizenship

By tailoring responsibility to the activities of the corporation, the PDE is narrower than the principle of corporate citizenship, defined thus: "It is not only governments that can stand accused of failing to uphold fundamental freedom. Citizens, be they individuals or corporations, can also be complicit if they fail to acknowledge or take action on known violations.... If corporations are citizens, from which we derive the concept of corporate citizenship, then they bear witness just as individuals do. If it is wrong for a person to turn away in the face of injustice, it is wrong for a corporation to do so."[17]

Although the idea of corporate citizenship is certainly appealing, I believe the narrowness of the PDE is an advantage. Corporations are not analogous to human beings. They are responsible *insofar as they act*, but they do not have the same range of moral duties and responsibilities as humans in their capacity of citizens. The definition of corporate citizenship presupposes too much by implying that our moral expectations toward the one are transferable to the other. Corporations may well be citizens, but they are a different kind of citizen. We need to recall what DeGeorge points out, namely, "[c]orporations and other artificial entities are human creations ... not ends in themselves".[18]

The PDE may narrow the scope of companies' responsibilities to the sphere of their own activities, but this does not mean that it weakens the strength of this responsibility.[19] The strength is upheld precisely because the PDE ascribes *mandatory* responsibility to take action to prevent or minimize side-effect harm within the company's sphere of impact. In this way, the PDE defines the scope of responsibility for companies, avoiding the shifting expectations that make it difficult for a corporation to establish stable and attainable ethical standards for its operations. As such, the PDE "fixes the goalposts" of corporate moral responsibility.

Although I agree with many NGOs that companies ought to protest against human rights violations and also seek to influence regimes that abuse human rights, the PDE sets limits on how far we can go in accusing a company of being complicit in such abuses if it does not raise its voice. Exercising pressure outside of the company's sphere of activity seems to respond to a kind of expectation that is supererogatory rather than mandatory; hence failing to protest cannot warrant justified blame.

To illustrate this argument, let us consider a case in Nigeria. In 2002, Amina Lawal was sentenced to death by stoning in a Nigerian local court. Amnesty International Norway wanted the Norwegian oil company Statoil, which operates in Nigeria, to take action by allowing for a campaign on its website. Statoil was not in any way involved – the case against Lawal was not even issued by the Nigerian state with which Statoil collaborates – but Amnesty International Norway believed good corporate citizenship in this case required a protest.[20] In the debate that followed, however, Arild Hermstad of the Norwegian NGO The Future in Our Hands pointed out that a duty to interfere in this case would equally oblige Norwegian companies operating in the United States to protest against the execution of convicts who commit crimes while still minors – a duty that it would seem almost absurd to impose.[21]

The PDE may help us assess whether Statoil, by refusing to protest, could be considered to be complicit. The case was not one of benefit from a negative framework, nor was it a case of contributing to wrongdoing. The verdict against Amina Lawal lay outside Statoil's sphere of activity and therefore its scope of responsibility (in the sense of being involved). If we were to hold Statoil responsible, we would also need to consider whether Norwegian companies in the United States are obliged to exert pressure on the US government regarding capital punishment of minors. If failure to object in one case renders the company silently complicit, then bystander responsibility would also apply in the other.

It follows from the PDE that merely *being there* is not sufficient to make a company an accomplice. Contribution and benefit, not silent bystanding, define the scope of corporate involvement in terms of side-effects. In accordance with the PDE framework, a substantial link must be proven between the company's presence and either worsened or prolonged human rights abuses or direct benefit from such abuse on the part of the company.

This, of course, gives rise to a pertinent question related to the infamous case of South Africa. Were not companies that invested in South Africa during the apartheid era in fact complicit in the wrongdoings of the regime merely by being there? It is commonly agreed that they were, and this shared intuition certainly carries a lot of moral weight. Would this not, in the spirit of Rawls' reflexive equilibrium, be a clear indication of the shortcomings of the PDE in this context, perhaps even indicating that we should reject the principle as a servant of the concept of complicity? My answer is that the intuition that companies operating in South Africa during the apartheid era were in fact complicit in human rights abuses and racism is correct *and* that this assumption is also compatible with the PDE. It suffices to show that, if a particular international company operating in South Africa substantially contributed to or benefited from the illegitimate jurisdiction, it can be rendered complicit under the PDE. What we need to clarify is what must be the nature of such contribution (or benefit) for the PDE to warrant an accusation of complicity.

There are (at least) two possible responses. If we focus on side-effects proper, the most plausible reasoning is that the foreign companies in question did lend the regime *substantial moral support* by accepting its jurisdiction and by violating international sanctions intended to punish the regime and make a statement. Research has shown that this support was so significant as to in fact contribute to the prolongation of the regime.[22] Perhaps more importantly, apartheid is a crime against humanity under international law. Breaking an international boycott and investing in a country that is off limits seem to violate the very presumption upon which the whole PDE is based; namely, that the objectives and means chosen by the company must be legitimate (i.e. legal *and* moral). Operating in South Africa at the time was simply not in compliance with legitimate business purposes and means thereto – being in violation of international norms; thus no side-effects ensuing from the investments can be permissible.

Conclusion

I hope I have shown that there are several arguments in favour of choosing a PDE framework for assessing the responsibility of corporations. First, the PDE implies a distinction between deliberately committing wrongful acts and negative side-effects resulting from legitimate acts. This provides a good incentive for companies to try to act responsibly, because it allows us to discriminate between "good" and "bad" companies. Secondly, the PDE ascribes mandatory responsibility for companies to counteract such side-effects, thus making it impossible for a company to buy itself free through charitable acts while ignoring the effects of its own operations. (If you pollute the environment, don't build a hospital unless you are prepared to do something about the pollution.) Thirdly, the PDE narrows the concept of complicity, compared with what is implied in notions of corporate citizenship and is desired by most NGOs, in a manner that is fair and feasible in practice.

To be sure, the narrowing of the scope of corporate responsibility entailed in the PDE does not preclude discussion of supererogatory acts beyond what is explicitly called for under PDE. However, a major motivation for this project is to contribute to fixing the goalposts – to provide corporations with a stable normative framework as an aid to decision-making and to avoid shifting expectations that may ultimately harm the case for a more ethically concerned business.

Notes

1. By "ethical responsibility" I mean responsibility towards stakeholders beyond stockholders.
2. Geneva Convention, Protocol IV, Article 147.
3. Peter A. French, "The corporation as a moral person", *American Philosophical Quarterly* 16(3), 1979, p. 211.
4. Peter A. French, *Collective and corporate responsibility* (New York: Columbia University Press, 1984).
5. Richard T. DeGeorge, "Corporations and morality", in Hugh Curtler (ed.), *Shame, responsibility and the corporation* (New York: Haven Publications, 1986), pp. 60–61.
6. Ibid., p. 65.
7. Some weapons, such as anti-personnel landmines, cannot be used without violating the principle of discriminating between combatants and non-combatants.
8. As regards nuclear weapons, there is no international consensus on whether they are intrinsically evil; however, to the extent that these weapons – even if they are used in a theatre of war – have long-term effects that could cause harm to soldiers in the future when they are no longer combatants, as well as to their offspring, I believe it is warranted to claim that nuclear weapons cannot be truly discriminatory no matter how they are put to use. They thus fall into the same category as other weapons of mass destruction, which are prohibited for use against combatants as well.
9. Gregory M. Reichberg, "The hard questions of international business: Some guidelines from the ethics of war", in Heidi von Weltzien Høivik (ed.), *Moral leadership in action. Building and sustaining moral competence in European organizations* (Cheltenham: Edward Elgar, 2002), p. 311.
10. Michael Walzer, *Just and unjust wars* (New York: Basic Books, 1992), p. 153.
11. Ibid., p. 155.
12. For example, to what extent was it reasonably foreseeable that the World Trade Center might be hit by hijacked airplanes? Would it be reasonable to expect the companies situated there to have taken that risk into account before 11 September? It is another matter entirely of course whether they should accept liability after the fact and compensate the families of their employees.
13. IPA, *Private sector actors in zones of conflict: Research challenges and policy responses* (New York: International Peace Academy, workshop report, 2001), p. 4.

14. Ibid., p. 4.
15. Lene Bomann-Larsen (ed.), *Corporate social responsibility in the Norwegian petroleum sector* (Oslo: INTSOK, 2002), p. 48.
16. Philippe Le Billon, "The oil industry and the state of war in Angola", in Asbjørn Eide, Helge Ole Bergesen and Pia Rudolfsen Goyer (eds.), *Human rights and the oil industry* (Antwerp: Intersentia, 2000), p. 124.
17. M. McIntosh, D. Leipziger, K. Jones and G. Coleman, *Corporate citizenship: Successful strategies for responsible companies* (London: Financial Times Pitman Publishing, 1998), p. 221.
18. DeGeorge, "Corporations and morality", p. 65.
19. Lene Bomann-Larsen and Oddny Wiggen, "Addressing complicity: Legitimate business objectives vs. harmful side-effects", conference paper presented at Acuns 16th Annual Meeting, New York City, 12–14 June 2003, unpublished.
20. It should be added that Statoil in this particular case felt it would harm Lawal's case if the company supported a protest against the court's decision. The argument, however, can still be made as a general one.
21. "Sjekkliste for bedrifter i konfliktområder", *Ukeavisen ledelse og næringsliv*, no. 34, 27 September 2002, pp. 4–5.
22. Arvind Ganesan, "Human rights, the energy industry, and the relationship with home governments", in Eide, Bergesen and Goyer (eds.), *Human rights and the oil industry*, pp. 65–68.

6

The principle of double effect, revised for the business context

Oddny Wiggen and Lene Bomann-Larsen

There are undoubtedly challenges related to adapting moral concepts from one context and one tradition to another. The attempt to adapt the principle of double effect (PDE) as it emerged within the just war tradition to the context of international business is no exception. Based on a consideration of the just war tradition, various discourses on corporate social responsibility and corporate governance, and international law as it relates to business, we have developed a revised PDE. We thus propose the following as a more suitable PDE for business ethical purposes:

Preamble: Negative side-effects do occur, even when businesses pursue legitimate objectives by legitimate means. In creating sustainable value for their stakeholders, businesses must ensure in dealing with the negative side-effects of their activities that:
1. consultation with affected parties, as well as risk assessment, is carried out prior to and during the business operation in order to identify negative side-effects;
2. negative side-effects that arise from a business's operations are not made to serve as means to achieving its legitimate objectives;
3. negative side-effects can be justified as proportionate to the legitimate objectives;
4. active measures are taken to prevent or minimize negative side-effects;
5. the negative side-effects are inescapable – it is not possible to achieve the legitimate objectives with fewer or no side-effects.

The preamble illustrates that we do acknowledge sustainable value creation as a legitimate aim for business, although it also implies that profit maximization at any cost is not acceptable and that a broader stakeholder perspective needs to be included. After all, the ultimate justification of the private sector is that it serves society at large through value creation, services, commodities, economic growth, job creation, and so on. The preamble further acknowledges the fact that, even if business is conducted for these legitimate purposes and by legitimate means, harmful side-effects will occur. Our underlying presumption is that the company does have a responsibility for these side-effects and that companies, *qua* actors, are under a duty not to do harm. The preamble ensures that the permissibility of side-effect harm is restricted and cannot even be discussed unless the operation is legitimate in ends as well as means.

The first criterion, requiring consultation with affected parties to be carried out prior to and during business operations, is included for reasons argued by G. J. (Deon) Rossouw in chapter 3; business is not like war on this point. As regards both what constitutes harm and the legitimacy of the decisions that are being made, stakeholder consultation is essential. In short, for purposes of legitimacy and access to knowledge, dialogue is a key. Further, where side-effects *appear* to be inescapable, a third way may be found and costs reduced significantly if consultation is conducted at an early stage.

Unfortunately, side-effects are often used as means, and means can often be disguised as side-effects. Benefiting from a poor framework may be easy, but a company must set higher standards for itself. Companies should at least adhere to international standards. The notion of *beneficial* complicity implies that the company is responsible not only for *causal* effects but for any kind of involvement in the wrongdoing of others; thus the company is obliged under the PDE to counteract benefiting from a negative framework.

Assessing proportionality is difficult, but it is important that the side-effects of the operation are at least *justifiable* to the stakeholders. Hence, the demand that side-effects have to be justifiable must mean that they can not only be justified in the eyes of the company, but proven to be reasonable and proportionate even to affected parties. One example is where the consequences of not laying off employees would devastate not only the company but the national economy. Making people unemployed must in this case be said to be a justifiable/proportionate side-effect of corporate activity. By comparison, letting people die is not.

Further, the criterion of proportionality is a reminder that, if there is no way to justify side-effects to stakeholders, withdrawal is perhaps the only responsible option. It is, however, also important to keep in mind that withdrawal may have unfortunate side-effects.

Finally, and most importantly, being responsible for the side-effect harm that ensues from its operations means that a company has a duty to prevent or minimize such effects as far as possible. To the extent that the side-effects are inescapable – i.e. no other course of action can be chosen – active measures to minimize harm must be taken, even if these are costly.

According to the PDE, side-effect harm is not permissible unless *no other way* can be found that does not produce side-effect harm, and it is only if side-effects cannot be avoided that the duty to minimize them becomes relevant. Ideally, however, a third way may be found that does not produce harmful side-effects at all, in which case the actor must choose this course of action in order to "do the right thing".

The case-studies in part II of the book all discuss this revised version of the PDE in relation to specific cases – some well known, others not. The case-study authors analyse the cases in light of the terminology presented in the PDE by *explicating* the objectives, the means, and the side-effects, including complicity in the wrongdoing of others, thereby indicating whether applying the PDE from the outset of the operations might have produced another outcome. They assess what is done to prevent or minimize side-effect harm. Most importantly, they evaluate the applicability and fruitfulness of the framework in relation to the case and give their feedback to the framework in light of the case. Taking account of the authors' feedback, a set of operationalizing guidelines for the PDE in the business context is suggested in the concluding chapter of the book.

Part III
Case-studies

7

The principle of double effect and moral risk: Some case-studies of US transnational corporations

Patricia H. Werhane

The classical principle of double effect (PDE) states that "in cases where a contemplated action has both good and bad effects, the action is [morally] permissible only if it is not wrong in itself and if it does not require that one directly intend the evil result".[1] The PDE revised and proposed in this volume rephrases the classic doctrine by claiming that "[n]egative side-effects do occur, even when businesses pursue legitimate objectives by legitimate means", but – this being so – it is a requirement that "consultation with affected parties, as well as risk assessment, is carried out prior to and during the business operation in order to identify negative side-effects" and "negative side-effects that arise from a business's operations are not made to serve as means to achieving its legitimate objectives". The revised PDE further adds three other qualifications: that "negative side-effects can be justified as proportionate to the legitimate objectives", that "active measures are taken to prevent or minimize negative side-effects", and that "the negative effects are inescapable – it is not possible to achieve the legitimate objectives with fewer or no side-effects". It is proposed that the PDE, with its qualifications, can become a tool to measure moral risk, particularly as companies venture into transnational relationships.

To illustrate the revised PDE proposed in this volume, in what follows I shall present and analyse two case-studies of American transnational companies operating in China and compare those cases with one case-study of an American transnational company operating in Africa. Before doing so, however, I want to add an addendum to the revised PDE that will complicate the qualifications that a side-effect harm is permissible provided that a risk assessment is carried out, affected parties are consulted, the negative side-effects are justifiable in achieving legitimate objectives and are not merely means, measures are taken to minimize negative side-effects, and these side-effects are unavoidable in order to achieve legitimate objectives. I use the term "moral risk" as an explanatory mechanism to describe and critique some corporate multinational activities. I define moral risk as follows: Moral risk entails choices where (1) one is uncertain about the outcomes, and (2) achieving what is morally right or good will, in all likelihood, entail doing some evil, engaging in activities that are harmful, that do not respect individuals and their rights, or are otherwise morally questionable. Moreover, ordinarily in these cases, (3) one is uncertain whether the outcome itself will produce a balance of benefit over harm or good over evil, erase the causes of corruption, or improve the occurrence of human rights violations, and (4) not acting itself entails moral risk.

The revised PDE, I want to suggest, is a good tool for analysing and measuring moral risk when negative side-effects are inescapable in order to achieve legitimate ends. But in many cases one cannot determine in advance whether or not legitimate objectives are justifiable in terms of being proportionate and necessary and thus outweigh the negative effects even if one takes active measures to prevent or minimize the negative side-effects. The risk, then, is prescient because one cannot predict beforehand whether the outcome will achieve more harm than good or even achieve the legitimate goals, and sometimes the positive or negative net effects of the outcomes can never be determined with certainty. Moreover, not engaging in the activity in question is usually morally risky as well, since the opportunity to achieve some propitious end is forgone. I shall present some case-studies where these challenges are evident.

Case-study I: Should Levi Strauss engage in doing business in China?

In 1992 the famous jeans manufacturer Levi Strauss was faced with the question of whether or not to continue and increase its business involvement with mainland China, one of the fastest-growing markets for consumer goods in the world. At issue for this company was whether it should do business with a country whose human rights practices did not meet the standards of the UN Universal Declaration of Human Rights or of Levi Strauss's own stated ethics principles and guidelines for business relationships.

Levi Strauss (LS) was founded in 1873 by a Bavarian immigrant, Levi

Strauss, as a family business making canvas trousers. Until 1971 the company was a wholly owned family business, but that year, wanting capital for expansion, the company became a publicly traded stock. However, the Haas family, descendants of Strauss, still controlled a majority interest. In the 1980s the company, responding to market declines, closed almost 60 plants worldwide and the company's name began to be identified with some questionable employment procedures. In 1985, after Robert Haas became CEO of the company, the family bought back outstanding publicly held shares at a cost of US$1.6 billion. Despite the cost to the family, their reasoning was that, since the family name was on the jeans, they should control how and where these products are manufactured and sold.

Under the family leadership the company again regained its reputation as a values-oriented company. Still, profitability remained equally important, and in 1987 LS revised its mission statement to reflect its philosophy that doing good and doing well were intertwined, not conflicting, principles.

The mission of Levi Strauss & Co. is to sustain responsible commercial success as a global marketing company of branded casual apparel. We must balance goals of superior profitability and return on investment, leadership market positions, and superior products and service. We will conduct our business ethically and demonstrate leadership in satisfying our responsibilities to our communities and to society.[2]

As LS expanded into global markets, the company faced what it perceived to be new challenges, and in 1992 it developed what it called Business Partner Terms of Engagement, which spelled out how and with whom it would do business worldwide. These guidelines restricted the company and its divisions to partnering only with companies that engaged in the following practices:

- All employment agreements are voluntary.
- Employees are paid fair living wages.
- Working hours are limited to no more than 60 hours per week.
- Children under 14 years of age are not hired nor allowed to work.
- There is no prison or forced labor.
- Workers are employed on the basis of their abilities (rather than on an ethnic, gender, or other bias.)
- Corporal punishment and mental coercion are forbidden.

To implement these guidelines, the company even sent audit teams to its partner companies to determine whether they were adhering to these guidelines.[3]

By 1992 mainland China had become an important and inexpensive supplier of raw materials for LS, including fabric, buttons, thread, and labels. However, the company had made no investments in its supplier companies in China nor did it manufacture in China, although it had large manufacturing facilities in Hong Kong. Importing materials from mainland China was advantageous for Hong Kong jeans production, production that could be expanded, given the demand for jeans in Asia. Materials from mainland China were favourably priced, and few other sources for LS's Hong Kong manufacturers could match those prices for the same quality. Moreover, LS's competitors were beginning to develop manufacturing and sales facilities in China, a potentially huge market given its population and focus on economic expansion. Labour costs in mainland China were much lower than in Hong Kong and many other Asian countries. In 1992 China was the largest supplier of clothing to the United States. Not to participate in this growing market seemed an anomaly to the goals of a major multinational apparel manufacturer.

On the other hand, in 1992 Levi Strauss perceived that doing business with mainland China was not without its difficulties. Mainland China was well known for what the West considers to be trademark and copyright abuses. There are questions of human rights as well. Tiananmen Square remained on the minds of most Americans, and the Chinese government periodically clamped down on people who spoke out or printed literature critical of the government. Prison slave labour was sometimes used in manufacturing facilities, there were rumours of child labour in the remote provinces, and, in general, China did not have a good record in respecting human rights. Although Levi Strauss had no intention of using prison or child labour in any of its plants, by doing business with the Chinese government in joint ventures it was worried that it might be morally complicit or perceived as complicit by partnering with and contributing to a regime that did not abandon these practices.

According to Levi Strauss's information, in 1992 mainland China's one-child-per-family policy was expected to be enforced by companies themselves, and companies were expected to punish workers who became pregnant for a second time. This policy was important to control population growth. Levi Strauss did not dispute that conclusion, but it objected to the requirement that companies, particularly non-Chinese companies, had to police and enforce government policy. That was not within its purview as a company nor, it concluded, should it require expatriate managers to enforce a policy that to many of them interfered with free choice and personal privacy.

In rural China there was evidence of unequal treatment of male and female children, and female infanticide was not unheard of in remote villages. By engaging in joint ventures with the Chinese government, was

Levi Strauss implicitly endorsing these practices? The legal system governing business transactions was confusing, at best, and the question of joint venturing with Chinese partners might include partnering with the Chinese government or the military, relationships that reportedly involved elements of bribery or extortion.

In 1993, after over a year of deliberation, the CEO of the company, Robert Haas, overruled the advice of his executive committee, and stated,

> In countries that do not offer protection of basic legal and human rights, we potentially expose our employees who live and work there to unacceptable risks; and we subject the company to the claim of legitimizing and supporting governments whose practices are condemned.[4]

Haas then announced that Levi Strauss would conduct a three-year phase-out programme to withdraw business from its Chinese contractors, find new suppliers for raw materials, and transfer work done in China to other locations.[5]

Haas's deliberations and decision can be interpreted as using PDE to decide against expanding company business into China. The company and its leaders had good intentions, its products are obviously not intrinsically evil, and ties with Chinese partners, like alliances it had made in the past with other companies and other countries, appear in the first instance not to be illegitimate. Disengaging from the Chinese market was morally risky for a number of reasons. From a shareholder perspective there would be lost opportunities for inexpensive manufacturing and sales to the large Chinese population. There were also lost opportunities to provide good jobs and to become an exemplary role model of how business can be done with integrity as well as profitably.

LS concluded that it could not avoid the negative side-effects of such an enterprise, in particular, partnering with human rights abusers, competing with or buying from suppliers that use prison slave labour, and what it saw as a requirement to enforce a birth control policy in the companies it would operate in China. It was also unclear from its information whether or not establishing business partnerships in China would involve bribery or extortion. Levi Strauss did not envision how it could take active measures to minimize these particular problems, and it was impossible to determine whether its presence in China as a role model for how business could be conducted in an ethical manner would outweigh these negative elements, elements that it would be at least implicitly legitimizing by its partnerships with Chinese companies and/or the Chinese government. The Levi Strauss management, and in particular its CEO, decided that this was much too risky a proposition – morally risky – because it could not be sure that it would be creating a net positive effect and it recognized the negative side-effects of whatever action it took. It appeared to engage in PDE reasoning (although it does not refer to it as such), it concluded that its risk assessment precluded a justification of this business venture, and it opted out.

Case-study II: Motorola in China

Motorola, like Levi Strauss, was originally a family-owned business, although currently its shares are traded on the New York Stock Exchange. From the very beginning the Galvin family set high moral standards for the company, standards that are still in force today. Motorola operates from what it calls "Key Beliefs":

- To maintain the highest standards of honesty, integrity, and ethics in all aspects of our business – with customers, suppliers, employees, governments, and society at large – and to comply with the laws of each country and community in which we operate.[6]
- **Uncompromising integrity** means staying true to what we believe. We adhere to honesty, fairness and "doing the right thing" without compromise, even when circumstances make it difficult.
- **Constant respect for people** means we treat others with dignity, as we would like to be treated ourselves. Constant respect applies to every individual we interact with around the world.[7]

In addition, Motorola has adopted the manufacturing standard of Six Sigma Quality (fewer than 4 defects per million units) for all its operations worldwide.

Motorola has been doing business in China since 1986. Currently it operates a number of projects – 2 are wholly owned by Motorola, 8 are joint ventures, and 20 are operations with Chinese partners, with a total of over 10,000 employees in mainland China. Its Chinese operations generate 12 per cent of its gross revenues, and include local sourcing, manufacture, and sales. In 2001 its investments were US$3.4 billion and sales reached US$4.9 billion, making Motorola the largest foreign investor in China.[8]

How does Motorola manage these operations, keep within its Key Beliefs, and achieve Six Sigma Quality? The company does not discuss publicly the one-child-per-family policy, so it is unclear whether or not it enforced this policy or enforced it equally in all its operations. (The rumour is that it simply ignored the policy, "trading" non-enforcement for social benefits it provided its employees, so that Chinese officials pretended not to notice the non-enforcement; but that rumour is not confirmed.) Indeed, recently China rescinded this policy as a mandatory element of government and business operations.[9] What is known is that Motorola sees its mission in China to become engaged in and contribute to community development. The Chinese call this Quanxi: developing good connections and giving back to the community. It has set up what it calls Project HOPE, contributing over US$1 million to help educate rural children.[10] It has a home ownership programme for its workers. The company has provided over 3,000 university fellowships, and in 1995 it was the first foreign company to co-sponsor (with the Tianjin Environmental Protection Bureau) a symposium on the environment. Motorola University in China trains all workers at least one week per year. Motorola has also developed what it calls the Chinese Accelerated Management Program: a 10-month programme for selected Chinese managers, many of whom are also sent out of the country on work/exchange programmes for two months. Motorola has been able to achieve Six Sigma Quality in semi-conductor and paging devices manufacture in China.[11] These achievements have been accomplished with a workforce that Motorola had to train extensively. Motorola has also had to adjust to workplace habits that differ considerably from those in the United States: most employees bicycle up to two hours to work, they bring their laundry to do and hang it up in the factory, they bring food to be cooked on the factory floor, and an afternoon nap is considered part of normal work practice.[12]

Motorola's philosophy is that one must be engaged within a country – not simply trade with it – to achieve moral, economic, and political progress. It argues that setting up the company as a role model and encouraging open communication and free trade will be the best avenues for a democratic China. Robert Galvin, former CEO of Motorola, recalls how in 1986 he met with Chinese officials, including the current president Jiang Zemin (then mayor of Shanghai), and challenged Chinese officials to accept Motorola as an autonomous enterprise that could show China's industrialists the path to world-class manufacturing.

We think we are helping to "write the rules" in China. We have the most free-hand of anybody in China because we set the game plan in his or her interest, and we are out doing things of social benefit.... Jiang Zemin spent a day with us [in 1995] then came back to Beijing and sent about 200 members of the Politburo back the next week on buses and said, "Go see how Motorola treats people. That's how we want Chinese people treated." Now that's not civil rights, but that's human rights. Therefore, when we contribute something to the society that drives the society to a more progressive environment.... We and others are helping to set the base for the Chinese market; hence a place to have a very significant platform for our businesses.[13]

Analysing Motorola's decision to engage in business ventures in China in terms of the revised PDE, Motorola determined that it could adapt the operational principle of constructive engagement without discarding its mission of uncompromising integrity. It judged that engaging with the Chinese would, in the long term, be more advantageous to challenge the Chinese approach to human rights than if it avoided doing business in and with China. It saw itself as a role model for how business can be conducted in a morally legitimate way. Moreover, it took specific steps to minimize and, in the case of the child policy, avoid the negative side-effects of its partnerships with the Chinese, not by criticizing the Chinese but rather by developing educational and environmental initiatives that contributed to improving the situation of its employees and the country. At the same time, I would argue, this is still a very morally risky venture. It is not clear that in doing business with the Chinese and with their approval one is not colluding with the Chinese government or even corrupting one's own expatriate managers, and Motorola's operations contribute to Chinese governmental wealth. So the moral risks are not abated by constructive engagement; they are merely faced head-on. Moreover, Motorola cannot calculate with certainty that its operations create a net positive effect in China. As China moves toward free markets and changes its human rights policies, albeit slowly, Motorola will still never be certain whether its activities were part of the precipitating force for those changes. And, if China fails to make significant changes to these policies and activities, Motorola will continue to be morally challenged as it is at present.

Case-study IB: Addendum

On 9 April 1998, five years after the Levi Strauss decision to withdraw from its Chinese markets and suppliers, a headline in the *New York Times* read: "Reversing course, Levi Strauss will expand its output in China."[14] This time Levi Strauss would try a new tactic. It would use its own Business Partner Terms of Engagement as principles that would be guidelines for managerial behaviour in every setting, including China, despite local difficulties or anomalies, and it would attempt to enforce these terms with its Chinese partners.

Part of its reasoning was that enforcement of the one-child-per-family policy was no longer an issue. Another part of its reasoning was that it saw other companies such as Motorola operating successfully without giving up moral principles. But now it is faced with new problems. Simply to apply its own sets of standards without taking into account local conditions is morally risky for at least two reasons. First, such a tactic gives the appearance of moral absolutism, even if those standards are pretty much in line with the prescriptions of general codes such as the UN Universal Declaration of Human Rights. Is it creating more harm than good by insulting the Chinese and ignoring local customs? Moreover, by not taking into account local conditions, one wonders what the possible economic success of Levi Strauss's operations will be in that arena.

Case-study III: ExxonMobil in Chad and Cameroon

My third case is an ongoing one: ExxonMobil's exploration of oil in Chad and its pipeline to be built through Cameroon. Chad and Cameroon are two of the poorest countries in the world: per capita income in each country is less than US$1/day. According to Transparency International, Chad and Cameroon repeatedly come bottom of its annual corruption index.[15]

In 2001, Exxon's revenues were US$190 billion; Chad's yearly gross domestic product was US$1.4 billion. However, ExxonMobil, in partnership with ChevronTexaco and Petronas (a Malayasian oil company), is investing US$3.5 billion in drilling in Chad and in building a 600 mile pipeline through Cameroon. The project should generate US$2 billion in revenues for Chad and US$500 million for Cameroon over the projected 25-year drilling period.[16] Nevertheless, from ExxonMobil's perspective, carrying out this project is fiscally risky (owing to the history of oil drilling in Africa) and, I would argue, morally risky because, as *Fortune* speculates, the president of Chad, Idriss Déby, who "has a flair for human rights abuses,... could 'pull a Mobutu'".[17]

ExxonMobil is a company created by the merger of Exxon and Mobil, each of which, prior to the merger, was a multi-billion-dollar oil company. Exxon was best known for the Exxon Valdez oil spill, which cost the company millions of dollars and did some serious environmental damage to the coastline, flora, and fauna in Alaska. Mobil is not without blemishes either. According to *Forbes*, in the early 1990s, Mobil, interested in oil development in Kazakhstan, became involved with a certain James Giffen, known as a "fixer". It is alleged, but not yet proven, that Giffen, in collaboration with a Mobil executive, was engaged in a questionable payment scheme with the Kazakh government in order to get access to Kazakhstan's oil fields.[18] Thus, both Exxon's and Mobil's activities, now linked, are closely watched after these incidents.

ExxonMobil faces another challenge: the history of oil company exploration in less developed countries. There is a perception, at least partly true, that until very recently oil companies simply went in to a region with a team of expatriate "foreigners", drilled, created pipelines, and left (and this still sometimes occurs). Time and again, as Jerry Useem reminds us in an article in *Fortune*, there have been problems such that these companies could never meet the criteria of the revised PDE. The most publicized case is Shell's operations in Ogoniland in Nigeria, as Ogbonna Ike relates in chapter 9 in this volume. Although Shell claimed to have invested over US$100 million in environmental projects in Nigeria, there is little to show for this investment. Even the *Wall Street Journal* described Ogoniland as "a ravaged environment".[19] Despite US$300 billion earned from oil since 1975, Nigeria's per capita income has dropped 23 per cent.[20]

Given that history, what is interesting about the Chad/Cameroon project is ExxonMobil's approach. ExxonMobil has created a partnership – a four-way alliance with the Chad and Cameroon governments, the World Bank, and a number of non-governmental organizations (NGOs). The World Bank's interest is in improving the well-being of the people in Chad and Cameroon. The rationale for considering and then approving the project was that, according to the World Bank, "[t]his project could transform the economy of Chad.... By 2004, the pipeline would increase Government revenues by 45–50% per year and allow it to use those resources for important investments in health, education, environment, infrastructure, and rural development, necessary to reduce poverty."[21] The World Bank created a series of provisos to ensure that there is sound fiscal management of the revenues received by Chad and Cameroon, it set up strict environmental and social policies, and it consulted with a number of NGOs involved in the project. In 2000 it approved the project.

By the middle of 2002 the project employed over 11,000 workers, of whom at least 85 per cent are from Chad or Cameroon. Of these local workers, over 3,700 have received high-skills training in construction, electrical, and mechanical trades, and 5 per cent of the local workers have supervisory positions. In addition, local businesses have benefited from the project to a total of almost US$100 million. The Bank has developed micro-lending projects accompanied with fiscal and technical training. The aim is to establish permanent micro-lending banks in Chad and Cameroon. In partnership with ExxonMobil the World Bank has created new schools and health clinics, provided HIV education, vaccines against tuberculosis and medical staff to monitor the distribution, distributed thousands of mosquito nets for protection against malaria, and provided farm implements and seeds to develop indigenous agriculture.[22] The Chad and Cameroon governments, in turn, have pledged to use the profits they receive from the venture to improve the standard of living of their citizens.

NGOs that have partnered with the project have goals similar to the World Bank's: to improve the economies of Chad and Cameroon as well as to protect indigenous traditions and the environment. Before approving this venture, the World Bank conducted extensive environmental studies to determine if this project could be achieved without causing serious environmental degradation. It concluded that, with careful drilling and attention to the surrounding landscape, and with safety measures that would prevent illicit tapping into the pipeline, the project was environmentally safe.

It would appear that, at least on the surface, ExxonMobil is attempting to apply PDE reasoning with some success. It is partnering with the World Bank to reduce environmental fall-out; it is working with NGOs and local communities to minimize the harm created by its exploitation of the countryside and its traditions. The alliance is pressuring the governments of Chad and Cameroon to make good use of the monies they receive as oil revenues. Its approach, then, is holistic, envisioning the company as part of an alliance that takes into account and is responsible to multiple stakeholders, not merely shareholders and oil consumers.[23]

Will this ExxonMobil project produce net benefits? Concerning the question of producing a net "good", it is important to clarify the context and the recipients of that "good". Oil companies create jobs and almost always produce profits from oil drilling, and thus enhance the well-being of workers and shareholders. Oil is necessary, particularly in industrialized countries. So there is almost always some net overall good effect from oil drilling. However, as the editors of this book carefully point out, in cases such as these a multiple stakeholder approach is critical, particularly in global business development. This complicates any PDE assessment by requiring an analysis of harms and benefits to multiple stakeholders, not merely aggregation of the net benefits. Part of the equation to evaluate this "net good effect" is how the drilling affects the country or region in which it is carried out. What is the environmental impact in the short term and the long term? Do the drilling and pipelines interfere with indigenous traditions, land ownership, etc.? Does the drilling provide jobs for citizens of that country? Does the country benefit from the oil profits? And do we need more oil anyway?

What, then, are the down-sides, the negative effects, of this project? First, despite good intentions, environmental hazards are inescapable. In any oil drilling project, even with the strictest safety measures, there will be oil spills. According to World Bank estimates, annual spill rates will be between 1 and 4 per cent.[24] There will be increased greenhouse gas emissions, although the level of these has not been accurately calculated. There will also be forestry and bush product losses (e.g. nuts, herbs, and fruit), all of which have to be compensated for. ExxonMobil knows this, as does the World Bank.[25] They are both working constantly to improve safety measures and to prevent spills from sabotage. The question of local sabotage is tricky because, according to the Rain Forest Action Network, in 1998 government security forces in the Doba region, the area now being developed by ExxonMobil, killed about 100 unarmed Chad citizens. In addition, large projects such as these usually lead to an increase in disease, for example HIV infection and other health risks. Agricultural and livestock losses from displaced farms and the forest will occur, although ExxonMobil has guaranteed compensation and/or relocation.

Critics of the Chad/Cameroon oil project include Archbishop Desmond Tutu, who recently was quoted as saying, "The Chad/Cameroon project is not the help we asked for or needed. In the absence of the rule of law and respect for human rights [in both countries] and the environment, financing of large-scale development is destroying the environment and us."[26] According to the Cameroon Environmental Defence (CED) report, this project has a number of almost insurmountable negative aspects. ExxonMobil, the World Bank, and NGOs working in the region are well aware that no sound rule of law exists in either Chad or Cameroon, so that any contracts or promises are not backed with a well-developed legal system to enforce those agreements. Not only is this problematic in terms of agreements between the drillers and the government, but there is also no legal guarantee that monies given to these governments will actually be spent on citizen welfare. Indeed, despite World Bank protests, the President of Chad bought arms with his first payment of oil revenue. (He has promised not to do this in the future, but the notion of promising is not one with which he is familiar, and there is no legal framework by which to challenge his purchases.)[27] To quote the Rainforest Action Network, "Jean Ndih, president of Defense de l'Environnement Camerounais ... says that the pipeline will only serve to further impoverish the people of the two countries and benefit 'highly corrupt regimes'."[28]

The CED questions whether adequate compensation is being provided for land use and displacement of people. There have been some intertribal wars between Pygmies and Bantus concerning whose land is actually being compensated. This sort of quarrel upsets the delicate balance between these tribes, and, again, there are no enforcement mechanisms to remedy any injustices or thefts. So there are questions concerning the protection of the rights and cultural values of indigenous peoples in this region. *Fortune* reports that not every citizen will be satisfied with the company's efforts. Even as they begin drilling, local people are complaining that they are not getting jobs, and worries about Pygmy peoples' (the Baka and Bakola tribes) rights abound.[29]

Both the CED and the Rainforest Action Network question the environmental viability of the project, arguing that issues of water pollution and rain forest protection have not been adequately addressed, so that part of the ecosystem may be negatively affected. Many of the local tribes depend on the forest for food, and changing this ecostructure may not be conducive to preserving these traditional food supplies.

Thus ExxonMobil faces the moral risk of creating more harm than good in Chad and Cameroon. Because it is dealing with multiple stakeholders, some of whom are not perfectly honest, in a situation where there are no enforceable legal mechanisms, the company and the World Bank cannot control or mitigate all these risks, although of course ExxonMobil will profit extensively from this very rich oil source and expand the oil supply for its consumers. I would classify this as moral risk because it is hard to calculate, in advance, whether the good of producing oil and wealth will balance the harms; indeed, this may never be determined with certainty. Yet both the World Bank and ExxonMobil continue to contend that there will be a net benefit to Chad and Cameroon from this project.

Conclusion

These case-studies remind us of both the strengths and the limitations of the revised PDE and the assessment of moral risk in analysing short-term and long-term corporate activities and interventions. Thinking through PDE and taking into account moral risk are important elements in corporate decision-making, particularly in multinational settings. In 1992, Levi Strauss backed out of risk-taking. Motorola, on the other hand, not only engaged in double effect reasoning to its advantage in developing operations in China, it also pushed its decision-making to think more broadly about operating in a country where traditions and customs were very different from those in manufacturing operations in the United States. That is, it engaged in *moral imagination*,

... the ability in particular circumstances to discover and evaluate possibilities not merely determined by that circumstance, or limited by its operative mental models, or merely framed by a set of rules or rule-governed concerns. In management decision-making, moral imagination entails perceiving norms, social roles, and relationships entwined in any situation. Developing moral imagination involves heightened awareness of contextual moral dilemmas and their mental models, the ability to envision and evaluate new mental models that create new possibilities, and the capability to reframe the dilemma and create new solutions in ways that are novel, economically viable, and morally justifiable.[30]

When it first entered the Chinese market, Motorola never imagined that a company could achieve Six Sigma Quality with laundry and cooking taking place on the factory floor and afternoon naps eating up productive worker time. But it was surprised, and this surprise helped Motorola to think more creatively and imaginatively while still preserving its moral principles as it moves into new markets.

ExxonMobil is to be admired for its attempts to use PDE thinking and a systemic multiple stakeholder approach to new drilling in Chad. But is it thinking out of the box and using its moral imagination in projecting the long-term perspective of the company? It is investing US$3.5 billion in the Chad/Cameroon venture; but do we need more oil? According to the World Bank, a strong supporter of this project, "the project is expected to deliver to markets for consumption 800–1,000 million barrels [of oil] over the 28-year production life of the fields. *However, given existing consumption levels, this supply of oil is expected to have a minimal impact, if any, on the global level of oil consumption.*"[31] US$3.5 billion could be the break-even point for justifying development of new and renewable energy sources such as the sun and hydrogen. Thus, long-term calculations involving PDE should entail balancing the costs and benefits of developing new energy sources against those of the present investment in Chad. Those calculations would have to take into account the income loss to Chad and Cameroon if this drilling did not occur. But a careful risk analysis might conclude that cheaper solar and other renewable energies would, in the long run, be more beneficial in terms of both environmental impact and profitability than an investment in a traditional energy source where the income generated might simply feed corrupt governments rather than improve the well-being of its citizens. At least that should be included in ExxonMobil's calculations. The revised PDE and moral risk assessments are important tools in evaluating risky projects. But they are only part of that evaluation, and moral imagination is necessary if companies are to make moral progress in global business decision-making.

Notes

1. William David Solomon, "Double effect", in Lawrence Becker and Charlotte Becker (eds.), *Encyclopedia of Ethics* (New York: Garland Publishing, 1992), p. 268.
2. Jane Palley Katz and Lynn Sharp Paine, *Levi Strauss & Co.: Global Sourcing [A]* (Harvard University Graduate School of Business Administration, case #9-395-127, 1994).
3. Ibid.
4. Jane Palley Katz and Lynn Sharp Paine, *Levi Strauss & Co.: Global Sourcing [B]* (Harvard University Graduate School of Business Administration, case #9-395-128, 1994).

5. Katz and Paine, *Levi Strauss & Co.: Global Sourcing [A]*.
6. Motorola, "Statement of uncompromising integrity", internal document, 1991.
7. See http://www.motorola.com/code/code.html (accessed 2002).
8. "Motorola sees bright future in China", *CircuiTree* 80, 15 January 2002.
9. Elisabeth Rosenthal, "One-child policy, China rethinks iron hand", *New York Times*, 1 November 1998.
10. Tony Carter, "Strategic customer development in China", *Columbia Journal of World Business* 31, 1996, pp. 56–59.
11. http://www.motorola.com/China (accessed 2002).
12. From personal interviews with a former Motorola China manager.
13. Galvin, quoted in "Business interests, social concerns", *Industry Week* 245, 2 December 1996, pp. 26–27.
14. Mark Landler, "Reversing course, Levi Strauss will expand its output in China", *New York Times*, 9 April 1998.
15. See http://www.trans.de/index.html (accessed 1999).
16. See http://www.worldbank.org/afr/ccproj/project/pro_overview.htm.
17. Jerry Useem, "Exxon's African adventure", *Fortune*, 15 April 2002, pp. 102–114.
18. Rene Fisher, *The Chad–Cameroon oil and pipeline project: A call for accountability*, Publication of the Association Tchadienen pour la Promotion et la Défense des Droits de l'Homme (Chad), Centre pour l'Environnement et le Developpement, and Cameroon Environmental Defence (2002/2003), p. 23.
19. G. Brooks, "Slick alliance: Shell's Nigerian oil fields produce few benefits for region's villagers", *Wall Street Journal*, 6 May 1994; reprinted in William E. Newburry and Thomas N. Gladwin, "Shell and Nigerian oil", in Thomas Donaldson, Patricia H. Werhane and Margaret Cording (eds.), *Ethical issues in business*, 7th edn. (Upper Saddle River, N.J.: Prentice-Hall, 2002), pp. 522–540, at p. 526. In 1993, Shell shut down its operations in Ogoniland, but it still drills for oil and gas in other parts of Nigeria. Shell has dramatically revised its Code of Ethics, it has invested at least US$100 million in cleaning up Ogoniland, and it has pledged over US$500 million for exploring alternative energy sources. See http://www.shell.com (accessed 2003).
20. Useem, "Exxon's African adventure", p. 106.
21. See http://www.worldbank.org/afr/ccproj/project/pro_overview.htm.
22. Useem, "Exxon's African adventure", and http://www.worldbank.org/afr/ccproj/project/pro_overview.htm.
23. According to ExxonMobil, "[s]ustainability is a critical consideration in how we operate the company. We recognize the importance of sustainable development, a process that seeks to protect the aspirations of future generations. As a major energy supplier we seek to maximize the contributions we make to economic growth, environmental protection and social well-being over the long run. Through the use of advanced technology, we have continued to add to the known reserves of oil and gas at a greater rate than they have been depleted, greatly extending the time period when affordable petroleum resources can meet the world's demand for energy. We believe this approach to be consistent with sustainability.... Our operations continually seek ways to reduce the footprint that we leave" (see http://www2.exxonmobil.com/corporate/Notebook/Footprint/Corp_N_Sustain.asp).
24. AFTE1 Environmental Group, *Project appraisal document on a proposed credit in the amount of SDR 4.3 million to the Republic of Cameroon for a petroleum environment enhancement project*, World Bank report, No. 19627-CM, 2000, p. 74.
25. Ibid., p. 74.
26. Fisher, *The Chad–Cameroon oil and pipeline project*, p. 1.

27. Useem, "Exxon's African adventure".
28. See the Rainforest Action Network website at http://www.ran.org/oilreport/africa.html (accessed 2002).
29. Useem, "Exxon's African adventure", p. 114.
30. Patricia Werhane, *Moral imagination and management decision-making* (New York: Oxford University Press, 1999), p. 93.
31. AFTE1 Environmental Group, *Project appraisal document*, p. 76 (emphasis added).

8

An object lesson in balancing business and nature in Hong Kong: Saving the birds of Long Valley

Robert E. Allinson

Introduction

This chapter is divided into four sections. The first section briefly outlines an ethic of "do no harm", including nature as a potential object of harm, which may serve as a norm for individual and corporate activity whenever environmental impact is an issue. The second section discusses the threat to the ecology of the Long Valley area in Hong Kong, and to the bird life in particular, posed by the proposal by the Kowloon-Canton Railway Corporation (KCRC) to construct the Spur Line railway between Sheung Shui and Lok Ma Chau directly across Long Valley, an area of great importance for bird life. The third section provides a short history of the case, including a description of the original proposal to build the railway across Long Valley, the rejection of the proposal by the Director of the Environmental Protection Department, and a court ruling that rejected the environmental impact assessment report by the KCRC, thus denying permission to proceed with the project. This was a truly momentous occasion because it was the first time that green groups had managed to stop a corporate/government project in Hong Kong.[1] This section also includes a concise description of the revised proposal, which did, in fact, receive environmental endorsement to go ahead. This revised proposal, which avoids Long Valley by the device of building a tunnel underneath it, will mitigate most, although not all, of the environmental concerns. The fourth section is a theoretical discussion of the value of this

121

particular case-study as an illustration of the blending of criteria (1) and (4) of the principle of double effect (PDE) – that one should consult affected parties prior to embarking upon a business plan for the sake of minimizing or preventing the incidence of negative side-effects.

Do no harm: Respect for nature

It is important to consider the general ethical framework from which one is operating whenever one considers the importance of the natural environment or wildlife. This is not to detract from the importance of an ethic for fellow human beings.[2] It is only that this particular case-study illustrates the importance of widening a humanistic ethic to an ethic that extends to all sentient life. One may consider Hippocrates' ethical maxim in *Primum non nocere*, "do no harm", to extend to all life and to sentient life in particular. Although it may seem impossible to avoid harming others and the environment to some degree, the real question is to what degree and where we draw the line.

In humanistic ethics or human-centred ethics, humans are considered to be lords of the planet; the welfare of humans is normally taken into account, whereas the welfare of nature or the planet as a whole is not the primary ethical end. The earth is perceived of as a resource for humankind. If one is to be careful not to exploit the earth, the reason for this is to ensure a longer use time for humankind and future generations. For example, water is not to be polluted, not for the sake of the purity of the water, but to preserve drinking sources for human beings.

In Asian traditions, however, one can find an ethic that extends the "do no harm" maxim to all sentient life. For example, Mahayana Buddhism teaches compassion for all sentient beings. It could be said that Buddhist ethics regards compassion for all sentient beings as the supreme ethical virtue. In the *Anguttara Nikaya* it is said, "how astonishing it is, that a man should be so evil as to break a branch off the tree after eating his fill. Suppose the tree were to bear no more fruit."[3] Tibetan Buddhism essentially prohibits the killing of animals.[4]

In ancient Chinese philosophy, there is a built-in moral order to the universe. In the tradition of Taoism, precept 132 of the *One Hundred and Eighty Precepts* is "You should not disturb birds and [other] animals".[5] In the *Tao de Ching*, 25, it is said that Tao models itself after the natural. What is the natural? How do humans follow the Tao, which follows what is natural? It must be considered that, whereas all animals have a predator (it has been suggested that the hippopotamus is the sole exception), humans have no predator. Of course, we could argue that humans are the predator of humans. But apart from this, if humans have no predator then humans possess a special responsibility to take care of the earth. Otherwise, the great ecological balance of nature will be destroyed.

How can humans take care of the earth in practical terms, and how can humans' caring for the earth be a lesson for their caring for their fellow humans? One could wait for humans to destroy enough of their own species to maintain the ecological balance. The problem is that humans might destroy nature in the process. A further problem obviously is weapons of mass destruction: humans' efforts to destroy their own species may go too far and accomplish self-destruction. Hence, awaiting humans' intra-species predatory behaviour may not be an effective method. Nature may attempt to reverse the course of its destruction by restricting the human species through famine, drought, disease, and other forms of natural catastrophe. However, reliance on these methods could also result in the extinction of the human species.

According to ancient Chinese philosophy, humans play an integral role in the trilateral unity of heaven, humankind, and earth. It could be said that it is humans' role to create the balance between heaven and earth. There is even an explicit reference in *The doctrine of the mean*, one of the Four Books (a great Chinese classic), to humans' role in giving full development "to the natures of creatures and things".[6] Indeed, it has been said that "[t]he entire content of Chinese philosophy, particularly in its enunciation of ethics, metaphysics and ontology, is principally directed toward unity and harmony with the external world, in its search for a social and cosmic order, and in its promotion of the realization of the common identity of all apparently distinct realities. To quote Professor T'ang Chün-I, 'The unity of Heaven and Man is the central idea in Chinese philosophy.'"[7]

In passing, it is useful to comment briefly on the debate among philosophers today regarding the concept of humans' obligation to the environment under the principle "do no harm". It has been very difficult for many philosophers to accept the concept that humans possess an obligation to the environment per se. The philosopher Tom Regan is an exception. In a chapter entitled "What sort of beings can have rights?" Regan argues against Feinberg that having a right does not require having an interest. But whether or not one accepts the idea that other creatures of nature possess purposes, Regan takes the stand that they nevertheless deserve respect.[8] Other philosophers, such as Peter Singer, do not consider that nature or the environment possesses an intrinsic value that places a demand on humans to respect it as such.[9] Perhaps this is the culture of post-industrialized humans. Carried through to its logical conclusion, if nature possesses only use-value, then ultimately it could be completely replaced if an alternative source of utility can be found. Of course, it is better to possess some attitude of respect towards nature, if only for use-value, than to have no respect for nature at all.

We cannot keep from hurting or killing other animals. How then do we draw the line? It is useful to take a lesson from the North American Indians. When hunting, North American Indians would select an aged or wounded deer to kill and allow younger and healthier deer to escape. Before eating the meat of the animal, prayers were said about the spirit and energy of the animal being put to good use. This reveals an attempt to blend the needs of utility, of using nature as a food source, with a respect for the life of nature.

When one is concerned about the possible and imminent extinction of a natural species, such as certain bird species, it could be argued that one is valuing it as worthy of living in its own right, as a value in itself, not as a use object for humankind's pleasure (because humankind's pleasure needs can be satisfied short of the enormous variety of species that do exist).[10] One is reminded of Mencius, the Chinese philosopher of the fourth century BCE, whose ethic was one of compassion for human beings, an ethic that derived from the feelings of compassion and alarm at the prospect of the imminent loss of life of a child who was about to fall into a well. When one contemplates the loss of a bird species, similar feelings of compassion and alarm are aroused.

A balance is of course required between the needs of humans and the needs of nature. Otherwise, respect for nature can be taken to absurd lengths, as in the case of the Jains, who, fearful of accidentally swallowing an insect, wear masks over their mouths and, fearful of stepping on an ant, sweep the ground before them as they walk. Why favour one creature over another? Is not nature itself governed by tooth and claw? Singer criticizes Schweitzer for favouritism.[11] Nature is not worth saving at all costs; but the attitude of respect towards nature as a sub-category of the general ethical principle "do no harm" makes it clear that one would attempt at all times to apply criterion (4) of the PDE as regards preserving natural life as much as possible when accomplishing legitimate business objectives.

Although distinctions must be made, and we value the life of the human more than the bacteria that we kill with penicillin, this is not the end of the story. If sensitivity is properly aroused, and here the aesthetics of beauty play an important role, then we will do all that we can to preserve the beauty and being of the environment simply because it is there. What right do we have to destroy something we did not make? Animals kill other animals for food and sometimes for territory, but they do not engage in the wanton and cold-blooded taking of fellow animal life. The reported cases of higher primates (the closest animals to humans) killing other higher primates seem to involve the motive to assert a territorial or leadership imperative. No vertebrate animal except for humans kills for the sake of killing. If the behaviour of a particular species is destructive of the environment, then a predator exists to limit the destruction caused by one species. In nature, so it seems, there is a marvellous ecological balance, a balance that is upset in a consistent, persistent, and high-risk fashion only by humans.

It is important in today's world of shrinking natural resources to resurrect an ethics of "do no harm", and to include nature in the category of that which is not to be harmed. Birds, although they serve important ecological functions, such as eating insects, also are a symbol of the non-utilitarian beauty of nature and of all life. Life cannot simply have a utility function or one day it might be possible to justify replacing life itself by another form of existence. Making an effort to save bird life provides a standpoint from which to take a stand for all life, even the seemingly least useful. Indeed, it is the least useful that functions best as a symbolic reminder of the value of all life. One remembers the stanza from Coleridge's poem:

He prayeth best who loveth best
All things both great and small;
For the dear Lord who loveth us,
He made and loveth all.

It is all too easy for a corporation to consider ways of compensating people for what it takes from them, but who will make restitution to nature? When a natural species becomes extinct, it can never be replaced. Although this may change in the future with the advent of cloning, it is not clear that this is an adequate answer because the destruction of habitat is the means of destroying the species. When a unique animal species is lost, something precious is lost that can never be regained.

What I wish to propose in this chapter is that, in pursuing the goals of corporate activity, one must think from the very beginning about how to do this without disrupting the environment. Thus, a combination of criteria (1) and (4) of the PDE adapted for business is of special importance. Business must consult with relevant parties before embarking on an enterprise in order to minimize or prevent harm that might be done to the environment. If a company's goals are initially set not to disrupt or damage the environment, one important consequence of the double effect – damage to nature – can be guarded against. To gain the motivation to take nature into account from the start, it is vital to have recourse to an ethics of "do no harm", including harm done to nature. Of course there is an issue of proportionality here – one may cause a population of insects to die in clearing swamp land – but there is an issue of ethics as well. It is crucial to introduce the issue of ethics here because extinguishing bird life may be perfectly legal. The only resource available to justify saving bird life is an ethical viewpoint. What is ethical or unethical becomes a crucial part of the debate and not merely what is legal or illegal.

Buckminster Fuller, whom I had the privilege of meeting on several occasions, wrote much about the importance of protecting the planet earth. It may be that this notion now needs to be expanded to protect the universe. For the moment, we must at least consider the needs of the whole planet in every activity in which we engage, whether individual or corporate. The case of saving the precious Long Valley bird habitat in Hong Kong illustrates a general principle that we need to take into account when we consider projects that make an impact on the world as a whole. Hong Kong is hardly environmentally pristine but this case is hugely significant both when taken in the context of the small land mass of Hong Kong and as an example for mainland China, which needs to be more sensitive to environmental concerns. In the case of migrating birds, the concern is for the bird life of the world. The loss of one key transit station can have an overall impact on the capacity of birds to migrate south to sustain their life. We must use our imaginations to consider how we can preserve our natural heritage. As in the title of Professor Werhane's book *Moral imagination and management decision-making*, we must enlarge our moral imagination.[12]

The case of Long Valley and the proposed KCRC Spur Line

The threat to ecological welfare

According to the Hong Kong Bird Watching Society (HKBWS), Long Valley is the largest remaining freshwater wetland in the north-western part of the New Territories – one of the three areas of Hong Kong, a Special Administrative Region (SAR) of China, which is made up of Hong Kong Island, Kowloon, and the New Territories.[13] According to the HKBWS, "it is a unique place where farming activities still thrive. Within the 25 hectares of farmland, more than 210 bird species have been recorded, nearly half the Hong Kong list. Of these, three species are 'vulnerable' and eight are 'near-threatened' by global standards. There have been breeding records of Painted Snipe at this piece of wetland." There are only 20–30 bird species resident in Hong Kong, and Long Valley is the last remaining site for Painted Snipe in Hong Kong.

The potential destruction of Long Valley would reduce the chance of birds' survival. According to the HKBWS, habitat destruction is permanent and cannot be compensated for. As Dr. Ng Cho Nam of the Ecology Department at the University of Hong Kong explained to me in a private interview in December 2002, when an alternative habitat is presented there is no guarantee that the birds will even select this habitat. During the time gap between the destruction of a habitat and the construction of an alternative site, bird population may already be lost. As regards technical details, the impact involves not only a reduction in the space of survival for wildlife, but also a deterioration in soil and water quality. There are also more far-reaching consequences for farming activities and relationships between flora and fauna. According to Dr. Ng, the unique location of Long Valley in conjunction with its famous counterpart Mai Po Marsh creates a unique biodiversity of bird life because different kinds of birds inhabit Mai Po Marsh from those that inhabit Long Valley (though there are some overlapping species). Another unintended consequence of the Spur Line project was that, as soon as the farmers who owned the land that they had abandoned to the marsh became aware that the government was planning to build a railway link, they began cultivating the land in order to obtain a better price when it was purchased by the government (cultivated land would fetch a higher price than abandoned land). Such cultivation, which did not produce any viable or needed crops, was already beginning to destroy the birds' habitat. This was an example of a double effect beginning to mushroom.

The ecological significance of Long Valley

According to the HKBWS, "[t]he ecological significance of the valley as the last area of wet agricultural land in Hong Kong is beyond dispute, not only for Painted Snipe, but also for Japanese Quail, Bluethroat and as a site for over 200 other species." The appeal by the Society during the 30-day period allowed for public discussion resulted in letters from members, bird tour companies, and respected conservation organizations throughout the world attesting to the value of Long Valley. What is important about this is that the action in the case of Long Valley is a model for action that might be taken by other groups in other parts of the world where environmental protection and species preservation are at issue.

Why is Long Valley an important site? According to the HKBWS,

Due to its hydrology and water supply, it functions as a freshwater wetland. As a freshwater wetland it works in combination with its famous counterpart, Mai Po Marsh which is both a salt water and a freshwater wetland. Thus, the two areas together provide a high degree of micro-habitat diversity. This is the reason why different kinds of birds inhabit these two nearby sites. In addition, Long Valley has minimal habitat fragmentation and low levels of human disturbance. Both minimal habitat fragmentation and low levels of human disturbance are important factors for bird habitation.

This combination of features makes Long Valley unique in Hong Kong. The only similar wetland is Kam Tin, which is facing even greater levels of development. Although there are protected freshwater wetlands in Hong Kong, none that are important for birds are protected. Many similar areas have been lost to or substantially damaged by development (Ha Tsuen, Fairview Park, Lok Ma Chau, and Yuen Long marshes).

Fragmentation

According to the HKBWS, fragmentation is a key issue. "From the ecological point of view, the smaller the area of habitat, the lower the number of species can be found. In Hong Kong, there are no small wetlands that support avian communities of any ecological value. For example, Lok Ma Chau has suffered serious fragmentation because of the drainage works there; as such, it is now very poor for freshwater wetland species. For example, the Gallinago Snipe are far less common there now, and although it once bred there, Greater Painted Snipe no longer occurs there."

Human disturbance

Long Valley is a relatively undisturbed area. Many of the species that are found in Long Valley and Kam Tin are easily disturbed, for example the Grey-headed Lapwing. Such species require large, open areas with low levels of disturbance. Long Valley is the only remaining site that satisfies these criteria.

Micro-habitats

The mix of micro-habitats at Long Valley, although unplanned, helps support a whole range of wetland specialists, from Greater Painted Snipe to Bluethroat. It is important to understand that many of these species are either absent from the Ramsar site (another bird habitat), or present in much lower densities, because that area is either the wrong habitat or sub-optimal for these species.

Globally threatened species

The problem that is created by the potential destruction of Long Valley is not one that is limited to Hong Kong. Certain species are globally threatened. If a habitat is destroyed, it has consequences not only for that location but for the world existence of the species. Thus, the concern for wildlife is not strictly speaking just a local affair; it is a planetary affair.

Landmark decision

On the basis of the above arguments, the Director of Environmental Protection made a landmark decision to refuse an environmental permit for the KCRC Lok Ma Chau Spur Line. This was an extraordinary event, especially when one considers the resources available to a group such as the Hong Kong Bird Watching Society compared with the immense resources of a corporation the size of the Kowloon-Canton Railway Corporation and its sole owner, the Hong Kong government.

BirdLife International Asia Council Meeting

The BirdLife International Asia Council Meeting held in Sri Lanka, 24–25 October 2000, passed a resolution calling on the Hong Kong government to ensure the future of Long Valley by declaring it a Nature Reserve. According to Mike Kilburn, chairman of the Conservancy Association of the HKBWS, "[t]his resolution is the strongest expression of international support for the Green Groups' campaign and the SAR Government's decision to save Long Valley. As a result, Hong Kong's commitment to protecting its natural heritage has become a model and an inspiration to conservationists and concerned governments throughout Asia."[14] The resolution of the BirdLife International Council illustrates the international importance of this case-study.

The history of the KCRC spur line

On 23 December 1998, the Kowloon-Canton Railway Corporation submitted to the Director of Environmental Protection a project profile with an application for a study brief. As required, it included information about the project, how and when it was to be implemented, together with its broad environmental implications.[15]

The study brief

The project profile was advertised and the Advisory Council on the Environment (ACE) was informed. Under the law, the Director of the Environmental Protection Department must consider comments received from ACE and the public in drawing up the study brief for the project.

On 10 February 1999, the Director provided the study brief to the KCRC so that it could undertake an environmental impact assessment (EIA) study and then provide an environmental impact assessment report.

Submission of the report for approval

On 28 January 2000, KCRC submitted a report to the Director, but the Director indicated that he wanted alternative alignments to be further investigated. After further study, KCRC submitted the report on 27 April 2000.[16] On 31 May 2000, the Hon. Christine Loh asked the Secretary of Transport "[r]egarding the construction of the East Rail Extension – Sheung Shui to Lok Ma Chau Spur Line which was gazetted on 8 October 1999 ... whether other alternative alignments that do not encroach on the ecologically valuable Long Valley have been considered?"[17]

The Secretary of Transport answered, "In June, 1999, we accepted a proposal from KCRC to construct the Spur Line ... To facilitate early consultation and discussion on key environmental issues at an early stage, the KCRC prepared and submitted an initial environmental assessment to the Advisory Council on Environment EIA Subcommittee in September 1999. On 27 April 2000, KCRC submitted a full EIA report to the Director of Environmental Protection for review under the EIA Ordinance."[18]

On 17 July 2000, James Blake, senior director of Capital Projects KCRC, presented the EIA report of the proposed Sheung Shui to Lok Ma Chau Spur Line to ACE. In this report, he argued that there could be one and only one routing: "It might appear strange that a connection point for the Spur Line with East Rail can only be found at one location." He argued further that "[t]he Spur Line is an Essential Infrastructure Project ... The urgency for the Spur Line stems from the doubling of boundary crossings during the past five years, reaching nearly 100 million last year." He stated that "[e]ngineering and operational constraints dictate that the Spur Line must connect with the existing East Rail at a point north of Sheung Shui, and be located on straight track alignment. Every effort has been made to find an alignment that causes the lowest impact in social and environmental terms, particularly minimizing ecological impacts." In particular one can take note of both his awareness of and his dismissal of an underground route: "An underground route cannot be provided below East Rail, due to space constraint and existing infrastructure alongside East Rail. Crossing above the railway and then going underground would mean a large tunnel portal structure in Long Valley and substantial measures to avoid flood risk during railway operations."[19] The justification of the Spur Line project was the claimed public interest of providing alternative rail travel between Hong Kong and the mainland of China. Such a railway would provide passengers with more choice than the existing railway link between Hong Kong and the mainland of China.

Although KCRC was the proponent, the construction of the Spur Line was the fulfilment of government policy. This policy was designed: to relieve congestion at the present East Rail crossing to the Mainland at Lo Wu; to provide a second rail crossing into the Mainland; and to provide access to rail transport for the proposed Kwu Tung Strategic Development Area.[20] The proposal called for the Sheung Shui–Lok Ma Chau Spur Line to cut across the Long Valley floodplain, located within the borders of Hong Kong. The motivation for this routing was simply that this was the shortest engineering distance between two points. Its proposed structure would utilize a viaduct, which would carry a train every few minutes across the centre of the marsh, which was considered the most important part of the valley from an ecological standpoint.

In order to obtain an environmental permit to construct the Spur Line, the KCRC was required by law to submit an environmental impact assessment to the government, in this case the Director of the Environmental Protection Department (EPD) and the Agricultural and Fisheries Conservation Department. In this submission, 30 days were given for public discussion. During these 30 days, 225 objections were lodged and the Hong Kong Bird Watching Society was active in eliciting and organizing these objections. The decision was ultimately left to the Director of the EPD.

Rejection of the EIA report

The EIA submission for a viaduct option across Long Valley was rejected by the Director of Environmental Protection, Rob Law, on 16 October 2000 on the grounds of the adverse environmental impact on Long Valley, a key transit point for more than 200 species of birds. Mr. Law said that the rail developer had failed to explore all alternative alignments to the existing line and its proposed measures to offset the ecological impact of the project were inadequate. This was an amazing development when one considers that the Hong Kong Bird Watching Society had, relatively speaking, extremely modest resources. According to a private telephone interview on 8 January 2002 with Mike Kilburn, the Hong Kong Bird Watching Society spent approximately HK$20,000 (equivalent to US$2,500) on public relations during the 30-day discussion period and the KCRC spent approximately HK$1 million (equivalent to US$130,000). Although the Bird Watching Society was joined in a rare and unprecedented show of unity by 10 other green groups (the Conservancy Association, the World Wide Fund for Nature Hong Kong, the Department of

Ecology and Biodiversity, the University of Hong Kong, Friends of the Earth, Green Lantau Association, Green Power, Greenpeace, Kadoorie Farm and Botanic Garden, and Produce Green Foundation), the victory was nonetheless a victory of a David over a Goliath.

In the Appeal Board decision, the reasons of the Director of the EPD for turning down the original EIA were summarized by the Board as follows:

The high ecological value and high diversity of birds in the area affected by the project. The high direct environmental impact during the construction stage and the likely residual impact from the lengthy construction phase having regard to proposed mitigation measures which were unlikely to be effective or practicable. In the light of comments from the public and ACE, the KCRC had not proved the absence of other practicable or reasonable alternatives. The environmental impacts were likely to be prejudicial to the well-being of the flora, fauna or ecosystem in the areas affected.

In his detailed reasons, the Director refers, *inter alia*, to the following:

The impact upon the high diversity of threatened species of birds of conservation importance caused in particular by the lengthy fragmentation effect of the linear construction site which will cause significant disturbance and habitat destruction. In Long Valley about 2.4 hectares will be subject to direct habitat destruction. Additionally, during construction disturbance sensitive birds will be disturbed. The mitigation measures proposed during construction for minimizing habitat fragmentation, silt runoff, hydrological disruption, concrete washing and other pollutants are unlikely to be practical or effective.

The Director did not accept that these problems could be overcome. Further, because of the need for storage, handling, and transportation, construction impacts were likely to be greater than predicted, particularly because lack of a proper drainage system in Long Valley and the likelihood of heavy rainfall or flooding would exacerbate silty run-off and cause problems with other pollutants. Therefore the Director concluded there would be significant adverse impacts during construction.

The proposed 1.8 hectares of temporary wetland are unlikely to be effective to compensate for habitat loss during construction. That having regard to Annex 16 of the Technical Memorandum this project will result in adverse ecological impacts in an area of ecological importance and it should not normally be permitted unless it has been shown to be necessary and that no other practical or reasonable alternatives are available. The Director was not satisfied that all alternative means had been explored nor did he believe that all constraints claimed by the

KCRC are insurmountable. The Director noted the key principle stated in section 4 of the Technical Memorandum that methodology proposed for mitigation should give priority to avoidance of impacts.[21]

The EIA report under appeal

According to the Appeal Board, "The Report concerns the whole of the 7.3 kilometer Spur Line from Sheung Shui to Lok Ma Chau, but the issues concerning its approval or rejection are now narrowed to the 700 meters of line or viaduct where it passes over Long Valley. Further, as we have pointed out, the real concerns are that during construction of this section, by the methods and program proposed and with the mitigation suggested in the report, the adverse impacts will be irreversible."[22]

The unanimous opinion of the Appeal Board was to uphold the decision of the Respondent, the Director of Environmental Protection, which was to reject the EIA report:

Faced with these completely new proposals which are not in the report or the assessment it is not open to the Appeal Board to properly exercise its discretion ... and approve the report with a raft of conditions as a substitute for amendment and proper assessment and (if appropriate) approval and registration of an amended report, which the public can access and rely upon. The reasons for this decision are as follows: The report cannot be approved without it being amended to include new and significant proposals of this kind. [The Board sits as an appellate tribunal not as a tribunal of enquiry] ... Because of the lack of knowledge, the success of ecological mitigation cannot be predicted with certainty. For these reasons, avoidance of adverse environmental impacts is preferred over mitigation.[23]

What is especially interesting for the purposes of the next section of this chapter on cooperative planning are the conclusions of the Board with regard to communication:

At all stages of the process there should be open, ready and frank communication between the Director and the proponent. Cooperation in achieving projects which are environmentally acceptable is the essence of the process.... Good communications between the Director and the proponent at this stage [i.e. an early stage] will often resolve future problems. Amendments to the report and a re-submission at this stage will assist the decision making process and cause little delay. Further, this may avoid delay and expense later in the process. If the report is allowed to go to the next stage by default ... or by a mistaken decision when it does not meet the necessary requirements, the following public consultation and submission to ACE will be a waste of time and money. A report cannot be approved unless it meets those requirements.[24]

The KCRC eventually presented a new proposal, which involved a route that avoided Long Valley (the chief objection of the Bird Watching Society) by tunnelling underneath it. This proposal was granted an environmental permit. The tunnel proposal was satisfactory to the Bird Watching Society and hence represented a great victory for this group and, more importantly, for bird life. It was not problem free, because the western-end station at Lok Ma Chau will still be built inside the wetlands, but it nevertheless represents a major change in that it mainly avoids the precious Long Valley.

The court costs of this entire procedure have been estimated at HK$100 million (equivalent to US$12 million). The tunnelling requires an additional outlay of HK$1.5 billion over the original budget.[25] It is of key importance to point out that this tunnelling option had been dismissed as impossible by KCRC in the original EIA.[26]

Placing the Spur Line in a tunnel has eliminated any direct impacts on Long Valley and thus removes the need for compensation. This is a major benefit of the tunnel option. Avoidance of impacts at Lok Ma Chau, however, was not possible because of the need to connect to Huanggang Station in Shenzhen.

Cooperative planning and PDE

It is noteworthy, as pointed out above, that the solution of tunnelling beneath Long Valley was initially rejected by the KCRC on 17 July 2000. The KCRC thus knew of this alternative at least a year prior to the final decision of the Appeal Board on 30 July 2001.

As noted in the Appeal Board decision, strong statements were made that prior consultation and communication could have resulted in cost savings. It is my opinion that consultation and communication would have been considerably enhanced if the KCRC had adopted a more holistic ecological ethic. For example, when the KCRC decided that it needed to build this railway to achieve its economic goals and satisfy public infrastructure needs, it could have considered more widely how to achieve these goals without endangering the environment. Such considerations could have led to consultation and communication with relevant green groups. The tunnelling solution, or an even more economical alternative, could then have been adopted and made the year-long adversarial procedures unnecessary.

One good result is that the government of Hong Kong is now approaching green groups in advance of putting forward proposals for projects.[27] This is an extremely good sign of the beginnings of a cooperative process. I suggest that this case could be a model for international study of the consultation of environmental groups before private or government organizations plan public projects that would have an impact on the environment. To make such early communications and consultation more likely, I suggest that criteria (1) and (4) of the revised PDE be seriously considered by private corporations and governments alike.

The avoidance of negative effects altogether would seemingly require an exercise of moral imagination in Professor Werhane's sense. The choice of tunnelling under Long Valley to avoid affecting rare bird species could be considered as an example of planning that avoided negative effects for the environment. Although this was not a case of advanced, cooperative planning, it could have been.

In the case-study presented, the inefficiencies resulting from the practice of corporate planning in the absence of criterion (1) of the PDE (prior consultation with affected parties) were enormous – a year of intense public debate, expenditure of public energy, and public relations and court costs amounting to an estimated HK$100 million (approximately US$12 million) could potentially have been saved. The problem is that unilateral corporate planning tends to result in a confrontational decision-making model rather than complementary group interaction. Not only is such a model costly, it is by its very nature antagonistic and adversarial in the way that it achieves its results. Moreover, these results may not be optimal and may involve great costs in terms of time and the efficiency of operations.

Conclusion

With respect to the phenomenon of double effect, this case-study shows that attempts to mitigate negative effects on the environment were considered at various stages in the process, but were considered to be ineffective. As a result, the only viable solution was avoidance of the ecologically precious area. This more comprehensive mitigation did not (on the whole) produce the negative side-effect of destroying the habitat of globally threatened bird species.

My conclusion is that the opposition to the Spur Line railway demonstrates the minimization of the incidence of double effect and thus serves as an excellent illustration of the application of criterion (4) of the revised PDE. In the case under study, the original proposed routing of the railway line through Long Valley violated criterion (2) because the negative side-effects (disturbing the birds' environment) were part of the legitimate objective of building a new railway line to relieve passenger congestion. However, by applying criterion (3), measures were eventually taken that minimized the negative side-effects as proportionate to the legitimate objective through finding a viable, alternative course of action that achieved the same goal without producing the harmful side-effects. The result of the protest was the alteration of the proposal of the KCRC to build the railway underneath the Long Valley, thus greatly minimizing its ecological impact on the area.

If the KCRC had initially consulted with green groups in order to adopt criterion (4) from the start, could huge costs totalling some US$12 million have been saved? Could the long delays in the completion of the project have been prevented? Could a huge expenditure of public time have been avoided? Could the adoption of criterion (1) have made a great difference to the outcome earlier on? If prior consultation had been carried out with the relevant parties (in this case, green groups), it is highly probable that another and perhaps even more economically viable solution could have emerged. Criterion (5) proved to be inapplicable in this study because the negative side-effects were escapable – it was possible to achieve the legitimate objectives with very few side-effects. The progress of this case and its ultimate solution thus provide clear support for the validity of the PDE.

Notes

This chapter is dedicated in memoriam to Charles Hartshorne, philosopher, ornithologist, author of *Born to Sing*, and my doctoral director.

1. This case is largely based on the work of the Hong Kong Bird Watching Society (HKBWS) in the course of its successful protest against the initial proposal by the KCRC to build the Spur Line. I wish to thank the HKBWS for the data it provided and two individuals in particular, Dr. Ng Cho Nam from the Ecology Department of the University of Hong Kong and Mike Kilburn, chairman of the Conservation Committee of the HKBWS.
2. For an outline of an ethic that places fellow human beings as the primary ethical end, see Robert E. Allinson, *Space, time and the ethical foundations* (Aldershot: Ashgate Publishers, 2002).
3. *Anguttara Nikaya, Gradual sayings*, vol. 3, p. 262, quoted by Chatsumarn Kabilsingh, "Early Buddhist views on nature", in Allan Hunt Badiner (ed.), *Dharma Gaia. A harvest of essays in Buddhism and ecology* (Berkeley, Calif.: Parallex Press, 1990), p. 10.
4. Stephanie Kaza and Kenneth Kraft (eds.), *Dharma rain. Sources of Buddhist environmentalism* (Boston: Shambala, 2001), p. 223.
5. See Benjamin Penny, "Buddhism and Taoism in the 180 precepts spoken by lord Tao", *Taoist Resources* 6(2), 1996, pp. 17–28.
6. See *Doctrine of the mean*, trans. James Legge, in *The Chinese classics*, vol. I (Hong Kong: Hong Kong University Press, 1960), pp. 415–416.
7. Paul Y. M. Jiang, "Ethics in cosmology: Variations on the theme of 'unity of heaven and man' in neo-Confucianism", in Robert E. Allinson and Shu-hsien Liu (eds.), *Harmony and strife: Contemporary perspectives, East & West* (Hong Kong: Chinese University Press, 1988), p. 271.

8. Tom Regan, *All that dwell therein: Animal rights and environmental ethics* (Berkeley: University of California Press, 1982).

9. See Peter Singer, "Not for humans only: The place of nonhumans in environmental issues", in Andrew Light and Holmes Rolston III (eds.), *Environmental ethics* (Oxford: Blackwell Publishers, 2003), pp. 55–64.

10. In preparing this case-study, which is focused on preserving the life of the birds in a particular site in Hong Kong, it became evident to me that I was committing myself to an ethical stance that values the existence of the birds as such and the entire system of nature that supports them, not their use to mankind. Although at first I thought "I want to give back to the birds something for all the pleasure they have brought to me", I discovered that my sympathies for unseen bird species went far beyond this notion of recompense. This case-study was useful in the sense of expanding my ethical viewpoint both beyond a payback for past pleasure and a focus on a dominantly human-centred ethics.

11. See Singer, "Not for humans only".

12. Patricia Werhane, *Moral imagination and management decision-making* (New York: Oxford University Press, 1999).

13. This section incorporates material from the website of the Hong Kong Bird Watching Society (http://www.hkbws.org.hk) interspersed with my own comments.

14. See http://www.hkbws.org.hk.

15. I am indebted to a private telephone interview on 8 January 2002 with Mike Kilburn for this brief history of the Spur Line.

16. Judgment of Environmental Impact Assessment Appeal Board, No. 2 of 2000, between Kowloon-Canton Railway Corporation, Appellant, and Director of Environmental Protection, Respondent, Before: Mr. Barry Mortimer, GBS, QC, Chairman, Prof. Joseph Hun-wei Lee, Member, Mr. Stanley Cho-tat Yip, Member. Dates of Hearing: 10–12, 17–20, 24 April, 2–4, 8–10, 16–18, 22–25, 29–30 May, 21–24 June 2001. Date of Handing Down Judgment, 30 July 2001, p. 5.

17. LEGCO [Legislative Council] Question No. 19 [For Written Reply], Date of Sitting 31 May 2000, p. 3.

18. Ibid., p. 4.

19. Presentation to ACE by Mr. James Blake, pp. 1–3.

20. Judgment of Environmental Impact Assessment Appeal Board, No. 2 of 2000, p. 2.

21. Ibid., p. 9.

22. Ibid., p. 11.

23. Ibid., pp. 21, 23.

24. Ibid., p. 28.

25. This figure was given by Mike Kilburn in a telephone interview on 8 January 2002. It had also been mentioned in conversations held with Dr. Ng Cho Nam in December in Hong Kong.

26. Judgment of Environmental Impact Assessment Appeal Board, No. 2 of 2000, 30 July 2001, p. 13; see p. 130 above.

27. As learned from Mike Kilburn in a telephone conversation on 8 January 2002.

9

Shell in Ogoniland

Ogbonna Ike

Introduction

In 1993, the Shell Petroleum Development Company of Nigeria (SPDC), a subsidiary of Shell Oil, had to stop its oil-prospecting operations in Ogoniland, a community in the Niger Delta which hosted about 10 per cent of Shell's oil wells. This decision was taken in the face of protests against its operations in the area, which culminated in violence against Shell staff and employees. The accusation against Shell is that its operations have had side-effects that it could have avoided if it had taken a more responsible approach to its operations. The side-effects include harm to the environment, pollution, and harm to the human population. Critics claim that Shell did not apply suitable environmental standards. Shell is also accused of complicity in the human rights abuses of the government in power at the time.

Whether there is a responsibility, and the extent of that responsibility, are difficult issues to determine. The PDE framework is thus applied here to enable the delineation of Shell's responsibility in specific instances. Lastly, we evaluate the framework for robustness and make suggestions for improvement.

Background

Nigeria

Nigeria is currently Africa's most populous nation, with about 130 million people in 2001, and an annual population growth rate of 2.3 per cent. About 55 per cent of this population is rural.[1] The populace comprises about 250 ethnic groups.

Nigeria, as it is today, was formed in 1914, when the British protectorates of the North and South were merged to form the colony and protectorate of Nigeria. In 1960 the country was granted independence and became a republic. Six years later, the civilian government was overthrown by a military coup and this was followed by another coup in 1967 and a civil war, which ended in 1970. The military regime in place at the beginning of the war continued until 1975, when it was ousted by another coup. The new regime lasted barely one year before the head of state was killed in an unsuccessful coup. Leadership then passed to the next in command, who organized elections in 1979 and handed power over to a civilian government. In 1984 the civilian government was overthrown, and the country went back to a military regime, which was replaced in 1985 after yet another coup.

Elections were organized in 1992, but were annulled after announcement of the results. In August 1993, the military leader resigned, handing power over to a transitional government led by a civilian. Several months later, General Sanni Abacha, then the head of the army, forced the transitional government to resign, assumed the function of head of state, and jailed the winner of the annulled election for treason after he declared himself the rightful head of state. Abacha promised to restore constitutional government in October 1998, but died suddenly in June, reportedly of a heart attack. He was replaced by the head of the army, who organized elections in 1999 and handed power over to the winner of the election, Olusegun Obasanjo, who had been the military head of state from 1976 to 1979.

Nigeria is the tenth-largest producer of oil, with a daily production of 2.9 million barrels, and is the seventh-largest oil exporter. Prior to the discovery of oil in Nigeria, Nigeria's GDP per capita was about US$200. By the early 1980s it had reached US$800, but it had declined to about US$290 by 2001.[2]

Nigeria's economy is largely dependent on oil, which accounts for about 90 per cent of its foreign exchange income and 65 per cent of its GDP. The oil windfall from the 1973 Yom Kippur war was the beginning of Nigeria's complete dependence on oil. The huge revenue from crude oil sales caused the government to pay little attention to other sources of revenue. As a result, non-oil sectors of the economy, agriculture in particular, were unable to compete as independent spheres of economic activity. From being an exporter of food products, Nigeria became a net importer.

In spite of its oil wealth, Nigeria remains one of the poorest nations in the world. The country had also earned a name for itself as one of the most corrupt countries. The Transparency Index published by Transparency International had Nigeria at the top of the list as a matter of course.

The Nigerian oil industry

Oil exploration in Nigeria is carried out by six major companies, of which Shell is the largest. The others are ExxonMobil, Chevron, Agip, TotalFinaElf, and Texaco. There are several other smaller companies, most of them indigenous and operating with foreign technical partners.

The Nigerian Petroleum Act of 1990 is the main law governing the rights to oil prospecting in Nigeria. This law, based on a similar law that dates to the colonial government, gives the rights over all petroleum resources (as well as other mineral resources) to the federal government. The government then grants the rights to oil-prospecting companies by issuing oil-prospecting and oil-mining licences. More importantly, through the Nigerian National Petroleum Corporation (NNPC) and its subsidiaries, the government is a senior partner in all the major upstream ventures, with a 55–60 per cent stake. The NNPC also enjoys a monopoly in refining and petrochemicals.

The origins of the oil industry in Nigeria date from 1937, when a joint venture of Shell and British Petroleum (BP) was given exclusive rights to prospect for oil. In 1958, oil was found in the Niger Delta. The Nigerian government took up a 35 per cent stake in the joint venture in 1973, and in 1979 it appropriated BP's 20 per cent stake in the venture. In 2002, the Nigerian government owned a 55 per cent stake, Shell owned 30 per cent, Elf held 10 per cent, and Agip held 5 per cent.[3]

The joint venture was managed by Shell, and its operations were funded through capital contributions by the partners in proportion to their holdings. Shell prepared a five-year plan of exploration and development, which was reviewed and ratified by the partners. When ratified, Shell then made cash calls on the partners as their commitments fell due.

The venture operated an oil-mining lease area of about 31,000 km^2 in 2001. It had over 6,000 kilometres of pipelines and flow lines, 87 flow stations, 8 gas plants, and more than 1,000 operating wells. In 2001, the joint venture accounted for 39 per cent of Nigeria's oil production and about 55 per cent of Nigeria's crude oil base.[4] The venture employed

5,000 people, of whom about 7 per cent were non-Nigerians. SPDC's operations in Nigeria represented about 12 per cent of Shell's worldwide crude oil production and about 7 per cent of its crude oil production profits.[5]

According to the memorandum of understanding that governed the joint venture, SPDC and the other companies received a fixed margin if the oil price remained between US$15.00 and US$19.00 a barrel. To illustrate this, at an oil price of US$19.00, the government share in taxes, royalties, and equity was US$13.92. Of the remaining US$5.08, operating costs and future investment took US$4.00 and US$1.08 was shared between the companies. At US$10.00 per barrel, the government's stake fell to about US$5.00, and the margin to be shared declined to US$0.88. At US$30.00 per barrel, the government's share increased to US$24.79 and the private operators' share increased to US$1.21.[6]

In addition to SPDC, which engaged in onshore exploration and managed the joint venture operation, Shell also had a number of affiliated companies in Nigeria. These companies were engaged in various businesses, including deep-water exploration, gas, marketing of Shell-branded products, and services. In addition, Shell had a 26 per cent shareholding in the Nigerian Liquefied Natural Gas Project. Its partners in this company were NNPC (49 per cent), Elf (15 per cent), and Agip (10.4 per cent).

From 1988, the Federal Environmental Protection Agency Act (Decree No. 58 of 1988) vested the authority to issue standards for water, air, and land quality in the Federal Environmental Protection Agency (FEPA). The Department of Petroleum Resources, a subsidiary of the NNPC, also issued a set of Environmental Guidelines and Standards for the Petroleum Industry in Nigeria (1991), which overlap with and in some cases differ from those issued by FEPA. The legislation has been held to be largely ineffective owing to lack of enforcement. The reasons for lack of enforcement include overlapping responsibilities among different institutions, as well as inadequate support with market-based incentives.[7] There are also issues of lack of expertise and corruption.

The Niger Delta

More than 75 per cent of Nigeria's crude oil production, representing over 50 per cent of the national government's revenues, comes from the Niger Delta.[8] However, the region's GNP per capita is below the national average. "Urban and rural infrastructure is poor – electrification, potable water supply, and sanitation levels are very low.... The extensive flooding makes transportation difficult in rural areas."[9] Health and education indices in the Niger Delta are also significantly lower than national averages.

Under a scheme set up in 1983, 1.5 per cent of the government's oil revenue was supposed to be returned to the Delta for development. This amount was increased to 3 per cent in 1989 and, in 1993, a body named Oil Mineral Producing Areas Development Commission (OMPADEC) was set up to manage and deploy the fund. In 1995, the Constitutional Assembly recommended increasing this allocation to 13 per cent when the new constitution took effect in October 1998. The new civilian government scrapped OMPADEC and, in 2000, set up the Niger Delta Development Commission in its place. The activities of OMPADEC are largely seen to be failures, which have generally been attributed to lack of focus, mismanagement, and corruption.[10]

According to a World Bank report, "oil activities have undoubtedly caused significant and extensive environmental degradation in the [Niger Delta] region".[11] The most glaring impact comes from gas flaring, which was the cheapest way to dispose of natural gas that Nigeria was not equipped to utilize. The degree of flaring in Nigeria significantly exceeds that in any other country: 76 per cent of the natural gas that is a by-product of oil exploration is being flared in Nigeria; the corresponding figure for Saudi Arabia is 20 per cent, Iran 19 per cent, Mexico 5 per cent, Britain 4.3 per cent, Algeria 4 per cent, the former Soviet Union 1.5 per cent, the United States 0.6 per cent, the Netherlands 0 per cent.[12] Flaring contributed significant quantities of carbon dioxide and methane to the atmosphere. It also filled the air with smoke, covered the land in soot, and contributed to the incidence of acid rain.

The impression this phenomenon made on a foreign correspondent who visited the Niger Delta region is instructive: "In the nearby Obagi community, open flares of natural gas, a by-product of crude oil, are burned off daily, emitting a pungent smell that tingles the nostrils.... New galvanised rooftops are caked with rust within two years, thanks to acid rain."[13]

The Niger Delta had many small oil fields interconnected by pipelines and by networks of flow lines – small-diameter pipes that carry oil from wellheads to flow stations. The high pressure in these pipes made them susceptible to leaks.[14] Many of the pipes in the Niger Delta were not buried, as is the case in most countries, but were laid above the ground. Apart from the fact that this reduced the quantity of land available for agricultural purposes, the pipes were more susceptible to physical damage and corrosion.

Oil spillage was another issue, arguably the most controversial. According to the World Bank report, the Department of Petroleum Resources claims that 2,300 m^3 of oil – from at least 300 spills – contaminate the Niger Delta region annually.[15] Human Rights Watch believes that the actual amount spilled annually "may be 10 times higher".[16] Between 1970 and 1982, 1,581 incidents of oil spillage were documented in Nigeria. Shell reported 130 spills in 1997, attributing 53 to equipment failure, 23 to human error, and 54 to sabotage by those frustrated with the government and the oil industry.[17] These leaks and spills contaminate groundwater and destroy the soil, significantly reducing crop yields.

Punctuating the chronic small oil spills, there have been significant large-scale spills that placed surrounding communities in immediate danger of starvation. In 1998, 840,000 US gallons spilled at one of Shell's flow stations, killing large numbers of fish. The spill was a result of what Shell called "a pipeline failure". Shell officials claimed that relief materials such as food, water, and seeds were distributed to the affected communities.[18]

The search for oil in the Niger Delta also caused large-scale deforestation as local populations moved in search of arable land uncontaminated by oil.[19] Clearing of mangrove swamps led to the erosion of riverbanks, which in turn led to flooding.

Claims that SPDC's operating standards in the Niger Delta were far lower than standards in other countries seemed to be substantiated by its former head of environmental studies in Nigeria, Bopp van Dessel. After resigning from SPDC, van Dessel made the following statement in a television documentary: "They [Shell] were not meeting their own standards.... Any Shell site that I saw was polluted. Any terminal that I saw was polluted. It is clear to me that Shell was devastating the area.... It also keeps the door for dialogue and co-operation with other involved parties firmly shut."[20] The same day, Shell issued a news release stating that the company had never denied that there were environmental problems in the Delta: "While many of these are not attributable to the oil industry, we accept that oil operations in general, including Shell's, do have an impact." SPDC also stated that many improvements had been put into place since van Dessel's departure.[21]

Communities in the Niger Delta also claimed that oil companies introduced major distortions into the social and economic fabric of their societies. Oil companies, they claimed, perpetuated regional and class inequalities by creating oil colonies in local areas where oil executives lived lavishly in contrast to the impoverished conditions of local communities. Because of the high skill requirements of the oil industry, local villagers were forced either to migrate to urban centres after being economically displaced, or to become low-skilled workers dependent on the oil company.

The relationship between SPDC and these communities has been tenuous since the early 1980s. On several occasions SPDC has called in the police to stop demonstrations against its operations in the Niger Delta. Police action has in some cases led to deaths and injuries among protesters. A document by Environmental Rights Action alleged that, in 1987, when the Iko community in the Niger Delta held a peaceful demonstration against Shell, the police, called in by Shell, destroyed 40 houses.[22] In 1990, the Umuechem community held a demonstration against Shell. The divisional manager of SPDC allegedly made a request to the state Commissioner of Police for "security protection", which was provided in the form of the paramilitary mobile police. Police action to stop the demonstration allegedly led to the death of up to 80 people. The official inquiry into the event indicted the police.[23]

The Ogoni uprising

The Ogoni tribe is one of the 20 minority tribes occupying the Niger Delta. The population of the tribe is estimated to be about half a million, roughly 7 per cent of the Delta's population. The Ogonis inhabited a 70,000 km^2 area of land and had farming and fishing as their principal source of livelihood.

In 1995, Ogoniland housed about 100 wells – 96 belonging to Shell and a small number to Chevron. Also located there were a petrochemical plant, a fertilizer plant, and two refineries. Ogoniland's contribution to Nigeria's oil was about 5 per cent in 1973, and declined to 1.5 per cent in 1993. According to information from the Shell website, 364 million barrels of oil had been produced since 1958, valued at US$5.2 billion before costs. Of this, Shell claims, investment and operating costs accounted for 15 per cent, 79 per cent went to the government, and 6 per cent to the foreign partners including SPDC. The Ogonis for their part claim that Shell has extracted an estimated US$30 billion worth of oil from their land since 1958.[24]

A British journalist who visited Ogoniland under cover had the following to say:

Oil fields mottle the landscape, their rigs ceaselessly pumping crude and natural gas from deep underground. The gas burns incessantly in giant geysers of flame and smoke, and at night the flares that ring the city of Port Harcourt and fishing villages deep within the mangrove cast a hellish glow. As the smoke from the flares rises above the palm trees, methane and carbon dioxide separate from the greasy soot. The gases rise but the grime descends, coating the trees, the mud-dabbed huts and the people within.

He continued:

Here was a place and a people utterly subservient to the production of oil. High pressure pipes snaked amid plots of yam and cassavas, past mud-brick huts, even through people's yards; I watched as one woman climbed over a tangle of pipes to get to her front door.[25]

In the early 1990s, the Movement for the Survival of the Ogoni people (MOSOP), one of the many activist organizations in the Niger Delta, began campaigning for a greater share of oil revenue from the government, for political self-determination, as well as for ownership of the oil beneath Ogoniland. It published the "Ogoni Bill of Rights", which started with the statement: "The Ogoni case is of genocide being committed in the dying years of the twentieth century by multi-national companies under the supervision of the Government ... of Nigeria."[26]

In November 1992, SPDC's then managing director received a letter from MOSOP demanding US$6 billion for damage caused by its operations in Ogoniland and US$4 billion in lost revenue from the sale of Ogoni oil abroad, which should rightfully have accrued to the Ogoni people. The letter, which had also been addressed to NNPC and Chevron, made no explicit threats. However, in January 1993, SPDC had to withdraw its entire staff from Ogoniland in the face of increasing intimidation from the communities and attacks that included physical beatings, theft, and destruction of personal belongings and equipment. Production ceased in mid-1993.

In 1994, the military government in Rivers State constituted the Rivers State Internal Security Task Force (RSISTF), with members drawn from the police, the army, and the navy. The task force was given a mandate to restore order in Ogoniland. A memo sent in May 1994 by the RSISTF commanding officer to the military administrator of Rivers State contained the following: "Shell operations still impossible unless ruthless military operations are undertaken for smooth economic activities to commence." To counter this, he recommended "wasting operations during MOSOP and other gatherings making military operations justifiable ... wasting operations coupled with psychological tactics.... restrictions of unauthorised visitors, especially those from Europe, to the Ogoni".[27] MOSOP claimed that, between late 1995 and 1996, the RSISTF carried out 36 extra-judicial executions, detained 28 people, and conducted brutal raids on 19 communities.[28]

In May 1994, four moderate Ogoni leaders were murdered after a meeting. Ken Saro-Wiwa was arrested and jailed the same day on charges of inciting the murders of the four chiefs; 18 others were arrested on the same charges and indicted. Only a few weeks earlier, Saro-Wiwa had reportedly told Greenpeace, "They are going to arrest us all and execute us. All for Shell." Amnesty International made a plea for his release, expressing its belief that the charges were unfounded.

The trials were held in 1995. Witnesses testified that Saro-Wiwa had said to those around him, "The vultures are meeting there. Go get them." Saro-Wiwa denied the statements. As the trial proceeded, a campaign for the release of Ken Saro-Wiwa was mounted by a number of human rights and environmental groups, including Amnesty International, the European Parliament, and Greenpeace. Shell was besieged by pleas from within and outside Nigeria to speak out against the trial, which was widely seen to be unfair. Other than a statement by Shell's managing director to the effect that the defendants were entitled to a fair trial, medical treatment, and lawyers of their own choosing, Shell officials said nothing publicly.

In November 1995, Saro-Wiwa and eight others were executed. Many independent observers felt that Saro-Wiwa and the rest had not received a fair trial and the execution was seen as an outrage by the international community. It led to the suspension of Nigeria from the Commonwealth of Nations and to sanctions against Nigerian government officials.

In January 1996, a large number of Ogonis celebrated Ogoni day, during which soldiers and police allegedly fired tear gas and ammunition, killing four youths. A report by the United Nations High Commission for Refugees stated that about 1,000 Ogonis were forced to flee to Benin Republic that day. According to one of the refugees, the military clampdown was accompanied by widespread looting, shooting, and rape.[29]

Pressure on SPDC

A report prepared by Pensions & Investment Research Consultants (PIRC) and sent to Shell's 1995 AGM reflected the points of criticism raised by environmental groups and the company's response to them. This report caught the attention of several important shareholders. That year, PIRC met with representatives of SPDC to discuss the issues and issued a report, which stated that, although the Nigerian situation was more complex than sometimes portrayed, SPDC's conduct and operations highlighted serious shortcomings in its Statement of General Business Principles and environmental policy. The report went on to recommend that SPDC should:

1. set out a plan for implementing its environmental remedies and investment programme in Ogoni;
2. make a public commitment to review its Statement of General Business Prin-

ciples and set out a general group-wide support for human rights and judicial principles with specific reference to relations with oppressive regimes;

3. make a public commitment to review its environmental policy in order to demonstrate a commitment to operating to the highest international environmental standards on a group-wide basis and a commitment to full disclosure of environmental targets, auditing mechanisms, and environmental impact data;

4. set out plans for the implementation and monitoring of new policies arising from these reviews;

5. set out clear procedures and remits for these reviews that enable monitoring of their progress and input into them by shareholders;

6. report to shareholders on the outcome of these reviews by the end of 1996.

The report conceded that Shell had initiated a review of its General Business Principles and its environmental policy. However, it stated that the procedure for these reviews had not been transparent. The report was sceptical about any change in the attitude and actions of SPDC management and concluded that there seemed to be little doubt that Shell's environmental management standards had been less stringent in Nigeria than elsewhere.[30]

Shell's response

Shell officials maintain that the company had always built its flow stations to standards set by the American Petroleum Institute. Since 1992, SPDC had been working on a series of projects, costing US$100 million a year, to upgrade infrastructure and make environmental improvements. Prior to the passage of environmental legislation in 1991, the managers said, the company had found it difficult to persuade its government partner of the need to upgrade the deteriorating infrastructure – much of it dating to the early 1970s – and to invest in environmental improvement.[31]

With respect to the environmental devastation it is accused of, Shell has this to say:

The replacement of ageing flow lines is reducing the number of oil spills we experience due to corrosion. However, today the biggest single impact by spills on the environment is caused by sabotage. We video [sic] and photograph evidence of sabotage and show it to communities. Representatives from the department of petroleum resources, communities and the police are also invited when sabotage incidents are investigated. Where spills happen, we stop the leaks and clean them up while assessing the damage. We pay compensation to communities only if spills are caused by operational failure, not by sabotage. Compensation for oil spills throughout the company's operations between 1992 and 1996 came to $16.6m.[32]

Shell managers point out that most of the spills were due to sabotage by local people. The absence of eyewitnesses willing to give testimony made it impossible to prosecute such cases. Since Shell did not pay compensation for damage caused by sabotage, the damage was often disguised to look as if it had been caused by technical failures. The individuals and communities then allegedly approached SPDC seeking compensation for the damage. Besides, oil spills created opportunities for contracts to clean up the spills.[33]

Dealing with gas flaring also constituted a major challenge. The company's response was that, when Shell operations began in the 1950s and 1960s, gas was not a popular energy source because it was more difficult to produce and transport than crude oil. Besides, the company says, there were few markets for gas in Nigeria and there was little environmental awareness of the consequences of gas flaring. In addition, fiscal and gas pricing policies did not encourage investment. The solution lay in building a gas plant. In 1995, the Nigerian government agreed to co-invest with Shell, Elf, and Agip for the construction of a liquefied natural gas plant. Shell states that it is committed to end gas flaring by 2008.[34]

In response to charges that SPDC had driven pipelines through the Delta's villages, officials exhibited a time sequence of pictures showing that, instead, villages had grown up around the pipelines as Nigeria's population had expanded.

According to Shell, its approach to community development "focuses on long-term development, especially through education and training, encouraging partnerships between communities and the company using non-governmental organisations and other outside parties with expertise in rural development". The company claims that it is reconstructing and handing over basic amenities to communities, including water schemes, roads, school buildings, and clinics. The company claims to have spent US$36 million in 1996 on development in the Niger Delta and US$220,000 on humanitarian aid to Ogoni and Andoni people in 1993/1994.[35]

In addition, the company claims to have developed a network of agricultural extension officers in communities in the Niger Delta to help and advise farmers on new crop hybrids and varieties, farming techniques, and financing methods. Up until SPDC withdrew staff from the area, two of these officers were based in Ogoni. New high-yield, disease-resistant crop varieties were developed at Shell's five research and seed multiplication farms, one of which was at Bori in Ogoni and was established in 1978. The company claims that about 6,800 Ogoni farmers had benefited from the agricultural programme. Further, the company claims that there were more than 200 SPDC-inspired cooperatives in the Delta, involving about 9,500 farmers; 21 of these were in Ogoniland, involving more than 1,600 farmers.

The company also claims that the Ogonis have benefited from SPDC's annual scholarships to children at secondary school and university levels. Every year, it says, 1,600 scholarships are awarded in the Niger Delta area, of which 85 went to Ogonis in 1996. In addition, the company awarded 550 university scholarships each year to Niger Delta indigenes; of these, 12 went to Ogonis in 1996. Between 1993 and 1996, the company claims to have given 228 secondary school scholarships and 37 university scholarships to Ogonis. Moreover, the company had vocational training programmes helping unemployed people start their own businesses. Four such schemes for 900 students were completed in 1996 throughout the Niger Delta and another nine schemes for 2,000 students were to be launched in 1997.

The company also had a policy of using local contracting companies from oil-producing areas where possible and 43 Ogoni companies were registered. Out of a total workforce of about 5,000, 85 Ogonis were employed by SPDC.

The company also sponsored 66 science teachers at 14 community schools throughout the area of operations. In 1996, the company carried out refurbishment work in seven existing hospitals, including a hospital in Ogoni, where it supplied equipment and took responsibility for maintenance. In 1997, it rehabilitated three Ogoni government health centres and supplied drugs to three others.

Information from the Shell website says that, between 1985 and 1992, SPDC spent more than US$2 million on the Ogoni area, about 16 per cent of the total community budget for the Eastern division of Shell's operations. This money went to the provision of 5 water schemes, 7 school blocks of 6 classrooms each, 17 sets of school furniture, 11 sets of science equipment, hospital equipment for 2 health centres, 6 kilometres of roads, and security fences for 2 schools.

The road to reconciliation

On 8 May 2002, Shell issued a press release offering a "plan of action in Ogoniland if agreement is reached with all Ogoni communities that company staff can return to the area in safety. The first priority will be to clean up all oil spills ... and to make safe all facilities. At the same time SPDC will begin to rehabilitate its past community projects. . . It will also investigate with communities the need for further development projects in the area."[36]

In 1996, SPDC had commenced work on upgrading and building more than 15 hospitals in the Niger Delta. The company also took responsibility for the maintenance of these hospitals as well as the supply of drugs. A youth training programme for about 300 youths was also commenced.[37]

In a 1996 report, the PIRC held the view that there remained a significant gulf between Shell and the local communities and there did not appear to be any imminent prospect of the company returning to Ogoniland. The PIRC believed that winning reconciliation with the Ogoni people would require considerable extra effort and demonstration of good faith. According to the PIRC report, SPDC appeared to be approaching the problem of reconciliation in a piecemeal way and not solving the environmental situation in Ogoniland. The report went on to say that Shell appeared to consider that winning a public relations battle was as important as addressing concerns on the ground.[38]

A subsequent report, issued in 1998, however admitted that SPDC had made significant changes in its environmental and corporate responsibility policies. Changes highlighted include the company's effort to reduce gas flaring, its increased investment in community development activities, and its publication of annual environmental and social reports.[39]

Applying the PDE framework

The PDE framework comes in useful for discussing corporate responsibility for the unintended effects of otherwise legitimate business activity. The framework is intended to resolve the problem of determining a company's responsibility when its activities create negative side-effects on other parties or when it contributes to or benefits from the wrongdoing of others. This case presents dilemmas under both aspects, with the additional complication that the activities that create the negative side-effects are carried out in concert with other parties.

Applying the PDE framework to this case will help to determine the extent of SPDC's responsibility for the identified side-effects of its activities, as well as the extent to which SPDC was complicit in other parties' wrong actions and which responsibilities arise therefrom. The side-effects to be discussed fall into two broad areas: environmental degradation and human rights abuses. I shall discuss these issues in the context of the PDE framework and, where I have adequate data, attempt to determine the extent of SPDC's responsibility in each case. It is not within the scope of this chapter to determine whether or not SPDC actually lived up to these responsibilities, because I do not have information on all the circumstances facing the company's management at that time. In spite of the limited data, I shall also attempt to make broad recommendations about alternative actions that SPDC's management could have taken.

The PDE framework, adapted for business purposes, essentially holds that side-effect harm of corporate activity is justifiable only if a few conditions are met:

Preamble: Negative side-effects do occur, even when businesses pursue legitimate objectives by legitimate means. In creating sustainable value for their stakeholders, businesses must ensure in dealing with the negative side-effects of their activities that:
1. consultation with affected parties, as well as risk assessment, is carried out prior to and during the business operation in order to identify negative side-effects;
2. negative side-effects that arise from a business's operations are not made to serve as means to achieving its legitimate objectives;
3. negative side-effects can be justified as proportionate to the legitimate objectives;
4. active measures are taken to prevent or minimize negative side-effects;
5. the negative side-effects are inescapable – it is not possible to achieve the legitimate objectives with fewer or no side-effects.

The framework, as adopted in this book, stresses the importance of risk assessment and consultation with the affected parties, prior to and during the business activity in order to identify negative side-effects. In many cases this would be a strong demonstration of good faith on the company's part and would give stronger legitimacy to its efforts to minimize or prevent, where possible, the side-effects in question.

Also intrinsic to the framework is the notion of complicity as a side-effect. The notion of complicity is well used in law and ethics. Complicity in this context refers to a situation in which a company unintentionally, by action or by omission, lends support to or encourages another's wrong action in pursuit of its legitimate objectives. From the application of this concept in law and ethics, the conditions that need to exist for a case of complicity to be built against a company are as follows:
1. The wrongdoing that is carried out by the other party must be reasonably foreseeable as a consequence of the company's activity.
2. The company's action or inaction encourages or lends support to the perpetration of the wrong action in question.
3. The support referred to above has a substantial effect on the perpetration of the wrong action.
4. A company knowingly accepts benefits that arise out of the wrong action of another party.

As stated in the preamble, a precondition for accepting negative side-effects of business activity is that the business objectives and activities in pursuit of these objectives be morally legitimate. Shell creates economic value by exploiting and selling petroleum resources. Creation of economic value is per se morally legitimate, and the value created is important for the Nigerian economy, its importance enhanced by the fact that petroleum accounts for 65 per cent of GDP and more than 90 per cent of Nigeria's foreign exchange income. SPDC, being the manager of a joint venture that contributes 39 per cent of Nigeria's crude oil production, plays a major role in the oil economy. The economic value created is multiplied as jobs are created along the entire value chain. The importance of oil to the world economy is obvious, as it continues to be the main source of energy for commercial and personal use.

It is, however, well known that oil exploration creates harmful side-effects. Some of the side-effects that have particular relevance in this case are environmental degradation and harm to the host population as a result of oil spillage, gas flaring, and physical alteration of animal and human habitats.

There seems to be considerable evidence that exploration activity in the Niger Delta did not meet environmental standards prevailing elsewhere in the world. The level of flaring was higher than that generally accepted in other countries, pipelines were laid above the ground, and they were apparently not maintained in line with standards elsewhere, considering the more-than-usual number of oil spills. According to the PDE framework, for a side-effect harm to be morally acceptable, the moral agent must make a reasonable effort to minimize it. The environmental laws in place in any country usually constitute a benchmark for the company's efforts to minimize these negative harms. This responsibility is not, however, eliminated when there are no environmental laws, as was the case in Nigeria up to 1992. It simply implies that the company in question must seek some other acceptable standard for benchmarking its efforts to minimize the harmful side-effects. Thus, this particular side-effect cannot be justified within the PDE framework and SPDC has moral responsibility, with its joint venture partners, for the environmental degradation and the consequent harm to the host communities.

However, we must discuss SPDC's responsibility within the context of its operating in partnership with other entities, including the NNPC, a corporation owned by the government of Nigeria. Nevertheless, SPDC's position in the joint venture as manager gives it a greater degree of responsibility than its partners. Officials of SPDC claim that the company had tried to improve the operating standards but this had been met with resistance from joint venture partners. Determining whether SPDC lived up to this responsibility is beyond the scope of this chapter and would require more information regarding the specific efforts SPDC made in this regard, and whether its efforts to overcome the obstacles were reasonable.

SPDC (together with the other joint venture partners) was also accused of not contributing to the development of the Niger Delta, in spite of the social and environmental harm its operations caused. The argument of the host communities is essentially that they bear most of the externalities of production but do not have a proportionate share in the proceeds of the natural resources derived there. SPDC for its part admitted that not enough money was put into the development of the Niger Delta.

Considering that it is the government's role to ensure a just distribution of the wealth created in any economy, the case here is not so much one of a harmful side-effect as complicity in the wrong action of another – in this case, the government. The question is, if the government was not fulfilling its duty to ensure that the Niger Delta got a just proportion of the proceeds from resources derived therein, what responsibility did SPDC, as a major operator in the industry, have to change the situation? SPDC's responsibility has to be evaluated from the point of view of its dominant position in the industry and the fact that it was the manager of a joint venture that produced most of Nigeria's oil. SPDC claims that it, with the other operators, did a lot to change the situation, including putting pressure on the government to increase the allocation of the federation account to oil-producing areas. It also points to its investments in community development. The apparent lack of appreciation by the host communities of Shell's efforts points to the possibility of flaws in SPDC's approach. One of the possible flaws is inadequate stakeholder involvement, an issue that is examined in further detail below.

There also seems to be considerable evidence that there were human rights abuses by security agents engaged by SPDC for the protection of its employees and property. Peaceful demonstrations were sometimes met with violence and demonstrators arrested, firearms were in some cases used against unarmed civilians, resulting in deaths and injuries, and villages were sometimes destroyed. In these cases, although it is not likely that SPDC ordered, or even intended, that these acts take place, the question is whether or not SPDC was complicit in these abuses of human rights. The question of complicity arises not only because SPDC benefited from these actions but also because there seems to be considerable evidence that the company provided material support to these agents. In addition, these actions were reasonably foreseeable, if not the first time, at least subsequently. All these factors point towards SPDC's complicity in the actions of these security agents.

On the other hand, one could ask what options the company had to protect the lives of its employees as well as the safety of its assets. It seems that it had little choice, because private armed security forces were not allowed in Nigeria. The police force, even when engaged by SPDC, was outside its control once deployed. This fact certainly mitigates SPDC's responsibility for the actions of the security agents. It is not possible to determine here whether SPDC did everything it could within its scope of influence to stop these abuses. However, after cases of human rights abuses, the company usually made public comments distancing itself from the actions of the security agents.

The activities of the Rivers State Internal Security Task Force (RSISTF) also involved massive breaches of human rights. There is substantial evidence that the RSISTF conducted several extra-judicial killings, carried out mass arrests, and destroyed villages in some cases. There are also reasonably substantiated allegations that RSISTF members carried out acts of looting and rape during their raids. Although there is no evidence that SPDC engaged the RSISTF, in contrast to the case with the security agents, there is an issue of beneficial complicity. SPDC was most likely aware of the activities of this body and gained benefits from it: the activity of this task force helped SPDC continue its activities in the Niger Delta. Evidence seems to show that SPDC even contributed to the financing of this task force. Again, these are strong pointers to complicity.

The trial of Ken Saro-Wiwa and the other Ogonis presents another issue with which to discuss SPDC's responsibility. In this area, too, there seems to be evidence that the trial involved many abuses of basic human rights. There was some pressure on SPDC to intervene in the trial, which the company declined, saying that it could not take a political stand or "get involved in internal processes". A senior Shell executive actually sent a letter to Abacha asking for clemency for the accused persons. The question is what responsibility SPDC actually had to intervene in the trial, and the extent of this responsibility. The issue of responsibility arises because SPDC featured prominently in Saro-Wiwa's activism that led to his arrest, and so would be a beneficiary, at least on the face of it, of Saro-Wiwa's neutralization. Some claim that SPDC had a responsibility to make a public statement on the human rights abuses that were evident in the trial, or even, as some suggested, threaten to pull out of Nigeria. The question here is whether it is sometimes counterproductive for a corporation such as Shell to criticize a repressive government publicly. In this particular case, one doubts that a public statement by Shell criticizing the government would have had a significant influence on Abacha's decision to execute the accused. The allegation of complicity is difficult to uphold in this case.

In making a final review of SPDC's responsibility and coming up with broad recommendations, it is important to note that the first solution is not always to stop an activity that has negative side-effects.

In a case where the issues get to a head, as they did, this is a pointer to the failure of stakeholder dialogue. This has been identified in this volume as a major component in dealing with the negative side-effects of business activities. If the activities of a corporation lead to harmful side-effects in the host community, it is important to consult with the affected parties and to carry out a proper risk assessment in conjunction with those parties in order to identify and weigh the negative side-effects. This consultation will also involve seeking ways of minimizing these side-effects, also in conjunction with the affected parties. SPDC's responsibility in a situation in which environmental standards were low and causing unacceptable levels of damage to the host community was to look for ways to communicate to the joint venture partners the risks of continuing to operate with such low standards as well as to the host communities the difficulties of meeting those standards. This would have enabled the company to lead the joint venture with a plan to improve the operating standards over a period of time.

The community protests that escalated to violence against SPDC staff and equipment would clearly have been avoided if there had been a proper and sincere dialogue with the communities concerned. Even after the protests had commenced, the escalation to violence might have been avoided if, at that point, a sincere dialogue had been opened up. The problem, of course, is that, by the time the protests began, there was already a lot of distrust and scepticism towards the company's efforts. Accordingly, it would have been even more difficult to win the confidence of the host communities. Still, it is better late than not at all. Although Shell had a duty to protect its installations and people from harm, this protection need not have taken the form it did – trying to stop the demonstrations, etc. It would have been enough to stop production at trouble spots and accept the costs involved, while at the same time making an effort to understand the reasons for the protests and to come to some sort of agreement with the representatives of the host communities.

The activities of the RSISTF were outside the control of Shell, but the notion of complicity arises mainly because Shell allegedly made contributions to the activities of this force. Shell has denied that it ever did. Assuming it did, the complicity would have been avoided if it had not made such contributions. Shell should also have refused to accept the benefits of the activities of the RSISTF, as well as making a serious effort to put an end to them. Shell claims it did just that.

With respect to the human rights abuses in the trial of Ken Saro-Wiwa, Shell had a responsibility to state its position on the matter. There are several pointers to the fact that the abuses at the trial were politically motivated. The company's statements on the matter seem to me to have been prudent, not dragging the company into the political issue while at the same time making its position clear. It is doubtful that public criticism of the trial would have been very effective. At the same time, it would have damaged Shell's relationship with the government, and even reduced its ability to influence the situation. Assuming that the letter to Abacha was sincere and followed through, my view is that the company did not have any additional responsibility for the trial and the subsequent execution of the accused.

Of course, my recommendations are made with an awareness of the practical difficulties involved; however, resolving these practical difficulties is beyond the scope of this chapter.

An evaluation of the framework

The PDE framework has been shown to be quite useful in determining responsibility for the side-effects of corporate actions. When an action is an outright abuse of human rights, assigning responsibility is an easy matter. The problem is that many corporate actions are performed in a context that includes other participants. Many times, therefore, it is a case of complicity. This produces a thorny issue that the existing PDE framework does not adequately address. The current framework does not incorporate clear criteria for determining when complicity is a side-effect, and how to assign responsibilities among the different parties. This has been brought out by this case in many respects – the fact that Shell's business in the area was carried out in a joint venture with other partners, as well as the fact that Shell did not in itself engage in human rights abuses.

The framework will thus be enhanced, incorporating criteria for determining the responsibilities of a company when its actions or inaction lead to complicity in the wrongdoing of others. According to my application of the concept of complicity in this case, a company is responsible for the wrongdoing of others when its actions or inaction encourage or lend substantial support to the perpetration of the wrongful act or when it knowingly benefits from the wrong action of another. Of course, the fact that the wrongful act will take place as a result of the company's action or inaction must be reasonably foreseeable by the company. It is also necessary, as we have seen from the application of the framework to the case, that the company should have sufficient influence to prevent the wrongful act or mitigate its effects.

Notes

1. http://devdata.worldbank.org/external/CPProfile.asp?SelectedCountry=NGA&CCODE= NGA&CNAME=Nigeria&PTYPE=CP.
2. Ibid.
3. Shell Petroleum Development Company (SPDC), at http://www.shell.com.
4. Ibid.
5. M. Moldoveanu, L. Sharp Paine, and R. J. Crawford, "Royal Dutch/Shell in Nigeria (A)", *Harvard Business School*, 9-399-126 (2000).
6. SPDC, *Annual business review, 2001* (2002).
7. D. Moffat and O. Linden, "Defining an environmental development strategy for the Niger Delta", Report to the Industry and Energy Operations Division, West Central Africa Department (World Bank, 1995), unpublished, vol. 1, p. 55.
8. Ibid., p. 1.
9. Ibid., p. 3.
10. Ibid., p. 82.
11. Ibid., p. 81.
12. Ibid., p. 82.
13. A. M. Simmons, "Tensions simmer above oil deposits in Nigeria, Africa: Many call foreign firms' exploration a menace", *Los Angeles Times*, 29 April 1998.
14. Center for Health and the Global Environment, *Oil: A life cycle analysis of its health and environmental impacts* (Boston: Harvard Medical School, 2002).
15. Moffat and Linden, "Defining an environmental development strategy for the Niger Delta".
16. Human Rights Watch, *The price of oil: Corporate responsibility and human rights violations in Nigeria's oil producing communities*, 1999, http://www.hrw.org/reports/1999/ Nigeria/Nigew991-02.
17. T. Susman, "Oil-rich but still dirt-poor: Nigerians angry as dreams fade", *Newsday*, 13 October 1998.
18. Human Rights Watch, *The price of oil*.
19. Moffat and Linden, "Defining an environmental development strategy for the Niger Delta".
20. B. van Dessel, statement on Granada Television documentary, *Shell Nigeria, World in Action*, 13 May 1996.
21. Shell Petroleum and Development Company, "Shell responds to environmental allegations". Statement on allegations of Bopp van Dessel, 13 May 1996; see http://www. search.shell.com/cgi-bin/rsearch.cgi.
22. Environmental Rights Action, *Shell in Iko – The story of double standards*, 1995; cited in A. Rowell and S. Kretzmann, *All for Shell: The Ogoni struggle – A Project Underground Report*, 1997; see http://moles.org/ProjectUnderground/motherlode/shell/timeline.html.
23. *Report of the Commission of Inquiry into the causes and circumstances of the disturbances that occurred at Umuechem in Etche Local Government Area of Rivers State* (Port Harcourt, 1990).
24. Movement for the Survival of the Ogoni People (MOSOP), *Ogoni Bill of Rights* (Bori, 1990).
25. J. Hammer, "Nigeria's crude", *Harper's Magazine*, June 1996, p. 58; quoted in Moldoveanu, Sharp Paine, and Crawford, "Royal Dutch/Shell in Nigeria (A)".
26. MOSOP, *Ogoni Bill of Rights*.
27. Restricted memo from the chairman of RSISTF to His Excellency, the Military Administrator, 12 May 1994, http://www.sierra.com.

28. Rowell and Kretzmann, *All for Shell: The Ogoni struggle.*
29. Human Rights Watch, Nigeria, "Permanent transition", in *Human Rights Watch/Africa* 8(3) (A), September 1996, p. 42.
30. Pensions & Investment Research Consultants, *Environmental and corporate responsibility at Shell: The stakeholder role in promoting change* (London: PIRC, 1998).
31. Moldoveanu, Sharp Paine, and Crawford, "Royal Dutch/Shell in Nigeria (A)".
32. See http://www.shellnigeria.com/info.
33. Moldoveanu, Sharp Paine, and Crawford, "Royal Dutch/Shell in Nigeria (A)", p. 8.
34. See http://www.shell.com.
35. See http://www.shellnigeria.com/info.
36. Ibid.
37. Ibid.
38. Pensions & Investment Research Consultants, *Shell and Nigeria: Analysis of the company's response to PIRC's recommendations* (London: PIRC, 1996).
39. PIRC, *Environmental and corporate responsibility at Shell.*

10

Del Monte Kenya Limited

Florence J. A. Oloo

Introduction

Business corporations all over the world are increasingly becoming aware
of their responsibilities towards their stakeholders. How to conduct business in a more responsible manner in countries where human rights
abuses are widespread, where war is being fought, or where the environment is being degraded is one of the serious challenges facing business
communities today. Even though the business enterprise may be pursuing a legitimate objective, the means are not always legitimate, and, even
when the means are legitimate, the side-effects of the means may still be
harmful. The principle of double effect (PDE) as outlined in the intro-
ductory chapters of this volume provides a solid framework of reference
in dealing with the negative side-effects when businesses pursue legitimate objectives by legitimate means.

This chapter examines the case of Del Monte Kenya Limited (DMKL)
and analyses morally dubious means as well as negative side-effects resulting from the means employed – including any complicity in the
wrongdoing of others – under the framework of the given PDE. Note
that some of the expectations of DMKL may seem far-reaching compared with what one would reasonably expect from business companies
elsewhere, especially as regards health care and housing. However, it is
important to keep in mind that certain welfare conditions must be met in
order for people to be able to work at all, and in a country such as

Kenya, where scarcely no public welfare system exists, foreign companies that enjoy staying in the country can be expected to give something in return to the workforce from which they benefit.

Del Monte Kenya Limited

Background

Del Monte Foods International Limited has a worldwide reputation for quality. It has a commitment to growing and using only the finest, freshest produce. It is one of the most respected names in the food industry and a brand leader in the canned fruit and fruit juice market sectors. The Del Monte label guarantees quality to those who consume it.

Del Monte Kenya is owned by Del Monte Royal, one of several Del Monte companies formed after the sale in 1965 of the US Del Monte Corporation. From the sale, several new companies were born: Del Monte Fresh Produce, specializing in the production of bananas and other fresh fruit from Latin America; Del Monte Foods Corporation, specializing in the preservation of fruit and vegetables destined for the American market; and Del Monte Royal, specializing in the production of pineapples and other preserved fruit, with production sites in Europe, Africa, the Philippines, and Latin America. Del Monte Kenya became Del Monte Royal controlled by two South African families (Oppenheimer and Immerman) each owning 30 per cent of the company, while the remaining 40 per cent was divided up between numerous small shareholders. Later, Cirio Alimentare S.p.A went on buying shares in Del Monte Royal until it bought up the group completely in February 2001.

Del Monte Kenya Limited owns the productive complex at Thika, one of Kenya's industrial towns with a population in excess of 200,000. Del Monte has had a presence in the region for 35 years and has a long-term commitment to the area. It is Del Monte's employment policy to transfer international technical expertise to develop local management. This approach has been successful in Kenya, where almost all of the management is local.

The plantations cover an area of about 5,000 hectares (about 7 km^2) and are patrolled by a large corps of security guards in jeeps or on horseback accompanied by dogs. Between 5,000 and 6,000 farm labourers work on the plantations, taking turns in a variety of jobs in order to guarantee a steady production the whole year round. Women comprise 60 per cent of the workforce. About 250,000 tons of pineapples are harvested every year, earning over KSh 4 billion in foreign exchange and KSh 10 billion invested in fixed assets.

The plight of Del Monte workers

When Lorenzo Bertolli took over as the new chief executive of Del Monte Kenya Limited in November 2000, his brief from the Del Monte Group headquarters was very straightforward – change the management style. There were a couple of pressing problems that needed to be addressed. The most immediate was the negative publicity arising out of various labour disputes in which the company found itself facing the wrath of human rights groups.

Claims by workers and human rights organizations that a senior manager at the firm had made it clear that profits, not workers, mattered at Del Monte were confirmed on 3 August 1998. A seasonal employee, Peter Mutiso Kamolo, reported to work as usual. At 11.00 a.m. he fell ill with malaria symptoms. He reported to his boss at the plantation and was allowed to go to the company's health centre, where he was given painkillers and asked to go back to work.

Two days later, his condition worsened while he was off-duty. He reported severe throat pains. Kamolo's brother, Bosco, who also worked at Del Monte, took him to the company's clinic. But a nurse denied him treatment, saying it was the company's policy that seasonal workers are not treated at the centre, especially when they are off-duty. Frustrated, Bosco left his brother by the gate and dashed out to look for a vehicle to take him to Kilimambogo Hospital, two kilometres away. The Del Monte factory is not located on the main road and it took Bosco more than two hours to get transport to take Kamolo to hospital. When he returned at 1.15 p.m. it was too late – Kamolo lay dead at the company's gate.[1]

In 1999, an audit report compiled by the quality standards monitoring organization Société Générale de Surveillance (SGS) said that Del Monte routinely threatened shop stewards with dismissal and that employees were not free to join trade unions.[2] Union leaders were intimidated and prohibited from communicating with fellow workers. The SGS said Del Monte had no proper contingency plans to ensure the safety of workers in the event of an emergency, such as fire, and no first-aid kits. Workers were exposed to high-decibel noise without any protection. The budget allocation for contingency plans was minimal. Only the factory floor workers wore boots to prevent foot contact with harmful chemicals. People using sprays were not provided with gas masks.[3]

The SGS monitor also uncovered low salaries and compulsory overtime that the company listed as voluntary. In Kenya, the minimum hourly wage is KSh 14.40/hour and employers are required to provide medical assistance for all workers. The Kenya Human Rights Commission (KHRC) reckons workers need to earn KSh 305.66 a day to cover the basic needs, including food and rent, of a family of six in Thika. According to the audit report, casual workers at the Thika plant earn KSh 12.60/ hour.

As these abuses continued at Del Monte, arousing anger and criticism both locally and abroad, managing director Barry Twite, who has since been fired, maintained that everything was all right.[4] He said the campaigns threatened the firm and the livelihood of its 5,000 employees. Twite said Del Monte was competing for markets with rivals in Thailand, Indonesia, and the Philippines. The campaigns, together with poor infrastructure, threatened the company's survival in the competitive world of fruit juice production. He said the company was a committed and responsible employer in Kenya and had spent KSh 100 million on community services. The management said at a press conference that the human rights groups concerned were free to make unannounced visits to the firm, but, when the groups did visit, the management declined to give them an audience.

As campaigns mounted against his firm, Twite sent out a memo to workers reminding them that, when the spotlight finally moved away and the dancers had left the show, it would be they who would be left to continue with the job of building the company through hard and honest work.

After researching conditions at the Thika factory, the Italian human rights group Centro Nuovo Modello di Sviluppo (CNMS) launched a campaign in November 1999 calling for a consumer boycott in Italy of Del Monte pineapples under the slogan "Say No to the Del Monte Man". The group asked COOP Italia, which markets the pineapples in Italy, to exert pressure on Del Monte to improve working conditions. The Kenya Human Rights Commission backed the campaign and said in a letter to COOP Italia:

• wages for casual workers and some seasonal workers at the Thika plantation are not enough to meet basic needs;
• toxic pesticides classified as Extremely Hazardous (Ia) and Highly Hazardous (Ib) by the World Health Organization are being used on the plantation;
• sanitation and living quarters in the villages built by the company are disgraceful;
• inadequate medical benefits and housing allowances are being paid to workers;
• internal trade union leaders are being intimidated;
• many workers' wages are being cut as they are downgraded from permanent to seasonal status under a restructuring process.

For several months the Del Monte group endured an unprecedented hate campaign and negative publicity that highlighted the allegedly poor working and living conditions of its workers. In Kenya, the campaign members constituted themselves into a group called the Solidarity Committee, which comprised human rights NGOs and trade unions representing workers at the multinational's subsidiary in Thika.

CNMS claims there have been no courses to inform workers about the dangers of pesticide use at DMKL, and precautions and health protection measures used in the industrialized countries are not taken.[5] The United Nations Food and Agriculture Organization recommends that pesticides in Class Ia and Ib should not be used in developing countries because of lack of proper training, protective clothing, and equipment; and Class II pesticides should also preferably not be used unless the user is trained and supervised.

In March 2000, water treatment at a plant close to the factory backfired when a worker added more hydrated lime than necessary. Workers, who had scarcely no training in chemical poisoning and industrial disaster management, detected a bad smell in the air. But it never occurred to them that it could be poisonous. Some started sneezing and feeling dizzy but continued working. Then thick fumes wafted into the factory from the water treatment plant. The workers ignored this and went on working. Nobody made attempts to evacuate them. As the smell got stronger and the smoke thicker, the workers covered their noses with cloths and handkerchiefs. Some held their noses with one hand while they went on working with the other. When the white acrid smoke turned black and even thicker, the cowed workers could take it no more and finally raised the alarm.[6]

The incident highlighted the fact the Del Monte plant was an unsafe place to work and that workers and supervisors were too afraid of being fired to halt work for a second – even to flee obvious danger. Apparently the Kenya Human Rights Commission called for an investigation, but it was ignored; in its report on the incident it said that doctors never disclosed what harmful gases the workers had inhaled.[7]

Del Monte's response

Del Monte Royal refuted CNMS's claims regarding pesticides. It said DMKL took part in the Global Crop Protection Federation, an international association of agrochemical manufacturers, which runs a programme for the responsible use of pesticides. Use of chemicals to control pests is restricted to the target host and is carried out only after thorough field surveys and where other methods of integrated pest management have failed. This, DMKL said, resulted in the bare minimum usage of pesticides. But the SGS audit report found that training records for the use of protective clothing and information about the health hazards of pesticides were not available for all personnel involved at the Thika plant. For example, the pesticide store signs and labels were in English only. The plantation's list of toxic substances also did not appear to be either approved or dated.[8]

No research has been carried out among workers at the Thika plant into the incidence of tumours, congenital malformations, or other health effects that might be related to pesticide exposure. Del Monte Royal said that, contrary to CNMS reports, there had been no evidence to point to any illness or disease or fatalities at the site arising from unsafe industrial practices.

In December 2000, Del Monte fired Mr Twite, scrapped the post of managing director, and appointed a new head, the current chief executive, Lorenzo Bertolli. The firm admitted that certain things had gone very wrong. In March 2001, Del Monte signed an agreement with all the organizations that had put pressure on the firm to change (KHRC, ChemiChemi Ya Ukweli, Kituo Cha Sheria, the Kenya Women Workers' Organization, shop stewards at the firm, and CNMS) in which it committed itself to invest in social facilities such as schools and hospitals for the workers and the local community and to work in closer partnership with the community. This favourable compromise led to the ending of the Kenyan "Say No to the Del Monte Man" boycott. The pressure groups pledged to hold an annual review meeting to ensure that the firm adhered to the agreed plan of action. Initiatives have already begun, especially in the company's Ndula Settlement Scheme. The company has also opened the Corina School at Kahinguro.

Willy Mutunga, executive director of the KHRC, which spearheaded the local campaigns, said that they did recognize that these commitments would take time to be realized. They had set up structures and would keep Del Monte on track. Construction of new staff houses had begun, together with a programme that will see Del Monte distribute clean drinking water to the workers and the neighbouring villages.

In another agreement signed in July 2001, the company pledged to support the campaign for workers' rights. Shop stewards at the firm agree that positive changes are taking place. For example, the process of job evaluation has started, which will define all jobs in the company and assign the correct grades and remunerations.

In December 2001, Del Monte launched a tree-planting operation in the neighbourhood as part of its pledge to protect the environment and promote sustainable land use. The firm supplied 3,000 seedlings to residents of Gachiki village to plant on their farms. A month earlier, Del Monte had planted some 30,000 seedlings at Gatuanyaga.

Application and analysis of the PDE framework to DMKL

The business activity of Del Monte in Kenya is legitimate in its twofold objective: to make a profit, which is the direct result of any business enterprise, and to produce quality pineapples and related products, which is a direct service to society (although one could argue that pineapple production is not a necessity per se for society). For its activity DMKL needs huge tracts of land, it needs to use pesticides to increase production, and of course it needs a large workforce. These *means* are legitimate and necessary for the type of activity in question.

The PDE states that an action that has harmful side-effects is permissible only if the chosen ends and means from which side-effect harm follows are per se legitimate and the side-effect harm is not part of the objective or made to serve as means to achieving the legitimate objectives. In the case of DMKL, not all the means were in fact legitimate; and, further, some of the *resultant side-effects* from the means are clearly harmful. Yet it appears that DMKL may have taken advantage of the situation and permitted these as means to achieve their objective. We need to ask if DMKL exploited the fact that Kenya has a poor legal framework, in which case we may be facing an instance of beneficial complicity. Indeed, the PDE does allow certain harmful yet unavoidable side-effects to occur but, even in these cases, responsibility is imputed. PDE strictly forbids using these harmful side-effects as means to the legitimate end. As we shall see, DMKL violated this requirement.

The criteria of the revised PDE that are most relevant to the present case are:

- negative side-effects that arise from a business's operations are not made to serve as means to achieving its legitimate objectives;
- negative side-effects can be justified as proportionate to the legitimate objectives;
- active measures are taken to prevent or minimize negative side-effects.

The landless

At the time when Del Monte was wanting to invest in Kenya, the government was seriously looking for alternative investments because the introduction of Nylon had adversely affected the marketing of sisal. The government was also looking for investment that was going to be labour intensive and export oriented because of the need to generate employment and foreign exchange. The government therefore acquired land that was formerly a sisal plantation and leased it to Del Monte. Farming based on the intensive use of chemicals is harmful not only to the workers and the population at large but also to the land itself, which gradually deteriorates until it becomes unproductive. Consequently, every so often Del Monte needs to expand to new land. The surrounding land is occupied by peasants who have been cultivating it for generations, but who now have to give it up, thanks to some corrupt government officials who do not do their job of protecting the people. Reduced to desperate straits, the landless will accept any kind of work on any terms. Del Monte may have taken full advantage of this situation.

The acquisition of land in itself is morally indifferent. What qualifies it as moral or immoral is the manner in which the land is obtained, i.e. with or without due consideration to full and proportional compensation to the previous owners. The harmful side-effect of landlessness could have been minimized if DMKL had exercised due diligence. As noted elsewhere in this book, companies such as Del Monte may not be able to control all the factors, but they can control their own responses and take responsibility for their decision to invest in a country whose laws are flawed in their application. I accept that companies cannot take full responsibility for the landless, this being a function of governments. However, if governments shirk this responsibility, and the companies are well aware of this, then companies should take this into account. Companies can to a certain extent use their resources to compensate people without compromising their profit margins.

I have mentioned beneficial complicity. The UN Global Compact's second principle states that companies must ensure that they are not complicit in human rights abuses. In Kenya, the law provides no buffer against abuse and, by simply choosing to benefit from the loopholes in the law of the land, DMKL can be interpreted as complicit in terms of this benefit.

Exploitative wages

Del Monte employs workers strictly according to production requirements. There are three different entry points to employment: as permanent staff, as seasonal workers, or as casual labourers. Being a permanent worker is a full-time job, consisting of 45 hours per week for an openended period of time. A seasonal worker may also work full time and have an open-ended contract, but when there is not much work the worker can be sent home. With casual work, the individual is taken on for a short period of time.

The permanent staff have the best conditions: they have a contract, holidays, sick pay, help with their rent, and even severance pay. Seasonal workers are also covered by a contract, but their situation is more precarious because they earn less and do not have the right to severance pay.

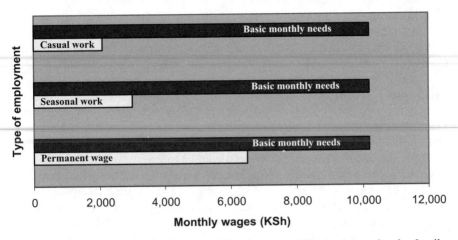

Figure 10.1 Comparison between monthly wages and the basic needs of a family of six in Thika District, Kenya, according to the 1999 Census.
Source: reproduced with permission from Willy Mutunga, Francesco Gesualdi and Stephen Ouma, *Exposing the soft belly of the multinational beast: The struggle for workers' rights at Del Monte Kenya* (Nairobi, Kenya: A Kenya Human Rights Commission Report, 2002).

As for the casual labourers, they have no contract and no benefits. All wages are in line with government laws, which stipulate a minimum legal wage of about KSh 2,800 per month.

Although Del Monte cannot be accused of not acting within the law, the law as it stands violates basic workers' rights (see fig. 10.1). I propose that this is a case of beneficial complicity because Del Monte is benefiting from the country's inadequate laws and doing almost nothing to minimize the harmful effects; it prefers the status quo. I am not in any way suggesting that it should invest elsewhere, but it should accept the cost of taking into consideration all the stakeholders in order to meet the criterion of proportionality. This entails offering higher wage standards than the minimum required by law.

Housing conditions

The housing conditions of most of Del Monte's workers were far from adequate, and were a *means* to maximize the company's profits. Certainly, housing conditions cannot be interpreted as a side-effect of corporate activity but, if it is necessary to provide housing for workers who must live near the plant, this should be done to acceptable standards. However, Del Monte does not want to make a reasonable investment in housing lest its profits are compromised.

A harmful side-effect concomitant with the housing conditions is the risk of contracting diseases. One could argue that Del Monte bears moral responsibility for this as well, because it should have known that bad housing conditions would naturally give rise to bad health effects.

Inadequate health care

From the foregoing, it is obvious that health care is inadequate. I should also point out that health care within Kenya is deplorable, so that whether the employees are working for Del Monte or not they would not have access to affordable health care. The question to be asked here is: did Del Monte shut its eyes to the health care of its employees because the government did not care anyway? I would suggest that perhaps more responsibility and conscientiousness are demanded of Del Monte. One cannot wholly absolve the company just because it happens to invest in a country that shows little regard for its people in health matters. On the contrary, in order to prove that the company is not in Kenya to benefit from the country's weak laws, Del Monte should actively set higher standards on behalf of its workers than the state and law demands.

If providing health care is necessary in order to treat workers properly in direct operations in a country such as Kenya, the lack of sufficient health care can be interpreted as an illegitimate means. Moreover, and more importantly in terms of this project, insofar as bad health conditions follow from bad housing conditions and bad working conditions, they are also a side-effect of the means by which Del Monte operates. As such, PDE requires that good health care is provided in order to minimize the side-effects. Further, insofar as the bad housing conditions and working conditions are illegitimate means, no harmful side-effects in terms of health damage can really be permissible.

Use of pesticides

The clearest example of harmful side-effects in the DMKL case pertains to the use of pesticides. To achieve the biggest possible yields and profits, extensive use of pesticides is required. Yet there are other factors that enhance yields (and thereby boost profit margins) much more than pesticides: timely seed bed preparation, planting certified seeds, having proven nutritional and water regimes in place, integrated pest management practices, in which pesticides play a minimal role, and timely harvesting of fruits. Del Monte's array of weed killers, insecticides, and fungicides includes Nemacur, Temik, Telone, Vydate, Diazinon, Gramexone, and others in categories I and II of the World Health Organization's classification of toxicity. These substances, besides causing cancer, sterility, and malformations in the unborn child in the long term, can also cause acute poisoning, with damage to the lungs, liver, kidneys, and nervous system. Nonetheless, tests carried out in Europe on DMKL products have found no detectable chemical residues.

At Del Monte, rigorous training to inform workers about the dangerous nature of pesticides had been minimal and the precautions and health protection measures adopted in industrialized countries had not been taken seriously. Del Monte did not deliberately aim to harm its workers, but it did permit them to be harmed as a result of its failure to provide training that is mandatory in the safe use of pesticides. Training implies investing in time and human resources. Del Monte may not have viewed this as beneficial to its profit-making goal. I would suggest that the company ought to have conducted a risk assessment of the use of pesticides in order not to worsen an already negative situation and to prevent and minimize the harmful effects of the pesticides. DMKL chose to ignore the foreseeable damage to workers' health, which as mentioned above also affects later generations. Under the PDE, DMKL is held morally responsible for foreseeable effects on the health of future generations who are also affected parties.

Kenya's environmental laws are loosely defined, which means that any multinational can readily harm the environment. However, environmental pollution is not necessarily linked to pineapple production in the same manner as it is to, for example, oil production. The harmful side-effects are not inescapable, because pineapple yields can be improved through integrated farming methods. Thus this is another example of a company benefiting from a negative legal framework that allows harmful side-effects while not taking the necessary steps to minimize them. The damage that has been caused to the soil is long term and will take decades to reverse. In order to minimize harm, Del Monte would have to invest in alternative farming methods to achieve the desired results.

Tacit denial of the right to association

The right to association is a basic human right confirmed by the United Nations in the Universal Declaration of Human Rights (Article 20:1). Respecting this right is conducive to choosing legitimate means. In Kenya, industrial peace is based on structures that bring together the Kenyan government, the Central Organization of Trade Unions, and the Federation of Kenya Employers as tripartite partners. The Trade Disputes Act set up these structures, including an industrial court that has two judges to hear industrial disputes. Any reading of the history of the trade union movement in Kenya, and indeed in East Africa, will confirm the genesis of repressive laws and how these laws have been used to weaken the trade union movement.

The Del Monte management became arrogant because of the support it received from the collaborative and exploitative trinity. What course of action could it have adopted in this instance? I would say that responsibility to one's fellow human beings should have been the overriding principle. One could expect DMKL to have different standards for its own operations in a country where the law is repressive – and, from a human rights perspective, illegitimate. The local communities, especially the most vulnerable ones, should be protected by the company's policies. When the right of association is denied, the voices of the oppressed are simply not heard.

Measures taken to prevent and minimize harmful side-effects

Events at Del Monte Kenya show that corporate social responsibility is not simply a luxury in which companies invest when they feel they can afford it. Good corporate citizenship entails contributing to the community, helping to build and strengthen it. Investments may be governed by international laws, but there comes a time when companies must rise above the profit motive and think about the people who toil to make it happen. This is a serious moral responsibility that multinationals can no longer ignore. It underlines that issues of corporate responsibility relate to how companies treat local communities as well as how they treat their employees. The Italian consumer boycott of Del Monte's goods was directed against the company's Kenyan operations, but the negative publicity undermined the Del Monte brand at large.

Action by Del Monte Kenya Limited appeased its critics. The boycott was ended in April 2001 but the damage done to the company is more enduring. Employee and community relations have notably improved, but profits remained down. Although Del Monte has learnt from its experience, it was a costly lesson. Expensive developments could have been spread over several years as part of company growth rather than as a large, unexpected capital outlay, and productivity is unlikely to have been harmed by better employee relations.

The new management style at DMKL is also a reflection of the new owners of Del Monte Food International. They have brought with them new market-oriented ideas, a more sensitive approach to dialogue, and a new degree of social responsibility, which are changing the focus of Del Monte worldwide. The positive responses developed by Del Monte

Kenya include the areas of: social development; workers' rights and trade union rights; environmental rights, health and safety; wages and benefits; corrective measures and monitoring.

Social development

Del Monte recognizes that, in pursuit of its objective and the production of pineapples, it has to establish and maintain a good working relationship with the neighbouring communities. DMKL also appreciates that its workers are entitled to social development, and it acknowledges its obligations by investing in social facilities such as schools and health care facilities. In addition to the investments that the company has undertaken so far, DMKL management has committed itself to:
- support local community initiatives that aim at improving their living standards;
- develop a working structure between the company and neighbouring communities;
- address the grievances of the local communities in regard to the activities of DMKL, including issues of land, environment, water, and security;
- address the various issues raised by individuals against DMKL with the intention of reaching fair and amicable solutions.

Workers' rights and trade union rights

DMKL recognizes the right of workers to organize and to participate in the activities of recognized trade unions. The management is committed to ensuring a conducive working environment for the trade unions and respect for the collective bargaining agreements. The management has already done the following to promote this:
- identified an office for the trade union leaders in the factory and the plantation;
- improved trade union leaders' access to the telephone;
- developed a management system that does not allow intimidation of trade union leaders;
- taken measures to tolerate and promote trade union leaders' access to other sources of information and training that would enhance their role as workers' leaders.

Environmental rights, health and safety

The company undertakes to ensure the protection and sustainable use of its environment. Efforts have been made to:
- provide all relevant workers in the factory and plantation with the correct and appropriate protective devices;

- ensure that all personnel receive appropriate health and safety training;
- ensure a safe and healthy working environment that is monitored by the safety committees;
- safeguard the land's biological integrity.

Wages and benefits

DMKL has signed a contract for a job evaluation exercise to ensure fair and adequate compensation for each employee. The company has also undertaken to:

- assess all cases of inadequate compensation in the factory and plantation and implement corrective measures;
- review all cases where permanent jobs were changed into seasonal jobs to make sure that this was done only when the nature of the job required it;
- rationalize overtime and encourage workers to participate voluntarily in it.

Corrective measures and monitoring

The company is also considering the following:

- highlighting its social and environmental activities over the year in the NANASI Newsletter;
- meeting with social and human rights organizations at least twice a year to be updated on the labour situation in Kenya and the world.

Assessment of corporate impact

The assessment of corporate impact is a complex process and no universal criteria for such an assessment can be established in advance. However, for both the corporate management and their critics, evaluation can be improved and dialogue promoted by the adoption of a shared framework for the assessment of responsibility.

Most of the obstacles to development in sub-Saharan Africa are not in a conventional sense the responsibility of business. Civil conflict, iniquitous trade rules, corruption, ineffective legal systems, and AIDS cannot be ascribed to corporate responsibility. Nevertheless, companies are finding ways to help address some of these issues. The problem of poverty too easily falls into the category of someone else's business. Even within the corporate citizenship movement, poverty has often remained an unspoken and unaccounted for issue below the bottom line. Countries where people enjoy good health, stability, and prosperity are better locations than those where disease, illiteracy, conflict, corruption, and environmental degradation have eaten away the foundations of the economy. How much can corporate responsibility therefore do towards ending poverty in Africa and elsewhere?

Many of the most-used business case arguments for corporate responsibility fall apart in the face of endemic poverty. It is true that companies that invest in the health, education, and prosperity of their local pool of staff, suppliers, and customers can reap the benefits in terms of improved productivity, lower costs, and increased sales. However, for internationally mobile capital there is often the alternative of investing in a less challenging business environment altogether.

The PDE framework provides a useful tool for judging the activity of corporations and their moral responsibility, especially in areas where the political authorities condone abuse of human rights and do not uphold the rule of law. Countries and regions with weak governments, civil conflict, and human rights abuses also demand more of the corporate sector in terms of responsibility and conscientiousness. According to the conceptions of complicity in the UN Global Compact, companies may have obligations to intervene with governments, even when they are not directly involved with the government in the sector concerned. According to the handbook *Corporate citizenship: Successful strategies for responsible companies*:

It is not only governments that can stand accused of failing to uphold fundamental freedom. Citizens, be they individuals or corporations, can also be complicit if they fail to acknowledge or take action on known violations....

If corporations are citizens, from which we derive the concept of corporate citizenship, then they bear witness just as individuals do. If it is wrong for a person to turn away in the face of injustice, it is wrong for a corporation to do so.[9]

DMKL benefits from the Kenyan framework with regard to the law, low wages and inadequate laws on pesticide use. To the extent that Kenyan laws are in violation of human rights and international standards for the treatment of employees, this renders DMKL beneficially complicit in the wrongdoing of the Kenyan authorities. Further, DMKL has the power to intervene and therefore the moral responsibility to do so.

Conclusion

Del Monte Kenya is a reflection of our complex "globalized" world. For several years now, multinationals operating in Africa have talked about their desire to tackle the myriad problems that afflict the region but, despite positive starts made by many companies, much still needs to be done. On the whole, multinationals remain too ambivalent about the misuse of tax revenues and foreign aid by corrupt or incompetent African governments. Multinationals now wield vast economic and social power, which gives them the opportunity to ensure that tax revenues and foreign aid are used to build infrastructures that have a positive impact on the environment, on sanitation, on health, and on economic development.

The hue and cry over human rights violations that rocked Del Monte Kenya is now over. Del Monte Kenya has acquired the ISO (International Organization for Standardization) 9002 certificate, the Kenya Bureau of Standards Diamond Mark of Quality, and the SGF/IRMA (Schutzgemeinschaft der Fruchtsaftindustrie/International Raw Material Assurance) Voluntary Control System Certificate 2001. It is in the process of acquiring ISO 14001, SA 8000, and ISO 9001/2000.

Notes

1. Dennis Onyango, "Dark days at Del Monte", *Daily Nation*, 8 April 2001.
2. SGS ICS s.r.l., International Certification Services, Audit Report, Del Monte Kenya Limited, SA/003/99 (Thika, Kenya).
3. Willy Mutunga, Francesco Gesualdi and Stephen Ouma, *Exposing the soft belly of the multinational beast: The struggle for workers' rights at Del Monte Kenya* (Nairobi, Kenya: A Kenya Human Rights Commission Report, 2002).
4. SGS Audit Report, pp. 1–10.
5. Mutunga, Gesualdi and Ouma, *Exposing the soft belly of the multinational beast.*
6. Onyango, "Dark days at Del Monte".
7. Mutunga, Gesualdi and Ouma, *Exposing the soft belly of the multinational beast.*
8. Ibid.
9. M. McIntosh, D. Leipziger, K. Jones and G. Coleman, *Corporate citizenship: Successful strategies for responsible companies* (London: Financial Times Pitman Publishing, 1998), p. 221.

11

The "just war" for profit and power: The Bhopal catastrophe and the principle of double effect

Upendra Baxi

Analytical concerns: Privileging a version

All endeavours to relate ethics, morality, human rights, or justice seem necessarily to founder when "efficiency" or wealth maximization provides the "theoretical foundation of contemporary corporate and commercial law scholarship" and of corporate conduct.[1] But, even in this milieu, the UNU/PRIO project to recraft the principle of double effect (PDE) provides a ray of hope. A viable framework for evaluating the "negative side-effects" of business and corporate cultures, practices, and decisions holds promise of some rapprochement between "efficiency" and "justice" and "wealth maximization" and "human rights".

However, because of its focus on the engagement of multinational corporations in ultra-hazardous processes, manufacture, and industry, this chapter overtaxes somewhat even this worthwhile enterprise. The already complex issues concerning the authorship, agency, incidence, aftermath, and amelioration of "negative side-effects" become even more complicated. The expression "negative side-effects" strains belief when extended to situations of archetypal industrial mass disaster such as the Bhopal catastrophe, even if we accept the notion that we all live in an "age of side effects".[2] What I am suggesting, however, is not that the recrafted PDE project is for these reasons unproductive in such contexts but that its inadequacies need to be further rigorously addressed.

The relationship between the recrafted PDE regime and its long enunciative habitats and history invites a side-glance even within the scope of this chapter. Originating in the context of the just war doctrine[3] and developed in the distinctive theological and secular discursive frameworks of *ius naturalis*[4] (for situations such as abortion and euthanasia), the PDE regime seems now to provide a general ethical theory concerning human conduct as a whole.[5] To enhance the potential of the present project's pragmatic (in the best sense) constructions of "legitimate" business practices, some genealogical regrounding may be both necessary and desirable. Undoubtedly, the new PDE must, if it is to engage the attention of captains of business and industry, almost wholly disinherit, as it were, the metaphysical overload of the multifarious PDE discourse. The question still poses itself: will such an attempt at normative cleansing altogether escape its recalcitrant residues?[6] The recrafted PDE regime avoids daunting questions that would otherwise arise – for example, the construction of the "good",[7] by its admirable recourse to "human rights", as providing a tolerable, consensually based intersubjective PDE ethic for corporate/business decision-making, governance, and culture. In turn, though, this raises some very distinctive questions.[8] In any event, talking human rights language to business remains a notoriously difficult enterprise, given the latter's overwhelming concern with efficiency and profit. At the same time, the recrafted PDE enables new configurations of what commonly passes as "business ethics".

This chapter also a raises a wider concern. Any retooling of the PDE regime summons some grasp of the problem of shifting bases of forms of social trust, a heavily contested terrain. The vertiginously complex globalizing world is rendered possible and sensible by everyday reliance on expert, and esoteric, knowledge systems. These systems are inevitably based on, and justified by, the webs of belief in their cumulative corrigibility and reflexivity.

Outside this frame, trust in expertise becomes ethically unsustainable; and this is the crux of the problem that poignantly arises in the context of the Bhopal catastrophe. Any extension of the PDE regime needs to encompass features of expertise on which contemporary forms of production rely:

First, expertise is disembedding; it is ... in a fundamental sense non-local and decentred. Second, expertise is tied not to a formulaic truth but to a belief in the corrigibility of knowledge, a belief that depends on methodological scepticism. Third, the accumulation of expert knowledge involves intrinsic processes of specialization. Fourth, trust in abstract systems, or in experts, cannot readily be generated by means of esoteric wisdom. Fifth, expertise interacts with growing institutional reflexivity, such that there are regular processes of loss and re-appropriation of everyday skills and knowledge.[9]

Clearly, the recrafted PDE regime is based on an implicit but never-theless pervasive belief in "institutional reflexivity". Minimization of negative side-effects, under the fourth criterion of the revised PDE, is a notion that speaks more clearly to managers of business than do the powers of "esoteric wisdom" of theistic and secular PDE discourse. Belief in the "corrigibility of knowledge" and the expertise of techno-scientific "communities" of risk producers clearly helps processes of risk pre-assessment and enables prevention in the first place, and amelioration in the second, of negative side-effects. I do not (for reasons of space) here directly address the debate about whether "non-know-ledge" rather than "knowledge" is the more crucial in dealing with the global risk society; in other words, whether popular reflexivity is more liberating than expert knowledge's systemic propensity to reflexive learning.[10] However, I note in passing here that the recrafted PDE seems to lean more towards the gestalt of Anthony Giddens than that of Ulrich Beck.

Leaving these larger issues out of consideration, this chapter invokes an understanding of the present project as postulating a distinctive kind of business ethics, specifically entailing the following:

- business associations and corporations may not be regarded as *amoral* agents;
- their conduct and operations can be and ought to be judged by ethical standards that define moral intentions and corresponding conduct that produces ethically the right result;
- even such right results may in real life be accompanied by positive as well as negative side-effects;
- a study of negative side-effects remains necessary to plan future business/ corporate social learning/reflexivity for corporations already inclined to a culture of business ethics and corporate governance that is ori-ented to human rights.

Given this, a number of pertinent consequences ensue:

- the problem of group identity and legal responsibility (liability) is rel-evant not in itself but only to the extent that it enables the study of negative side-effects;[11]
- the state and the law, as it were, do not end where corporations begin;[12]
- in stipulating liability, the state/law has itself to be ethical; it should remain concerned with issues of the relationship between moral *re-sponsibility* and legal *liability*. The state/law ought then to provide strong justification for the view that economic enterprises may be said

to be morally responsible without being legally liable or to be legally liable without being morally responsible.

The PDE in catastrophic contexts

Transnational corporate governance engaged in the production and management of ultra-hazardous processes, substances, manufacture, and industry raises a number of issues of concern. By definition, decision-making here entails the creation of huge risks, which proliferate and intensify in a situation where a number of dispersed corporate decision makers remain globally networked (through corporate interconnectivities between subsidiary companies and affiliates). These risks (in chemical, biotech, nuclear, and conventional defence production, for example) affect both living and future generations (in terms of their impact on existential life cycles and choices and of overall ecological consequence), and at times (as in Bhopal) they approach the dimensions of large-scale catastrophes and social disasters.[13] This raises a threshold question concerning the extension of the PDE regime: should it focus on the ethics in the *production* of risk, or on the ethics of its *distribution*, or *both*. The easy answer – that it must address both – is indeed superficially attractive, until we attend to understanding notions of risk in the circumstance of globality called provocatively "reflexive modernization",[14] which characterizes both the *politics of production* and the *production of politics*.[15]

Risks, as is well known, emerge where decisions have to be made under conditions of uncertainty. Thus arise constructions of risk-causing communities and risk-bearing communities in collective human conduct and experience. Because risk-causing communities do not usually directly suffer the risks caused by ultra-hazardous manufacture, processes, and industry, especially under multinational modes of risk production, the two communities remain both spatially and temporally distinct. This distinction causes a dilemma for the recrafted PDE regime.

Given the ubiquity of risk, the politics of describing the production and distribution of risk as production and distribution matters considerably in any extension of the PDE regime. There is a choice to make between using the language of "accident" and that of "catastrophe". Each and every sector of hazardous production remains viewed in terms of "normal accidents".[16] The PDE regime, however it is constructed, mandates an ethic of production that requires such production to be planned and carried out so as to minimize, and even avoid, accidental harm. "Accidents" are events that specifically injure and harm a determinate number of human beings; "catastrophes" are events that cause multiple, even generational, injury and harm to indeterminate human populaces and environment. "Accidents" may occur in spite of the best collective efforts in the management of hazardous/ultra-hazardous industry or manu-facture, and therefore invite description in terms of "negative side-effects". Because "accidents" constitute misfortunes, it would be rather odd to describe them in the language of injustice. Mass disasters (cata-strophes), in contrast, certainly for those affected, are experienced as in-justice.[17] If the language of "negative side-effects" remains apposite to doing business, this is indeed strained to breaking point in catastrophic situations, which in turn retrospectively raise large questions concerning the very ethics of ultra-hazardous production.

At least two threshold questions, in terms of the PDE-informed ethics of production, arise. First, do business/corporate decision makers have a human rights responsibility to avoid decisions that entail catastrophic consequences? Second, what concrete duties do they owe to the bearers of human and social suffering caused by actual catastrophes? This last question also points to the multitudinous issues concerning the ethics of the distribution of risks.

In these terms, the principal question concerns risk, responsibility, and redress. This question is posed and mediated in various ways in cata-strophic situations. In order that responsibility and redress become per-tinent to business conduct or ethical judgement, issues of the *authorship* (conventionally put, the causation), the *agent* (means), and the *extent* (incidence) of harm need to be clearly addressed. Assuming an agreed response to this, the issue of responsibility has at least two dimensions; first, the language in which the discourse about responsibility is con-ducted makes all the difference; second, the extent of the responsibility for catastrophic harm ensuing from the PDE.

The first dimension once again raises the distinction between legal and ethical languages (however contingent their relationships); legal liability and moral responsibility do not often comfortably merge. The second di-mension translates these issues into the corporate language of damage limitation, suggesting at least some minimal thresholds for responsibility/liability. In terms of redress, then, even the most minimalist version of the recrafted PDE regime rejects the notion of impunity that ordains that the costs should lie where they fall, on the submissive bodies and voice-less souls of those direly affected.

However, the culture and practice of corporate damage limitation raise further obdurate questions. What may be said to constitute the "floor" and "ceiling" obligations of redress for catastrophic impacts? How may the scope or limits of redress be conceptualized? Is compensation in the form of a one-off "negotiated" monetary quantum of "damages" suitable for mass disaster situations? If not, what medium- and long-term concrete obligations, in terms of human rights, to ameliorate massive human suffering may attach to corporations? How may we justify the corporation's capacity to pay as furnishing an ethical cap or ceiling that defines the limits of redressability? Does the invocation of penal law and sanctions relate to redress, and if so in what ways?

The Bhopal catastrophe, and its negotiated passage of risk, responsibility, and redress, brings alive, with some poignancy, these and related questions. I start by noting a bare fact: the Bhopal catastrophe[18] involved the release of nearly 45 tons of methyl isocyanate gas (MIC) on 2/3 December 1984 at the Bhopal plant of the Union Carbide Corporation's (UCC) Indian subsidiary, Union Carbide India Ltd (UCIL), which killed at least 2,500 people.[19] In the face of the scale of the disaster, the UCC, and the UCIL under its auspices, assiduously engaged in the logic of double denial concerning the agent (means) of harm and the author of harm.

As to the agent of harm, the UCC insisted the gas emissions were not of MIC; and that, in any event, the emissions were in no way harmful. On this scenario, the question simply did not arise for the UCC of corporate moral responsibility for the timely identification of the agent of harm and sharing any relevant toxicological, epidemiological, and therapeutic information. Instead, the UCC's propagandists advised people to stay indoors and hold a wet towel over their faces. Given the UCC's global monopoly of technoscientific information concerning the toxicity of MIC, these evasive moves successfully impeded appropriate therapeutic regimes that could have minimized the overall harm and mayhem. The recrafted PDE regime is sensible if and only if it casts corporate duties to minimize colossal human suffering in the wake of a mass social disaster.

The issue gets further complicated in terms of the authorship of harm. When assumption of any such humanitarian obligations is seen to entail acceptance of some degree of moral responsibility that may in turn attract a measure of legal liability, corporate decision makers become simply morally incoherent. This happens because modern corporate management styles and cultures of corporate "legality" encourage individual decision makers within networked corporate contexts to avoid confessional gestures of any sort. The "ethics" of risk analysis and risk management "taught" in the top business schools engrains the logics and rhetoric of *denial*. So does the "ethic" of the global insurance industry, which precludes any confessional gestures, save when consistent with losses duly insured.

Further, the postmodern (as well as a post-Fordist) transnational corporate governance form complicates acknowledgement of the authorship of harm. This form is flexible enough to make imputation of authorship vexatiously indeterminate. Although the UCIL was a subsidiary of the

UCC, and although the UCC held 51 per cent of the shares, it was also, under law, an autonomous corporate self. In the complex mass tort litigation that ensued, the UCC maintained that it could be held neither responsible nor liable for the acts of its subsidiary. It also argued before Judge Keenan that, as an American corporation with its headquarters in Danbury, Connecticut, it was not subject to the jurisdiction of the Indian courts, a position that the learned Judge did not accept in mandating UCC to appear before the Indian courts.[20] At the level of strict law, the UCC contended before the Indian courts that it was not liable for damages under the principle of multinational enterprises' absolute liability for mass disasters. How may one construct this denial of any legal liability under a PDE-oriented regime?

As we shall see in some detail in what follows, the UCC further maintained that the ultimate moral responsibility lay with the Union of India (UOI) and the State of Madhya Pradesh (MP): the UOI initiated the technology transfer agreement with the UCC; it allowed the location of the plant at Bhopal; its laws and regulation governed the UCIL; and, in particular, factory or onsite technical safety inspections were the responsibility of the MP government. The responsibility to minimize negative side-effects (if one may use this term without a moral shudder in the context of the Bhopal catastrophe) befalling hapless Indian citizens was thus said to be pre-eminently governmental. And the settlement amounts the UCC initially and then finally proposed did not betoken any singular notion of moral corporate responsibility; rather, these remained animated by the need to negotiate transaction costs between a "host" state and a multinational corporation. As we shall see later, the responsibility issues here are ineluctably constituted and related to a multiple-nested collective moral "self".[21]

Narratologies and PDE: A preliminary excursus

I have already begun the Bhopal narrative. But some threshold issues arise concerning narrative integrity: how "best", and from whose standpoint, may we construct and narrate stories concerning risk production and distribution in terms of the objectives of the action, the means employed to achieve this, and the results (including both positive and negative side-effects). As already hinted, the Bhopal case is laden with multiple stories concerning extremely diverse actors and comprising multifariously constituted intersections between governmental, corporate, and violated selves.

The UCC narrative path privileges the fact that the national government of the world's most populous democracy was the actual author of the key decisions to import an ultra-hazardous process, manufacture, and industry and its eventual location at Bhopal. The UOI, representing India's free, equal, and sovereign state, was the custodian of the rights and interests of Indian citizens. The UCC was then no more than a supplicant for state largess, with no real power to bend its sovereign will towards its own commercial ends. In this narrative, then, primary ethical responsibility lies at the door of the UOI and its constituent state, the MP. In a way, this responsibility narrative was also implicitly subscribed to by the UOI from the 1960s to the early 1980s, when the catastrophe occurred.

When this privileged narrative was disrupted by the massive release of 45 tons of MIC in the early hours of 2/3 December 1984, the UOI and MP constructed the narrative in terms of a model of action that vested pre-eminent, even sole, responsibility in the UCC, which it naturally then chose to contest all the way through diverse instrumentalities and forums of a unique global mass tort litigation. The UOI, as a sovereign plaintiff, sued the UCC, first in New York and subsequently in India, creating the epoch-making principle of *absolute enterprise liability*, which insists that ultra-hazardous processes, manufacture, and industry (national or multinational) remain absolutely liable, to the point where the enterprise is fully liable for the harm caused and does not even have the capability of invoking the standard defence that a mass/social disaster might have been caused by sabotage or (as lawyers call this) an Act of God. In this narrative genre, the Bhopal catastrophe becomes intensely juridicalized.

The Bhopal-violated Indian humanity offers a third and complex narrative path. The anguished survivors constructed scripts of responsibility that indicted the UCC and UCIL as well as the UOI and MP, co-equally but variously. They posed the issue of responsibility not merely in terms of causation and damages but also in the language of duties of care as justice entailing amelioration of here-and-now and long-term suffering via specific obligations of relief, redress, and rehabilitation. In this perspective, the "negative side-effects" become embodied selves. These are best measured not in terms of juristic principles of liability and quantum of compensation (assessed by the UOI at US\$3 billion and finally settled at US\$470 million) but rather in terms of collective human bereavement and grief, and whole encyclopaedias of the immediate as well as the indeterminate future physical and psychological hurt and harm, lived now for nearly two decades. The so-called side-effects signify for them the wholesale and continuing destruction of their life projects.

Any morally sensitive PDE-oriented articulation of "intended" harms and unintentional negative "side-effects" needs then to confront the stark issue: from *whose* and from *which* perspective may we choose to tell epic stories of human, and human rights, violation? The issue here concerns the very formation of a narrative self. How and where may we locate its origins and itineraries? Which narrative self, in its multiple unfolding, may we privilege? How may we periodize the various births and rebirths of this narrative self in the archetypal situations of mass/social disasters from Bhopal to Ogoniland and beyond?

Clearly, different narrative modes result in different emplotment of the ways in which we privilege both the *narrative* self and the *narrated* ones. After all, each and every narrative performance tends to distribute/redistribute constitutive narrative functions. Different narrative selves emerge; as does the great chain of events that constitute the being of the catastrophe and the variety of its aftermaths. The "narratees" (those who stand narrated) also vary, depending on the intentionalities of the narrative selves. Different narrative structures emerge in ways that privilege certain accounts of causation and of the moral responsibility and legal liability of the various actors (that is, those that singly and together produce a range of critical events). Different narrative ethics too emerge. Diffused distribution of responsibility and liability for unfortunate impacts thus characterizes critical events.

Furthermore, there is the problem (already noted) of the language of the chosen narrative style. For example, was what happened on 2/3 December 1984 at Bhopal merely a "gas leak", a "disaster", or a "catastrophe" equivalent to Hiroshima, earning it the name of "Bhoposhima" or the "largest peacetime industrial disaster in the world" (as Judge Keenan was to describe it)? What, if any, PDE-related consequences may then be said to ensue?

The problematic of adequate narratology continues to haunt us all the way. What narrative forms may be pertinent in terms of risk pre-assessment and prevention and of amelioration of negative side-effects? Were the diverse choreographies of corporate/business conduct, governance, and culture sufficiently PDE responsive? How are we to understand differential PDE ethics thresholds that led the UCC to acknowledge responsibility while altogether denying any legal liability? Does any preferred version of PDE help us to discover Archimedean points of narrative? If none may be established, how then may we tell, even as "chain novelists", the "best" stories concerning what actually happened? How then also might we adjudicate the inner narrative moralities thus conflicted? All one may say perhaps is that narrativist reductionism remains unethical in its irredeemably simplified (and reified) descriptions of complex and contradictory realities. Narrative integrity is indeed a virtue. The question, then, is what in the PDE regime may help us privilege any narrative form for the presentation of the critical events of a mass disaster.

Periodization remains central to fashioning "core" narratives of critical events because these occur and are experienced in differential space-time. The space-time of the UCC decision makers was intensely *global*; the space-time of those violated at Bhopal was irremediably *local*. Feats of periodization hover ambivalently across these catastrophic horizons; for reasons of space, I rather clumsily cluster the periods into three categories relevant to any PDE application: the pre-catastrophe period; the catastrophe period (the minor 1982 gas leak and its managerial after-math; the "management" of the immediate events on 2/3 December 1984); and the period of juridicalization of the catastrophe (from 1985 to the 1998 "settlement" and its aftermath).

The pre-history of a catastrophe

The background

The UOI, in the circumstance of post-colonialism, espoused a state-driven conception of development. In this form, it emerges as an ethical actor, a singularly burdened multiplex network of public decision-making, confronted by the perceived need to make India self-sufficient and self-reliant in food production. In the 1960s it decided it no longer wanted to be dependent on the United States aid programme for the supply of carbama-rates (pesticide and insecticide chemicals entailing indeterminate actual and future impacts on human life and the environment) and to commence a programme of chemicalized agricultural production under its own auspices (the first Green Revolution). It thus embarked on technology imports. The UOI floated global tenders for the manufacture of MIC-based pesticides, thus exercising toxic sovereignty. The wider aspects of the pre-UCC governmentality, which were important in the struggle for justice for the Bhopal victims, will not be pursued here.[22]

The UOI considered two offers/tenders, from Bayer and UCC, and, following the standard procedure, invited public comments on these. Both tenders were based on methyl isocyanate (MIC). Bayer followed the "best industry standard" in that its offer entailed merely production on demand, with no large-scale storage of MIC, even then known to be lethal in as yet unforeseen ways. The UCC, in contrast, saw no harm in large-scale storage of MIC as and when needed. Only one Indian company (Atul at Valsad, Gujarat) lodged an objection, based on the grounds of future endangerment – to no avail. The contract was awarded to the UCC.

Any appeal to the recrafted PDE version then raises the following issues:

- Did other concerned Indian corporations have the same PDE "duty" as Atul to raise objections? This involves the issue of the collective corporate pursuit of what is commonly known in business as the "best industry standard", an ensemble of business practices and trade customs that anticipate and limit the overall harm of negative side-effects. Two questions here arise: first, how may we glean the uncontested existence and provenance of the best industry standards; and, second, how may various human rights norms, standards, and values relate to the birth and growth of such standards?
- Was the UOI justified, under *any* PDE regime, in treating the Atul objections less deferentially? This question, lying perhaps outside the threshold of the recrafted PDE regime, remains crucial in any narratives concerning the Bhopal catastrophe.
- Was the UCC preferred because of objectives driven by American foreign and/or economic policy? If thus narrated, which set of moral actors may be identified, singly or jointly, as morally blameworthy (and legally consequential) for any catastrophic production and distribution of mass disaster risks?
- Did the UOI fully consider the hazards, given the state of contemporary knowledge, of large storage-based production of the two UCC products?[23]
- What fiduciary duties, under any PDE regime, were owed by the UCC in terms of obligations of full disclosure of the levels of toxicity and ranges of epidemiology involved in its modes of production? To whom were these owed?[24] And what was required by the PDE regime by way of coherent obligations of corporate policy/governance fulfilment?
- What, if any, PDE regime duties ought to have informed the insurance industry as regards known and foreseeable hazards in their underwriting of the UCC project? Because hazardous industry and manufacture are increasingly insured for catastrophic risks as well as for accidental harm, the PDE regime ought to address the ethic of the global insurance industry; all too often, the insured risks determine the modes of acknowledgement of responsibility/liability and the quantum of compensation in mass disaster and mass tort litigation and settlement.
- What human rights obligations, constitutive of a new incarnation of the PDE regime, ought to have informed decision-making by the UCC and its network affiliates? Because existing human rights regimes tend to exclude the application of human rights norms and standards to multinational corporate conduct, specification of applicable customary and treaty-based human rights remains vital to the recrafted PDE regime.[25]

The politics of location decisions

Location decisions in relation to ultra-hazardous industry, processes, and manufacture structure the nature of "negative" side-effects (they condition as well as determine). From a business standpoint, industry location invariably entails considerations of access to factors of production (land, labour, tax incentives, and access to infrastructure, especially transport and communication, the manipulability of executive discretion). Human rights considerations scarcely impinge on location decisions; "safety" considerations do matter but not decisively, at least when a multinational corporation operates in a populous developing country setting. In any event, in such settings the "technical" aspects often get associated with, even overlaid by, the "political" dimension within which the host governments necessarily function. The question then arises: in what ways may PDE normativeness speak to location decisions?

Bombay (now Mumbai) was thus obviously the first choice for the UCC plant, but the best available site also proved to be the worst: the proposed location at Chembur in Bombay was too close to an already ageing civilian nuclear power plant. The narratives of mass disaster and its historical impacts would have been spectacularly different had the plant been located on this site. Indian governance and politics, as well as multinational corporate conduct, would have been affected in far-reaching ways. Did any sense of business ethics (to put the best ethical face on corporate decision-making) guide the UCC acquiescence in the abandonment of this site? May it be credited with some scruples in not deploying its corporate power to persist in the original and more industrially favourable location?

It is doubtful whether any PDE logics/paralogics informed the choice of Bhopal, the capital city of the state of Madhya Pradesh. Was this choice (as compared with Bombay) justified on the basis of any pursuit of the "less harm" principle?[26] What corporate deference, if any, was owed to the vociferous and principled opposition by no less than the then Chief Secretary of the MP (M. N. Buch)? He opposed the location of the hazardous plant in the heart of the old city, where millions of impoverished citizens etched their ways of survival and livelihood. But this location was eminently convenient for the UCC and it prevailed; the Chief Secretary resigned in protest, but to no avail. What negative side-effects were thus considered ethically unproblematic?

Further, it goes without saying that the people affected had no say in the final locational decision, at least in terms of involvement in risk pre-assessment. Had a measure of due PDE-oriented diligence informed the UCC management, a less populous site at Bhopal would have been preferred, avoiding future catastrophic results. Ethically informed options concerning the avoidance of negative side-effects would have emerged for consideration had stakeholder consultancy been in place before, and during, the operations. However, any such meaningful participation would have required a symmetrical flow of information about the nature of the hazard, its foreseeability, and its short- and long-term impacts on life, health, and the environment. *What* ethical obligations did the UCC and its affiliates have, even within the mixed jurisdiction of public/private (governmental/corporate) decision-making, concerning public education about the potential hazard?

Informational asymmetries and monopolies

More to the point, how may this task be addressed where the flow of information is asymmetric? As already noted, the UCC had a near monopoly on technoscientific global knowledge concerning the toxicity and epidemiology of MIC-based pesticide production. Was its deliberate non-disclosure to the UOI, MP, and potentially concerned communities justified or justifiable under the PDE regime? Positive law regimes of trade secrecy and intellectual property provide almost full protection of rights of corporate non-disclosure. The UOI's tolerance of this monopolistic advantage is equally understandable, because ultra-hazardous technologies constitute a seller's market. But does full acceptance of these rights legitimate business practices that overtly or covertly amount to genocidal decisions? Denial of even *prima facie* PDE-related obligations adequately to conceptualize potential negative side-effects and to provide a state-of-the-art safety regime for the Bhopal plant, given the unprecedented storage of MIC, remains PDE impertinent.

How can we explain the fact that the same UCC management did not allow similarly large MIC storage at its West Virginia plant? No PDE-oriented regime may, in the abstract, sanction a racist corporate culture that differentiates between duties of care owed to co-nationals and non-nationals.[27] At the very least, PDE norms entail equally scrupulous solicitude for the human right to life and livelihood; locational as well as technical operational decisions in particular require the duty to avoid hostile indifference and ethnic discrimination in ultra-hazardous processes and manufacture. In addition, application of the PDE proscribes "economy" measures that might increase the risk – the UCIL management shut down the Bhopal refrigeration plant to minimize operating costs, a decision that greatly contributed to the catastrophe. A similar range of issues arises in terms of the prevention of negative side-effects occurring through accident and even industrial sabotage.[28] A PDE regime manifestly imposes a higher threshold for eliminating or at least minimizing such side-effects.

Likewise, in designing and maintaining efficient safety systems, the UCC management was clearly obligated by a PDE regime to maintain the same level of state-of-the-art safety systems across its worldwide MIC-based production. I say this for the simple reason that the PDE regime derives its cogency from the premise that business practices must be based on equal treatment and equal respect for all. The UCC's West Virginia plant had computerized safety systems providing for early warning, automatic fault rectification, and similar coping abilities for the avoidance or minimization of negative side-effects. The Bhopal plant, in appalling contrast, began operations with an already outmoded manual safety system, which was not redressed (as I note in the next section) in the wake of the 1982 gas leak by any attempt at conscientious implementation of its own safety audit report.

Routine managerial decisions at the local plant level, which were not subject to concerned scrutiny by the controlling multinational management, as well as policy decisions taken when setting up the plant, may be criticized on PDE grounds. Hazardous production should not be further aggravated by differential management of safety technology that devalues life, livelihoods, and minimal dignity in developing countries. Put another way, hostile ethnic discrimination, even when "justified" in terms of efficiency and profits, remains unconscionable under any PDE regime.

The catastrophe period

Decision moments

When investment and operational management decisions remain wholly "instrumental", the underlying rationality of business/corporate conduct invites the description "fly now, pay later". The "fly now" aspect concentrates mostly, even exclusively, on the needs of production and profit. The "pay later" mode, in turn, is enclosed by the risks that the global insurance market may "reasonably" and "rationally" be said to bear. It is also manifest in recourse to legal stratagems to avoid "paying" even *later*.[29] "Rational" business/corporate decision-making is thus at each stage carefully informed by profit maximization and avoidance of uninsurable liability. In real-time corporate/business decision moments, reflexive corporate governance translates human rights solicitude and imperatives, if at all, in terms of what the market will bear.

The catastrophic leakage of MIC in 1984 was preceded by a small leak in 1982 that killed two workers. This incident occurred despite periodic safety inspections by the state of Madhya Pradesh. The active pursuit of plant safety by the local trade union leadership was swiftly disciplined

and punished by the UCIL; the union unavailingly pursued the wrong-
fulness of the management action in a local labour court. However, the
UCC management was so concerned that it ordered a "safety audit",
which uncovered the alarming condition of safety systems and procedures at the Bhopal plant. The discovery proceedings before Judge
Keenan revealed that this safety audit report was not shared with the
UCIL management or the UOI or MP governments.[30] Worse still, far
from carrying out any participative exploration prior to and during the
business operation with a view to avoiding "negative side-effects" (in
terms of the revised PDE), the UCC *suppressed* the safety audit report.
Its irredeemably unilateralist business/governance conduct merits thor-
oughgoing PDE indictment.

The post-catastrophe managerial aftermath

What PDE-related considerations may inform cultures of corporate governance and conduct in the event of a catastrophe? I have already noted
the problematic logic and rhetoric of denial of the agents (means) of
harm. But the long aftermath of the catastrophe deserves brief analysis
here.

First, was the UCC justified in contesting that whatever emissions
ensued were not MIC laden?

Second, was it justified in not sharing all available epidemiological and
toxicological information with the UOI and MP governments and Indian
health care professionals? Were there *no* available means and methods
(even within management limitations on confessional gestures of moral
responsibility, which are perceived as liable to be translated into legal
liability) by which the UCC might have helped to ameliorate the enormous human suffering?

Third, was the UCC justified in arguing (in the mass media, in board-
rooms, as well as in courtrooms) that the negative side-effects would have
been less lethal had the levels of nutrition and community health been
higher, even if not comparable to those in the developed world? It
maintained, for example, that the adverse respiratory impacts of exposure would have been noticeably different had the smoking habits of
the affected populace been different or their nutritional floor richer! Such
archetypal damage limitation exercises, if taken at face value, seem to
rule that corporate investment and location decisions may be constrained
by the PDE *only* where communities are well fed and nourished and do
not indulge in health-damaging addictions. Investment decisions around
the globe would then indeed punish relatively less "worthy" communities. Such excesses in damage limitation exercises go against not just the
PDE regime but plain common-sense.[31]

Fourth, the PDE entails that, where suffering is a side-effect, the company is obligated not just to minimize it but to "take on the suffering as well".[32] This then answers in the affirmative the question: Did the UCC have any obligations, consensually crafted together with the UOI and MP, to provide any interim financial relief and assistance to the Bhopal victims? The UCC complained vociferously (in terms of a public relations exercise) that the concerned governments had closed down UCC/UCIL-maintained "facilities" (such as provision of sewing machines for female "victims"), but so far as is known made no effective attempt to provide a non-adversarial consensual platform for such cooperative endeavour. Instead, it contested all the way up to the Supreme Court the award of interim compensation by the MP High Court (of US$270 million) aimed at immediate amelioration of the victims' plight. The UCC may have been well advised to deny any legal obligation to pay compensation, but there was nothing to prevent a humanitarian gesture, consistent overall with its eventual non-liability position, to offer an equivalent sum for immediate relief and rehabilitation.

This raises an important question that PDE-oriented business management ought to consider. When judicial orders direct interim compensation in damage suits for mass torts, corporate management needs to have ethically sound reasons for opposing compliance. Such compliance may properly be accompanied by two conditions: first, that such aid and assistance do not preclude or prejudice the company's legal position or defence in ongoing legal proceedings; and, second, that the company may seek to deduct from a final settlement amount any interim compensation already paid. These conditions were in any event integral to the MP High Court's award of interim compensation.

Of course, a hard-nosed management may want to maintain that, were it to succeed on appeal and thus be found not liable for any compensation at all, it might be difficult to recover interim compensation already disbursed. Given, however, that most mass torts litigation is ultimately settled, rather than fully adjudicated, there is no legal or juridical reason for the interim payments not to be set off against the finally settled amount. Even if a settlement is not made, it is not clear why, as part of the principle of minimizing intense human/social suffering, ultra-hazardous manufacture and industry should not add suitable provision for interim relief to its overall insurance portfolio. For example, insurance portfolios already extend to "political risk", which covers losses arising from political circumstances and situations such as regime change or civic unrest and violence that adversely affect pre-existing contracts. There is no reason for business not to insure against measures of interim relief or compensation being judicially ordered. Likewise, toxic industries (for example, in the United States) have agreed to the legislative imposition of subscription to industry-wide environmental clean-up public funds (the

Toxic Superfund); is there any reason for the principle informing such legislative arrangements not to extend to interim relief payments in the event of a major industrial disaster? In any event, any PDE-friendly business ethic requires, at the level of both individual firms and business/ industry associations, morally imaginative innovations to address the amelioration of human/social suffering that may emerge on any reasonable scenario of the probability of a catastrophe occurring.

Fifth, what justifies the extraordinary self-presentation by the UCC of itself as a victim of Bhopal litigation? I have explored the multiple ironies this raises.[33] Here it should suffice to mention that the UCC presents itself as the *ultimate victim*, denied fair play by social action and human rights groups, the Indian media, and even Justices of the Supreme Court. On this presentation, actions for legal redress by the UOI and victim groups constitute a second Bhopal catastrophe. The UCC thus clouds, multifariously and mischievously, the issues concerning the authorship of mass disaster, the moral obligation to ameliorate human suffering thus caused, and allegiance to moral causes.

Sixth, although the criterion of immediacy of harm is not integral to the recrafted PDE, the recalcitrant residues of the original PDE raise the issue of how we may extend or apply the PDE criterion that beneficial effects must follow from the action at least as swiftly as harmful effects. This criterion of immediacy, which is well suited to just war or medical/ bioethics contexts, requires wholesale reconsideration in the context of corporate governance contributing to or causing mass disasters. Although I applaud the recrafted PDE regime, which dispenses with the criterion of the immediacy of harm because the harmful effects of mass disasters unfold over time and across generations (especially mutagenic impacts),[34] the issue of translation persists. By this I mean the ways in which business ethic formations may actually assume long-term responsibility for rehabilitation and redress. During prolonged litigation, as in Bhopal, corporations remain overwhelmingly concerned with denying any serious long-term effects and even immediate effects; upon settlement, they tend to maintain that the manifestly inadequate sums thus made available must be held to absolve them from any further responsibility and liability. The logic of dispensing with the criterion of immediacy in mass disaster situations needs to be put to work; as such it constitutes a problem that warrants future attention.

The juridicalization of the Bhopal catastrophe

The issues so far raised acquire further complexity and contradiction with the juridicalization of the Bhopal catastrophe. Juridicalization entails unequal and deadly combat between formidable networks of global technoscientific capital and numerous, usually impoverished, dispersed and powerless victims. The victims of the mass disaster have to bear the burden of proving the harm; they have not merely to show the authorship of harm (causation) but also to demonstrate that they have suffered compensatable injuries. What constitutes compensatable injury is further determined by the civil law of torts, which is not always and inherently inclined towards the justice of their cause. Its principles and standards of liability are not historically designed to empower the victims of mass disaster. Juridicalization commingles issues of legal liability and moral responsibility and the adjudicatory auspices follow its autonomous path and career. Most catastrophic mass disasters do not involve hot pursuit of the offending corporation by a sovereign plaintiff state. Bhopal was probably the only major mass disaster in which the state claimed to act as *parens patriae* for those harmed by the catastrophe.

The immediate trigger was provided by the swarm of contingency fee American lawyers that descended upon the Bhopal victims in the wake of the catastrophe. Within less than a fortnight, they had assembled powers of attorney and begun to institute as many as 118 civil mass torts suits in various United States jurisdictions. Incidentally, were we to conceive of the American Bar as a business, might PDE logic also extend to legal professionals?

Considered in necessary detail, juridicalization entails contestation by the defendant corporation of the facts, causes, and effects of a mass disaster. Further, corporate/business handling of mass disaster litigation systematically reveals juridicalization to be a war of attrition. Because legal services constitute a paradigm of a seller's market, corporations tend to suborn the best and brightest legal competence, which is thus never in full measure available to the "victims" of mass/social disasters and their next of kin, to the human rights and social activists, and in the Bhopal case even to a sovereign state plaintiff. The commanding heights are captured in juridicalization strategies by aggregations of techno-scientific capital. From these heights, immensely complex legal manoeuvring constantly takes place; every form of procedural and substantive complexity in the legal orderings is relentlessly marshalled (as the corporate conduct in the Bhopal case documented in my trilogy abundantly testifies). This invaluable strategic advantage is pursued in the undeniable values, languages, and rhetorics of the rule of law and due process.

The overall result is a huge "docket explosion", in which litigation moves through the judicial hierarchy in a constant game of "snakes and ladders". The Bhopal case furnishes a paradigm of the movement of issues and contentions through the appellate judicial labyrinth. Both the UCC and UOI remain engaged with the production of the docket explosion. The UCC corporate governance and culture are favourably disposed to delaying consideration of the real issues because delays favour relatively low settlements that fall within the range of insured amounts. The UOI, through the unique device of the Bhopal Act, which personified it as a collectively injured self, subrogating litigational rights and privileges, constituted itself as a sovereign plaintiff, which cannot afford to appear complicit or weak in the public political eye. It sued a multinational corporation for mass disaster, both in the New York court and in various Indian judicial forums, under an innovative regime of absolute liability of multinational enterprises. Thus began an extraordinary forensic saga that infinitely complicates the PDE-related narratives. Because global capital remains loath to accept a final judgment on legal liability or to accept operationally meaningful moral responsibility, institutional PDE reflexivity is hard to decipher and demonstrate.

How may corporate governance and business ethics address their PDE-constructed roles aimed at minimizing the repertoire of negative side-effects in the context of complex litigational strategies, each of which aggravates the plight of those victimized by the occurrence of the catastrophe? First, the UCC's denial of the jurisdiction of, or non-submission to, Indian courts led to the UOI suing the UCC before Judge Keenan; second, the UCC chose to appeal even the conditional submission to Indian jurisdiction; third, it used the litigation period to promote settlement within the parameters of the sum insured (around US$250 million); fourth, as already noted, it resisted all claims for an interim award of compensation. These strategies are not consistent with PDE-related obligations to minimize suffering.

Nor are such obligations ever fully borne in mind when proposing and negotiating settlement amounts. The final settlement of US$470 million (as against the UOI's claim for US$3 billion) is by no means adequate for the immediate and long-term relief, rehabilitation, and redress of over 200,000 human beings. UCC also inscribed in the settlement absolute immunity from all future civil litigation and criminal prosecution. The latter immunity was subsequently cancelled by a post-settlement judicial review, but the UCC does not recognize Indian criminal court proceedings, even acquiring in the process the status of an absconder (fugitive from justice). It further aborts all extradition proceedings.

To be sure, a PDE regime may not address all the foregoing aspects of a complex litigation process. However, the overall narrative thus far is unflattering in the extreme to notions of PDE-oriented institutional reflexivity. My task would have been amply done had all the foregoing addressed the principal issue, namely the relation between the ethical duty to minimize unintended harm (and negative side-effects) and the "effective" cancellation of this moral order with the preferred forensic and litigational strategies. The juridicalization of the Bhopal catastrophe further raises anxious questions about the institutional role and integrity in the adjudication of mass disasters; the Indian Supreme Court, despite a long and proud history of judicial activism, did not cover itself with glory in ordering an excessive and premature settlement, in its lackadaisical invigilation of the disbursement of compensation, and in its inability to prevent the revictimization of the Bhopal victims.[35]

Needless to say, juridicalization creates constitutive ambiguities for any extension or application of PDE criteria. These will simply be redundant in a business/corporate world where PDE norms have become a part of institutionally reflexive learning. Till then, legal defence positions in cases of mass disaster (these versatile corperate ways of instant damage limitation that present a catastrophe as mere accident) possess no ethical or juridical pertinence for future conduct.

Conclusion

This chapter has attempted to demonstrate both the importance of the recrafted PDE regime as well as the difficulties of extending it to human rights and social catastrophe caused by mass disaster. The importance of this regime, of course, lies in the animating impulse to subject business and corporate governance to critical morality, whose standards derive from existing human rights norms and standards. Its difficulties lie in the extension of the notion of "negative side-effects" to catastrophic situations and in the articulation of precise entailments of duties to minimize human suffering in mass disasters. I have tried to show that these difficulties are not insurmountable, but they do need to be more clearly addressed if we are to develop PDE normativity as a critical platform from which to assess business conduct and corporate governance. The task becomes infinitely harder because it deploys PDE standards not just as tools for moral judgement after the event but directly to address foundational and routine business and corporate decision-making before the event. Put another way, if the development of standards of critical morality is already a heavy task, the creation of standards of positive morality is even more formidable.

For such standards to emerge and to be internalized in business and corporate cultures, we need to develop overall acceptable ethical conceptions of the constitution of expertise itself. PDE normativity then needs to address the circuits of decision-making in the global risk economy that "regulate" forms of production, distribution, exchange, and consumption of risks (or "negative side-effects"). It needs to address (as partly shown so far) the networked nature of the expertise thus involved;

this directs attention not just to a named corporation and its affiliates but to entire submerged structures. The Bhopal case reveals inter-connectivities among the insurance industry (which defines insurable and therefore compensatable injury); medical, health, and science profes-sionals (epistemic classes necessarily involved in disaster management and damage limitation); the learned professions (including legal pro-fessions and the mass media); and the political classes (political actors, legislators, and justices). Are all these myriad agents and structures to be the addressees of the recrafted, or any other, PDE regime? Further, are there any areas of corporate/business decision-making free from the PDE regime? If so, how may these be identified and justified?

A more general question can now be bluntly put. How may we prevent the PDE discourse from being swallowed up by amoral or agnostic multi-national corporate culture and conduct in ways that further legitimate its insatiable hunger for power and profit? And how, in a post-9/11 world, do we invent a new discourse concerning the moral responsibility and legal liability of the group or collective? How may all this speak to the postulation of the ethical obligation to minimize and ameliorate human suffering?

I need also to conclude with a question about the fiduciary responsi-bility of our own project. Does our project, which is admirably addressed to the ethical corrigibility of business conduct and corporate governance, pose or harbour any potential for negative side-effects? Put another way, in this era of the struggle of the new multitudes against the despotism of the new minuscule, how may we escape the future indictment of our laudable project as contributing to forms of conversion of the PDE to-wards ever new pastures for plunder, profit, and power at the behest and on behalf of global multinational capital? Put yet another way, how may we seek altogether to avoid cannibalization of our precious project by corporate governance while crucially protecting the human rights of the wretched of the earth? In sum, how may we build on our initial work in ways that take both *human suffering* and *human rights* even more seriously?

Notes

1. Jody S. Krauss and Steven Walt, "Introduction", in Jody S. Krauss and Steven Walt (eds.), *The jurisprudential foundations of commercial and company law* (Cambridge: Cambridge University Press, 2000), p. 1.
2. Ulrich Beck, Anthony Giddens, and Scott Lash (eds.), *Reflexive modernization* (Stan-ford, Calif.: Stanford University Press, 1994), p. 175.
3. For example, the discursive traditions of just war (scarcely a unique Euro-American ethical heritage), killing in self-defence, abortion, euthanasia, human and animal cloning.

4. This divide between theistic and secular formulations furnishes some important residues and reminders that are especially worth noting. This is not a task I address here, even as helpful in grounding our choice of PDE regime enunciation. See, for example, G. E. M. Anscombe, "War and murder", in W. Stein (ed.) *Nuclear weapons: A Catholic response* (London: Merlin Press, 1961), reprinted in *Collected philosophical papers* (Oxford: Blackwell, 1981), vol. 3, pp. 51–61; F. J. Connell, "Double effect, principle of", *The new Catholic encycopedia*, vol. 4 (New York: McGraw Hill, 1967), pp. 1020–1022; R. A. Duff, *Intention, agency, and criminal liability: Philosophy of action and criminal law* (Oxford: Blackwell, 1990); Phillipa Foot, "Abortion and the doctrine of double effect", in J. Rachles (ed.), *Moral problems* (New York: Harper & Row, 1971/1978), pp. 28–41; Germain Grisez, "Towards a consistent natural law of killing", *American Journal of Jurisprudence* 15, 1970, pp. 73–79; Joseph Mangan, "A historical approach to the principle of double effect", *Theological Studies* 10, 1949, pp. 41–69; Warren Quinn, "Action, intentions, and consequences", *Philosophical Review* 98, 1989, pp. 287–312; Suzanne Uniacke, "The doctrine of double effect", *Thomist* 48, 1984, pp. 188–218; Joseph M. Boyle Jr., "Toward understanding the principle of double effect", *Ethics* 90, 1980, pp. 527–538.

5. Extending to, *inter alia*, suicide bombers, terrorists, dentists, and professors who grade students; see Allision MacIntyre, "Doing away with double effect", *Ethics* 111, 2001, p. 219, and materials cited there.

6. These "residues" involve moral languages of "good" and "evil" acts and intentions, "intended" and "incidental" effects, "benefits" and "harms", foreseeability and responsibility, deontic and instrumental ethics. Thus, we clear a significant amount of normative debris when we maintain that the PDE is unconcerned "with what the agents intend to bring about as ends or with their motives or ultimate aims". Rather, it "is limited to a contrast between harms intended as a means to a good end and harms foreseen as side effects of promoting a good end" (MacIntyre, "Doing away with double effect", p. 226). Quite simply, PDE "does not provide the grounds for condemning someone who acts with malicious aims" (ibid., p. 228). Indeed, as MacIntyre observes, the PDE, although addressed to well-intentioned agents who seek to realize good ends, "expresses ... something more specific: it singles out instrumental harming in particular and contrasts it only with incidental harming" (ibid., p. 228).

7. Is the "good" to be judged by outcomes, results, effects, and consequences or by the intention of act, behaviour, and conduct? Or is it the case that there is the good in itself, independent of the consequences thereof ("not intrinsically evil")? If "good" is to be approached in consequentialist terms, this raises at least the following issues:

   • How may we conceptualize the key notions of "benefits" and "harms"? When may we say that certain "benefits" may indeed be harmful and certain "harms" may be beneficial?

   • How may our ways of evaluating "benefits" and "harm" differ from routine cost–benefit analysis, which is not necessarily tethered to any ethical theory?

   • Where may we reckon with the time dimension in operationalizing the key notions? Is it possible to say that the short-term "harms" may be "beneficial" in the long term? Indeed, what are "short" and "long" horizons and what ethical construction of temporality may here be privileged? When is "harming" a present generation good grounds for securing "benefits" for a future one?

   • If the PDE signifies an ethical theory concerning decision-making, how does it guide decision makers acting under conditions of uncertainty? These include risk-taking, the etymological sense of the term "entrepreneur" – "risk" notions make sense only in contexts where it may be said with sincerity that no degree of foresight is able to offer a clue to all the potential "harmful" effects. Does the PDE seriously address notions of risk in a global risk society, as Ulrich Beck, *The risk society* (London: Sage, 1992), calls this?

- Is "foreseeability" quite the same as "foresight"? Is the distinction worth making? Does the former signify a pragmatic moral calculus, whereas the latter suggests powers of divination of a future state of affairs not quite open to rational ethical calculus? Or is "foresight" merely an accumulation of common wisdom arising from a large number of hindsights? In any event, sociologists (most notably Robert Merton) educate us in the distinction between *manifest* (foreseeable) and *latent* (unforeseeable in the present state of knowledge) functions. If the "latent" is by definition unforeseeable, does the PDE then offer absolution from moral responsibility? And, if so, in what measure? And at whose cost? Incidentally, it would be rewarding to explore the discourse on the precautionary principle, now ambivalently incorporated in the Cartegena Protocol on Biosafety; see, e.g., Karl Buechle, "The great, global promise of genetically modified organisms: Overcoming fear, misconceptions, and the Cartegena Biosafety Protocol", *Indiana Journal of Global Studies* 9, 2001, p. 263.
- Do these twin notions – benefit/harm – exhaust the ethic of the good or for that matter of evil? How may the PDE address what has been called "radical evil" (which Hannah Arendt describes as a state of affairs that we may never fully be able to punish or to forgive)?

8. Because of this threshold ethical perspective, the project assumes that human rights rules, norms, standards, principles, values, and ideals constitute an unqualified good; it privileges the notion of a "community of rights" superbly theorized by Allan Gewirth, *The community of rights* (Chicago: Chicago University Press, 1996). This creatively revisionist PDE suggests that "legitimate" business operations are those that are consistent with human rights norms, standards, and values; the duty to avoid or minimize "negative" side-effects (i.e. those that violate human rights) ought to inform corporate conduct, governance, and culture, and these side-effects may be justified only insofar as they are "proportionate" to the legitimate (business) "objectives". Further, human rights regimes do not address all agents of violation; by and large, human rights discursivity does not readily extend to civil society conduct, which at times is more abusive of human rights values and ideals. Notably, global and national corporations (aggregations of technoscientific capital) are not the primary addressees of internationally fashioned human rights obligations (see Upendra Baxi, *The future of human rights*, Delhi: Oxford University Press, 2002), as their exclusion from the Statute for the International Criminal Court and the extreme voluntarism of the United Nations Global Compact suggest. The basic grounds for anxiety remain: How may we best relate the PDE to "human rights"? For notable attempts to relate human rights to multinational corporations, see James Sterba, "Introduction", *The ethics of war and nuclear deterrence* (Belmont, Calif.: Wadsworth, 1981/1985), pp. 2–3; Henry Shue, *Basic rights* (Princeton, N.J.: Princeton University Press, 1980); Henry Shue, "Exporting hazards", *Ethics* 91, 1981, pp. 579–606; James W. Nickel, *Making sense of human rights: Philosophical reflections on the Universal Declaration of Human Rights* (Berkeley: University of California Press, 1987); Thomas Donaldson, *The ethics of international business* (Oxford: Oxford University Press, 1989), pp. 65–94.

9. Anthony Giddens, "Living in post-traditional society", in Beck, Giddens, and Lash (eds.), *Reflexive modernization*, p. 84.

10. Ulrich Beck, "Self-dissolution and self-endangerment of industrial society: What does this mean?", in Beck, Giddens, and Lash (eds.), *Reflexive modernization*, pp. 174–175.

11. Long before the important discovery by Greimas that corporations remain juridical semiotic productions (see Bernard S. Jackson, *Semiotics and legal theory*, London: Routledge, 1987), the issue of the personality of corporations was framed and formed

primarily by the rights discourse. Given the pre-socialist, laissez-faire insistence on near-absolute individual rights to property and contract as defining the concept of freedom (that is, autonomy from state incursion), the eighteenth/nineteenth-century discourse concerned itself with the issues arising from the "artificial" nature of the juristic personality. On the one hand, the foundational concepts of early capitalism (property and contract) authorized the collective/associational form of economic agency itself as a natural right; on the other hand, the law (both legislative and adjudicative) was expected to define various associational forms (such as partnerships, firms, joint stock companies) and regulate these (mostly by way of facilitating economic enterprise) in the long-term interests of "disorganized capitalism".

12. I present this below schematically, and in language that is not contemporaneous with the origins of this discourse:

   1. If we were to regard the legal personality of corporations to be a mere fiction, as a legal semiotic production, as some jurists do, we would be constrained to conclude that corporations do not exist in nature or society; they are brought into being by law as a fictive entity, both to facilitate and to regulate a certain type of economic enterprise. Accordingly, there is no law *beyond* the "positive" law that may address their constitutive ethic.

   2. As such, rights and responsibilities attach to these juridical beings only through the performance of a legislative (and, we may add, adjudicative) will to power. Accordingly, ethical discourse extrinsic to the logics of power that shape positive law may not have much purchase.

   3. If corporations are creatures of law, how can they be said to possess unlawful or criminal will? If they do, can mere legality restrain their Frankenstein powers? In more difficult terms, how may we speak about the ontology of corporations, especially the multinationals?

   4. The "bracket" theory of corporations sought a way out by denying the full force of "fiction" theory; it addressed the power of corporations within and against the law by insisting that the corporate form is just the functional equivalent of a bracket, which is a shorthand way of describing the additive and cumulative activity/conduct/enterprise of so many diverse and varied individual economic actors. In order to understand and regulate corporate activity (as well as challenge it from an external ethic), we need to address the moral logic or economy of group formation. Here, the question of course is: how may we understand a group? As *seriality* (to evoke Sartre) or as *excess* (to invoke Bataille), is a group merely additive, the sum of its various parts? Or is it cumulative – that is, some ineffable surplus is not thus exhausted? If the latter, how may law and human rights languages describe and locate this excess as the very site of PDE-type responsibility?

13. In an insightful analysis of the Bhopal catastrophe from a rights perspective, Thomas Donaldson distinguishes four types of risk: first-party risks (to members of the corporate organization such as officials and employees), second-party risks (to the citizens of a government), third-party risks (to persons and communities not members of risk-causing organizations), and fourth-party risks (to "entirely innocent" victims of future generations). The last two communities of risk await the invention of a language of moral responsibility (see Donaldson, *The ethics of international business*, pp. 110–128).

14. Beck, Giddens, and Lash (eds.), *Reflexive modernization*.

15. Michel Burawoy, *The politics of production: Factory regimes under capitalism and socialism* (London: Verso Books, 1985).

16. "Accident" waiting to happen; see Charles Perrow, *Normal accidents* (Princeton, N.J.: Princeton University Press, 1999, updated edition).

17. I here rely on the germinal distinction suggested by Judith Sklar, *Faces of injustice* (New Haven, Conn.: Yale University Press, 1990).

18. See Upendra Baxi (ed.), *Inconvenient forum and convenient catastrophe: The Bhopal case* (New Delhi: Indian Law Institute, 1986); Upendra Baxi and Paul Thomas (eds.), *Mass disasters and multinational liability: The Bhopal case* (New Delhi: Indian Law Institute, 1985); Upendra Baxi and Amita Dhanda (eds.), *Valiant victims and lethal litigation: The Bhopal case* (New Delhi: Indian Law Institute, 1990); Upendra Baxi, "Mass torts. Multinational enterprise liability and private international law", *Recueil des cours* (The Hague: Martinus Nijhoff), 276, 1999/2000, pp. 305–427, and the literature cited therein. Additionally, for a poignant literary and existential narrative, see Dominique Lapierre and Javier Moro, *It was five minutes past midnight in Bhopal* (Delhi: Full Circle, 2001); Don Kurzman, *A killing wind: Inside Union Carbide* (New York: McGraw Hill, 1987); David Weir, *The Bhopal syndrome: Pesticides, environment, and health* (San Francisco, Calif.: Sierra Club Books, 1984); Paul Shrivastava, *Bhopal: Anatomy of a crisis* (Cambridge, Mass.: Ballinger, 1987). A very useful periodic contemporary analysis by Will Lepowski appears in several issues of *Chemical and Engineering News*.

19. Though the official figure is about 2,500, contemporary eyewitness accounts suggest 10,000 fatalities. I myself saw hundreds of bodies piled up in a large number of municipal trucks for expeditious disposal (with no identification or regard for religious preferences for cremation or burial). This raises the basic issue of the nationalization/corporatization of truth relevant for measuring "negative" side-effects.

20. Baxi (ed.), *Inconvenient forum and convenient catastrophe*.

21. Obviously, on a "network" conception of multinational enterprises, ethical agency is widely dispersed, even to the point of the right hand not knowing what the left does; or, more accurately, to the point where the five fingers of either hand to do not quite know what each intends to do or in actual effect does or accomplishes. The attractions of a reductionist view remain seductively fatal indeed. Such a view assigns to the HQ (or *siège sociale*) a heavily concentrated collective moral and ethical agency/persona. It insists that every single act of commission and omission remains ruthlessly attributed to an imaginary "brains trust" of global capitalism. On this view, "good" and "evil" intentionality and impact scarcely pierce what lawyers call the "corporate veil". The distribution of the juridical personality of global and multinational corporations emerges as a series of ethical disguises; all collateral damage continues to be traced to forms of ultimate authorship that are completely uninhibited by legal forms (the "parent"/ "holding" company, its national and regional subsidiaries, and related assorted affiliates that "outsource" proportions of labour and capital). I have myself rather relentlessly pursued this imagery over nearly two decades of the struggle of Bhopal victims against Union Carbide and its successors. And I have to say I found it vigorously empowering in all manner of ways. Yet the issue remains: are juridical forms merely signifiers of the divestment of moral agency or are they something more that escapes activist meaning, at least in terms of the PDE discourse?

Second, we need resolutely to confront the issue of in what sense we may assert that "corporations" are moral agents. This is an extremely difficult problem, especially in the light of the formidably well-worked out thesis by David Gauthier (*Morals by agreement*, Oxford: Oxford University Press, 1986; but see Baxi, *The future of human rights*, pp. 132–166), which argues, in effect, that corporate/business conduct constitutes a "moral free zone". This, indeed, is self-evident in the very constitutive grammar of "free" market and enterprise that valorizes market competition. How may we extend the PDE language to business competition? Am I, as an economic agent in a free market, obligated to take into account any harm that my competitive success causes, even harm to the human rights of my rivals? Free market competition under capitalism necessarily entails a notion of the legitimacy of such harm to co-equally placed rival market agents. Indeed, property and contract rights postulate a human right to cause legitimate and lawful harm to business rivals (see Upendra Baxi, "From human rights to right to be human", in *The right to be human*, Delhi: India International Centre, 1987, and the reference therein to Guyla Eorsi in particular). Resituating the PDE remains then at odds with market competition and problematizes state/law justifications for coercive state capitalist regulation of immoral/illegitimate business practices that overall adversely affect the operations of free market, predatory, and perverse forms of corporate/business conduct, governance, and culture (e.g. "insider trading", business fraud, "creative" accounting, corrupt practices), extreme corporate/business practices that degrade and destroy the environment, reckless exploitation of labour markets, and impermissible forms of gender hostility via a free-for-all production/reproduction of the global sexual division of labour and business practices producing/reproducing slave-like labour exploitation.

Third, this raises the all-important question of corporate moral autonomy in the self-legislation of standards of moral conduct. From whence may they derive notions of "good", "evil", "intentions", collaterality", and "side-effects?" To whom, as economic entities/agencies, may they be said to owe any moral or ethical obligations? How may the PDE regimes justify the movement from forms of *shareholder* responsibility to *stakeholder* responsibility? How may they construct, in frankly human rights terms, the varieties of the logics of fiduciary obligations to concerned communities and incorporate profit and power considerations? Put another way, what levels of moral altruism may the PDE prescribe for corporate governance? When may state coercion to reinforce such normative obligations be justified, and on what possible or arguable grounds? What varieties of PDE may guide principled choice between self-regulation and justified state coercion?

22. Was the Green Revolution planning (which aimed to increase food grain production and economic self-reliance) conceived within the moral framework of the Indian Constitution? Was it conceived and pursued with solicitude for the constitutionally enshrined rights of all Indian citizens? What might justify overweening governmental monopoly over the definition of the "public" interest? What PDE-related ethic ought to have guided state policy-making?

23. Namely, its brand-name products Temick and Sevin.

24. Many of us appeared before the UCC, Danbury, Annual Meetings as stakeholders. As a stakeholder representing the American Union of Baptist Churches, and on the fifteenth anniversary of the Bhopal catastrophe, I raised the issue of whether, having settled all liability issues, the UCC might consider releasing information concerning the toxicity of MIC, information that would then facilitate governmental and non-governmental business community efforts at ameliorating the adverse impacts on physical and psychic health. The chairperson of the UCC simply ignored this request in his response.

25. See Anita Ramsastry, "Corporate complicity: From Nuremberg to Rangoon ...", *Berkeley Journal of International Law* 20, 2002, pp. 91–159.

26. The invocation of the "less harm" principle is not free from difficulties. True, the magnitude of death, injury, and harm would have been demographically much higher for Bombay. Further, one may only speculate on the overall impact of a massive MIC release on the nuclear power plant. And it remains arguable that in this location scenario the UCC would have been far stricter concerning safety design and operations. Would it have ensured greater vigilance had the 1982 incident occurred at the Bombay location? Apart from all this, any suggestion that the Bhopal location in itself remains PDE commendable on the less harm principle must rest on the unsustainable notion that human lives are worth more in Bombay than in Bhopal. The equal worth and value of all Indian citizens and other persons likely to be affected by a catastrophe prohibit comparisons between populaces exposed to catastrophic events.

27. See also Upendra Baxi, "Geographies of injustice: Human rights at the altar of conve-

nience", in Craig Scott (ed.), *Torture as tort: Comparative perspectives on the development of transnational human rights litigation* (Oxford: Hart Publishing, 2001), pp. 197–202.

28. The UCC argued the theory of terrorist sabotage before Judge Keenan; even he was constrained to dismiss this as a flight of fancy. Subsequently, the UCC floated the theory of a disgruntled employee who intentionally allowed the contamination of MIC that produced the catastrophe; the UCC has not been able to substantiate this, although its media campaign made it plausible for financial newspapers and cohorts of the global chemical industry. Dr. Ward Morehouse, the president of the International Council of Public Affairs, New York, has rendered inestimable service to the Bhopal victims by archiving a wholly different narrative of a UCIL worker.

29. Through legally permissible, though ethically impugnable, bankruptcy proceedings, as illustrated most pointedly in the aftermath of the Enron scandal and of various asbestos litigations.

30. Baxi (ed.), *Inconvenient forum and convenient catastrophe*; Baxi and Thomas (eds.), *Mass disasters and multinational liability*.

31. Thomas Donaldson expresses all this in terms of contrasting "cultural variables" and "extracultural vision". The latter allows us "to understand a trade-off between risk and productivity, between the dollar value of an increased gross national product on the one hand and higher dollar cost of medical care necessary to accommodate higher levels of risk". But this vision is "blurred for more ethnocentric trade offs. In many less developed countries a higher gross national product is only one of the handful of crucial goals informed by cultural tradition and experience" (*The ethics of international business*, p. 112).

32. I owe this striking formulation to Lene Bomann-Larsen.

33. Upendra Baxi, "Introduction", in Baxi and Dhanda (eds.), *Valiant victims and lethal litigation*.

34. There is simply no way in which we may apply this principle to the people in Bhopal affected by MIC, or the people affected by Agent Orange, or subjects identified by great realist fictional narratives such as Jonathan Harr's *A civil action* (New York: Vintage, 1997) or John Grisham's *The king of torts* (London: Arrow, 2003).

35. How may approaches/reconstruction of the PDE regime that favour human rights address conceptions of judicial autonomy, judicial integrity, and the human rights obligations of the judicial role and function? In the concrete context of the Bhopal litigation, this raises at least the following PDE-relevant issues (and not just for the Indian courts):

- What PDE/human rights friendly fiduciary obligations may justices and courts be said to have?
- How may we assess Judge Keenan's "technical" production/performance on this measure? See Baxi (ed.), *Inconvenient forum and convenient catastrophe*; Baxi and Thomas (eds.), *Mass disasters and multinational liability*; Baxi and Dhanda, *Valiant victims and lethal litigation*; Baxi, "Mass torts"; Baxi, "Geographies of injustice".
- Did the UCC have any PDE-relevant obligations to submit to Indian jurisdiction?
- If so, what PDE-informed perspectives may be said to furnish legal or forensic bases for its logics of argumentation concerning non-liability/responsibility?
- Does the PDE criterion of "participation" by affected peoples inform the province of adjudicative decision-making? If so, in what ways did the Indian Supreme Court violate the application of a PDE regime in ordering settlement of the case?
- How may the project to rework the application of the PDE address the outcome problem; that is, help us in judging the justice and efficacy of the eventual settlement amount and its careful disbursement?

12

Dealing with harmful side-effects: Opportunities and threats in the emerging Polish market

Julita Sokołowska

Introduction

This chapter demonstrates the difficulties involved in the moral evaluation of business in a transformation process. The principle of double effect is discussed in relation specifically to the Polish economy and to a typical Polish company in a phase of restructuring and adaptation from a planned economy to a market economy.

All companies are under a general obligation not to do harm to the communities in which they operate, including not violating anyone's rights.[1] But we need to keep in mind that running a business in the particular market reality of a troubled developing country such as Poland is different from running a business in a developed country. The Polish market situation is unique owing to the transformation process in the economy, which is still proceeding. The potential for harm is greater in an unstable and transforming economy, and the impact of business enterprises is greater too – as is their scope of influence. Naturally, in the Polish market there are a few democratic institutions functioning to safeguard the community against negative corporate impacts. But Polish democratic institutions are also still developing and are less experienced in dealing with the specific problems of the free market than are similar institutions in the old democracies.

It is important to remember that, since the turning point of 1989, Poland has undergone great political, social, and economic changes. The most important achievement in the early 1990s was the implementation of the so-called "Balcerowicz Plan".[2] The outcome of the programme introducing this reform was liberalization of every economic area, such as domestic prices, rising imports, a tightening of enterprises' pay structures and financial policy, the introduction of interest rates above the rate of inflation, the stabilization of the zloty against the dollar, and the introduction of zloty convertibility. As a consequence, the Polish economy stabilized and opened up to the world. The banking system and credit policy were also reformed. The process of ownership change started with the systemic reforms, making enterprises independent and building domestic competition. Capital and labour markets were also created in Poland.

The implementation of democratic structures, the move from a centrally planned economic system to a market economy, and wide-ranging systemic reforms were long drawn out and complicated, and resulted in a distinctive market situation. The developing process of legislation, administrative regulations, and business rules is not yet settled. This has resulted in unpredictable, imprecise, and ambiguous legislation on, for example, the fiscal system, labour code regulations, or consumer protection that exerts influence on business activity.

What is the applicability and functionality of the principle of double effect (PDE) to the Polish business context? The PDE is designed to assess and manage harmful side-effects of otherwise morally legitimate acts. The main discussion of this chapter will show that, in this particular context, there is an urgent need to assess the potential legitimacy of both means and side-effects in light of the goal of sustainable value creation. I will thus focus on the dilemmas and loopholes in the Polish economy.

In the process of analysing and judging examples of corporate behaviour in Poland, it becomes evident that there is an urgent need to take into consideration the specific economic character and unique historical features of this market. And although this chapter mainly presents one instance of side-effect harm on the part of corporate actors – the case of Polmo Łomianki S.A. – I shall suggest that the corporate behaviour displayed here is not exceptional. On the contrary, it is typical of the Polish economy.

Background: Distinctive features of Eastern Europe – Poland

To understand the problems related to Polmo Łomianki S.A. and the two other cases that will be treated briefly in this chapter, we need to see the distinctive features of the Polish economy in a broader context. Since

1989, Poland, like several other Central and East European countries, has been undergoing a core-shaking transition from a centrally steered socialist economy based on centralized distribution mechanisms and a command and quota system to a market-based, privatized economy.

Peculiarities of the Polish developing economy

The transition from a centrally planned system to a market economy and the restructuring processes throughout the country represent profound challenges for Polish business. Many sectors had to be totally transformed; for example, brown coal mining, power, oil, gas, steel, chemical processing, defence, and rail transport. The fundamental aim of restructuring was to make these enterprises and sectors profitable, which required new legislation on the national economy. The legal regulations are still in a process of being altered to fit the changing market circumstances. In particular, the Polish fiscal system and extensively developed bureaucratic rules are criticized for discouraging private business initiatives.[3]

Privatization and complete company restructuring were the only way for state-owned companies such as Polmo Łomianki S.A. to survive.[4] However, each company chose a different restructuring method in order to make production both effective and profitable.[5] Out of 1,600 enterprises that were transformed into joint stock companies, nearly 85 per cent declared insolvency and had to be closed. Over the five-year period 1998–2003, about 40 per cent of all Polish firms went bankrupt after privatization and restructuring.[6]

The Polish market situation

The turn of the century has not been favourable to Polish industry. The negative tendency of the growth rate in industrial output sold has continued, a tendency that first occurred in the second half of 1998 as a result of the deteriorating economic situation in West European countries and of the Russian and Asian crises.

At the end of 2002 there had been no significant increase in production, and the rate of growth of gross domestic product was rather low. Yet the slightly improved rate of growth in industrial production was accompanied by positive structural changes in industry, such as a decrease in the share of the mining sector in the production structure and a rise in labour productivity; a major share of production is now taking place in branches considered to be carriers of technological development. On the other hand, unfavourable phenomena in recent years have been deteriorating profitability, including a negative net balance for industry as a whole, a slower rate of growth in investments, and an increase in the debts of economic units. At the beginning of the twenty-first century, the liberalization and privatization of Poland's economy had still not been accomplished. Many sectors of Poland's economy are now in private hands: for example, trade, small- and medium-sized industry, and transport. However, the private sector is no longer on the dynamic path of development. It is confronted with the difficulties of imprecise and ambiguous legislation, widespread bureaucracy, and the particular mentality of the Polish population.

The development of the private sector was based on the inflow of foreign direct investment. The Polish private sector is now responsible for 75 per cent of the country's economic activities.[7] Dominant industries include metalwork, steel, and chemical and textile production. A few big enterprises, for example in heavy industry (coal and steel, railroads, ship building), are still largely in state hands, and their restructuring has not yet been completed. The state-owned sector continues to work according to centrally steered economic principles. It is inefficient because of the employment overgrowth typical of the old economic system; it is beset with high production costs and lacks the motivation to develop because of "handicaps" imposed by state regulations.

Legislation

The view that the Polish legal system and economic rules are not conducive to development is now widely acknowledged by entrepreneurs (including the owners of Polmo Łomianki S.A.). In particular, Polish fiscal policy is often criticized for its high tax rates, lack of comprehensiveness, and unpredictability. Tax regulations are imprecise, complicated, obscure, and ambiguous; and tax rates often change, thus creating unfavourable investment conditions. Furthermore, the Polish legal system gives wide authority to officials and civil servants. Legal regulations are rigorously specified and combined with an over-developed bureaucracy.[8] Particular decisions are often made at officials' or civil servants' discretion and, because there are many ways to interpret a particular rule, the way is open to straightforward corruption.

For these reasons, state intervention in the economic sphere is sometimes accused of not facilitating corporations in adapting to new market conditions, and even of preventing, hampering, or restraining corporate activity. Entrepreneurs often claim that current state policy discourages initiative and is an obstacle to development.

The significant role of Polish trade unions in the business environment

Trade unions play a fundamental role in the economy and in politics in Poland as a result of their significant historical impact and tradition. In fact, the trade unions were deeply involved in initiating and realizing the process of system change and opened the path to a free, democratic country for the Polish people.[9]

The strikes by Polish workers on the Baltic coast in August 1980 led to the establishment of "Solidarity", and many of its activists have helped to form subsequent governments. Trade unions and trade organizations are still very strong in Poland and their rights are widely protected in the Polish Labour Code. It states amongst other things that:

- a trade union can be established by as few as 10 people,
- a trade union has the right to oppose the strategic plans of a company,
- a trade union has the right to influence dismissals, wages, etc.[10]

No company in Poland wants to have a trade union in its structure, because of the many corporate problems caused by trade union activity. (The strikes and riots in the cable factory in Ożarów Mazowiecki and in the clothing factory in Szczecin, referred to below, are good recent examples of this.) Thus, companies often have no alternative but to take the ethically questionable step of limiting the activity of a trade union. Otherwise, the survival of the business might be threatened. The questionable actions of Polmo Łomianki S.A., as outlined below, directly resulted from structural features of the Polish market.

High labour costs and strong labour rights

The Polish Labour Code puts the employee in a very strong position. It lays down detailed procedures as to the terms and conditions of labour contracts, and it grants employees a wide range of rights and authority. The regulations are extremely elaborate, but also imprecise, complicated, obscure, and ambiguous and they often change. This gives employees the advantage and makes them very expensive for the company. Furthermore, costs connected with social welfare make up as much as 45 per cent of labour costs. This is especially critical for bigger companies, which employ many workers and therefore have to cover higher costs and as a result become less profitable. What is more, when the economic situation deteriorates and demand for the company's products and services decreases, it is difficult and very expensive to reorganize the company to adapt to new market circumstances through dismissals.[11]

The aim of the restructuring process is to increase the profitability and efficiency of companies under transformation through lower production costs and productivity improvements. Because of the high labour costs, however, the restructuring process is expensive and slow. As a result, the majority of companies have cash-flow problems. A side-effect of the slowdown in economic growth is an increasing rate of unemployment. Unemployment is also a negative effect of economic restructuring, which has led to the closure of many unprofitable large industrial plants and the liquidation of large collective farms.

The "homo sovieticus" attitude

One would have thought that, with the end of the state's protectionist policies in 1989, Poles would have learned that work is not something that is always readily available and that it is necessary to value it. However, despite huge changes in the attitudes of Polish employees, the so-called "homo sovieticus" attitude is still present, and not just among older people. Recent research reveals that this attitude is also characteristic of young people, who never experienced the old system.

The "homo sovieticus" attitude was a side-effect of the communist system. Employees did not have to make any individual choices because decisions concerning both production and consumption were made by the state. Moreover, the whole centrally steered economy operated for the sole purpose of employing every member of the state. Everybody was granted a job and an assured, albeit low, living standard. The requirement of equality ensured that, independently of one's contribution to the common work effort, everyone had the same income.[12] Hence there was no incentive for employees to work harder. That is one of the reasons for the unproductiveness of the centrally planned system.

Yet even today some people have problems realizing that the era of the old system has passed. Whereas, in a market economy, personal decision-making and responsibility for one's own activity are vital, the "homo sovieticus" attitude manifests itself in passive expectations of help. Employees believe that the government should guarantee them a job and a salary, even if the work is unprofitable and inefficient. It is a make-believe way of thinking that significantly contributes to the high unemployment rate in Poland. People will not take just any job; they are awaiting a better one. Today we see the true effects of the communist system's dysfunction – ineffective and unprofitable production and a high unemployment rate.

Two brief examples to illustrate the ethical dilemmas in the Polish market

Two short case-studies will set the scene and illustrate what is at stake. These examples show what can happen when a company does not take any social responsibility for its impacts on the community in which it operates.

The telecommunication cables factory in Ożarów Mazowiecki

The telecommunication cables factory in Ożarów Mazowiecki was a producer and distributor of telecommunication and electrical cables. It was located 2 km from Warsaw and employed a total of about 900 people.[13]

In 1999, the cable company was privatized and a 70 per cent stock package was bought by Electrim S.A. Typically for a state-owned company, the "package" included problems such as cash-flow difficulties, low productivity, and over-employment. After two years – because of an unprofitable investment strategy – Electrim S.A. proclaimed itself bankrupt. It then disposed of its stock package to Tele-Fonica S.A., a phone cable producer. After the contract was signed, the new owner promised that there would be no dismissals for a one-year period.

Then the general economic situation deteriorated. Demand for telecommunication cables decreased and the period of protection was coming to an end. The new owner – who was also a proprietor of two other cable factories in Szczecin and Bydgoszcz – decided to relocate production from Ożarów (2 km from Warsaw) to the factory in Bydgoszcz (200 km from Warsaw) in order to reduce production costs, and specifically *labour* costs, which are higher near the capital. Moreover, the new owner announced that he had to fire 500 out of the 900 employees, because keeping such a high number of staff would make the company less profitable, given the decreasing demand for the company's services.

The employees were not happy about the news. They called a strike and blockaded the road into Warsaw on which the factory was located. The strikes were organized by the factory's trade union leaders and lasted for about a year, threatening the sustainability and survival of the whole company.

When the proprietor decided to move machines and equipment from the factory to the other plants, the workers were determined not to let him do this. They believed that, as under the old system, the government had to guarantee them work and a salary no matter what. And they did not care that the demand for telecommunications cables was no longer sufficient to keep them all in work. Believing their rights were not being respected, they started riots and fights. They blockaded the front door of the company's building and organized five protest marches through the streets of Warsaw.

Six months after the first strike, the proprietor hired security personnel who began removing the equipment from the factory. In response the workers started destroying the equipment. They claimed they were fighting for the company's survival. After some time, the police intervened to stop them, and a few workers, security personnel, and policemen were injured. The investor estimates that the strike has cost US$9 million so far.

The government, having privatized the factory in the first place and thus being a party to the controversy, attempted to resolve the problem. It wanted to help negotiate between the company's owners and the employees, but every time the workers broke off the talks. The government's last attempt was to create a special economic zone for the Ożarów Mazowiecki area. The government wanted to get the unemployed back to work by retraining them for new jobs. But the majority of the unemployed were not interested in such offers. They wanted to continue producing cables and have their employment guaranteed for the next five years. At the time of writing, the situation has still not been resolved.

The clothing factory in Szczecin

The clothing factory in Szczecin was built in 1963. It was engaged in production for the Polish clothing trade and textile industry. Like the cable factory, the clothing factory had serious cash-flow problems because production was inefficient and costs were very high. Furthermore, demand for the company's products had considerably decreased. Consequently, the state started looking for an external investor – with no result. Finally, in 1999, the factory – in a bad financial state, with old equipment and poorly qualified personnel – was privatized and transformed into a joint stock company. In 2002, a majority of the shares (51 per cent) were bought up from the employees by a private investor, the remaining shares being divided amongst employees and the managing director.[14]

However, the new management strategy implemented after the privatization failed. The company's debts to the Treasury Office were increasing, and the employees were not paid for three months. Consequently, the workers decided to call a strike. First, they worked for only two hours a day, but the investor did not react. As a final measure, the employees of the clothing factory asked for help from the workers at the Szczecin shipyard, who were also on strike at the time. The dockyard workers – a total of 2,000 people – came to the assistance of the clothing factory employees, a majority of whom were women.[15]

The strikers marched through the streets of Szczecin to demonstrate their discontent. Then they all arrived at the clothing factory to confront the managing director, whom they held responsible for the whole situation. They forced him out of his office, took his clothes off, threw eggs at him, and hit him. Neither workers nor policemen – who arrived at the scene during the riot – did anything to help him. The press, TV, and radio stations were mainly concerned with covering the story.

At the end of 2002 the investor in the clothing factory in Szczecin declared the company insolvent. Now the employees wait only for references.

The case of Polmo Łomianki S.A.

Company profile

The case of Polmo Łomianki S.A. is the main case-study of this chapter. Polmo Łomianki S.A. is a medium-sized company involved in the production and distribution of metallurgy, electro-technical and plastic components used mostly in the automotive and nutritive sectors. The firm is situated in Łomianki, on the outskirts of Warsaw, near the main road connecting south and west Poland.

In 1949, two companies dealing with the production and distribution of powder metallurgy components were merged. After 1965, the company was known as a powder metal components manufacturer, named Fabryka Wyrobów z Proszków Spiekanych. The company's production at that time was largely used in the automotive industry. The development of sintering technology worldwide was closely connected with the automotive industry – 70 per cent of all products manufactured by these methods have been used in motor vehicles. The products manufactured by this department of Polmo Łomianki S.A. include components for shock absorbers, gear wheels for oil pumps, chains, belt timing, generators, gear box catches, etc. The other department of the company produced components for the household equipment industry and machine components industry (for example, slides, drivers, self-lubricating bearings, gear wheels, caps, and plungers).

In the 1960s, the company started manufacturing electro-technical components. These components, such as combined switches for indicators, headlights and wipers, reversing light switches, brake light contractors, and universal push-button switches, were used largely in the heavy and automotive industries. During the second half of the 1970s the factory was modernized. Two new production halls, a sewage treatment plant, a water treatment station, and new access roads were constructed. In the 1990s, during the economic transformation period, the company entered a restructuring process, directed at overhauling all aspects of corporate activity. This led to processing modifications, the launching of new products, and improvements in labour conditions.

But the company's production was still inefficient. The inefficiency was caused by over-employment inherited from the centrally planned economic system, high labour costs, poor management procedures, old and misused equipment, and poorly qualified employees. All these factors resulted in expensive production. The company's debts to the Treasury Office, the Social Insurance Office, employees and suppliers were continually increasing. At this time, a group of employees, who saw great potential in the enterprise, decided to profit from the prospects of economic transformation and applied to the Treasury Office for permission to lease the company.

In January 1995, the company was transformed from a state enterprise into a joint stock company called Polmo Łomianki S.A. The employee share ownership consisted of 402 people. However, the transformation of the company's name and legal status did not solve the problems of low productivity and high costs. The employee-owners realized that the only way for the company to survive would be a complete restructuring of every aspect of the company's production. But this required investment capital, which the company simply did not possess. Thus the employee-owners went in search of a strategic investor who could bring in fresh capital and help the enterprise to face the new market reality, but they were not successful. Not wanting to give up, the employee-owners decided to undertake the transformation gradually, with their own means.

The transformation process

The transformation was a landmark in the company's activity. In the first stage, the aim of the restructuring was to lower production costs in order to make the company's production efficient. Capital was indispensable for the restructuring, and the first capital was gained through a reduction in the most inefficient spheres of the company's activity – by decreasing stock-in-trade, by clearing out old and useless components, and by cutting down on the most inefficient production shops. Still, the capital gained through these procedures was not sufficient.

The only way to acquire the requisite capital and to lower the company's costs was to decrease employment, which was about 50 per cent higher than necessary. From the beginning of the transformation process it had been impossible to dismiss groups of employees, owing to the leasing contract between the company and the Treasury Office. There were strict regulations on employment policies, stating that, for three years from the date of the contract, the company could not carry out group dismissals amounting to more than a 10 per cent decrease in total employment.

Furthermore, more than half of the employees were organized in the strong and active trade union "Solidarity" within the company. The trade union was directly connected with the Independent Self-Governing All-Poland Trade Union "Solidarity".

The problem of side-effect harm

To cut down on production costs by decreasing over-employment was the only chance for Polmo Łomianki S.A. to survive. High labour costs have been an obstacle in the transformation of Polmo Łomianki S.A. and other companies across Poland; dismissals have been a difficult but necessary stage in the process.

Polmo Łomianki S.A. also came up against the barrier of a particular Polish mentality. Many of those dismissed would not accept any help from the company. The dismissals were especially damaging for the local population of the city of Łomianki, where the company was a major employer. On the other hand, the company's survival in the long term also benefited the local population, for example through capital contributing to the local government. A bankruptcy would have caused more unemployment and greater damage to the community.

The owners of the company realized that they had no choice but to reduce employment. Because they were legally restricted from implementing the dismissals rapidly – through group dismissals – they chose "creative" ways to limit employment. As long as Polish law is under development, the question of what is legal or illegal is a matter of interpretation. Nobody really knows which measures are in accordance with the law, so action can be taken purely on the basis of profitability. In this legal grey area, there is room for some questionable creativity in the search for solutions.

Using the corporate employment policy of Polmo Łomianki S.A. as an example, we can discuss corporate actors' responsibility for side-effects. In general, all business agents are under a moral obligation not to do harm.[16] If the corporate activity might cause any negative side-effects, these should be prevented or minimized as far as possible. Polmo Łomianki S.A. provides an example of dealing with side-effect harm that was foreseeable but inescapable, because the sustainability of the business was undermined.

Dismissals are not an illegitimate means in private market economies, although in Poland they have been considered as such owing to the legacy of the old system. Even so, dismissals always entail harmful side-effects. In the present case-study, the obligation to deal with the double effect of corporate means jeopardized the sustainability of Polmo Łomianki S.A. As such the case-study illustrates the aspect of value creation in the principle of double effect. Sustainable value creation is a legitimate objective – the actual purpose – of the business company, whereby it also produces value for other stakeholders, such as the community and the overall economy, and in the final instance also for the (remaining) employees. Seen in this context, the case-study challenges the principle of double effect in terms of its own criterion of sustainability. One could say that the negative side-effect (unemployment) is here a means to achieve the intended effect (sustainability). Laying people off is undoubtedly a means. But is it illegitimate? And what about the general case, where companies in a whole economic system have no choice but to lay people off because of government reforms and a transformation process of the Polish kind? No one would benefit from closing them all down. Looked at from the point of view of the sustainability of the company, the dismissals may be regarded both as means and as negative side-effects. As means, dismissals are legitimate but harmful because unemployment is harmful to the affected parties. The great challenge here is to summarize the concept of "legitimate means".

"Intended" and "unintended" effects of corporate activity

The PDE assessment of the Polmo Łomianki S.A. case-study can be compared to similar assessments in the field of applied ethics in medicine or war. It is about priorities. As regards medical ethics, doctors sometimes have to choose between lives (for example, choosing to save just one conjoined twin by separating them, or allowing them both to die). As regards the just war tradition, the permissibility of allowing protected civilians to die in order to achieve a necessary military goal must be evaluated according to the concrete situation.

The situation of Polmo Łomianki S.A. was complicated because of internal features as well as external environmental difficulties. The owners had a choice: either let the company go bankrupt, or help it to survive by decreasing production costs, for example by reducing over-employment by morally questionable methods. It was a question of saving the company and causing harm to some of the employees, or permitting the whole company to crash, harming all of the employees. A compromise was required, and not because of potentially lower profitability but because the survival of the business was threatened. The owners of Polmo Łomianki S.A. decided to find a sustainable way of modifying the side-effect harm.

Assessment of the ethical issues arising from the transformation process

In identifying the harmful side-effects of Polmo Łomianki S.A.'s activities, we must primarily address the impact on labour rights, although corruption has also turned out to be a problem. The corporate wrongdoing resulted here from the transformation strategy and its employment-reducing activity. The first stage of the process was to weaken the position of the trade union operating within the company. The second stage was to reduce employment by about 50 per cent not only to make the company efficient and competitive in the future, but, most of all, to secure its survival at the time. This policy would significantly affect the local community and its labour market.

First stage: Preparing the ground for dismissals

As stated above, the position of trade unions is very strong in Poland. Since the beginning of the "Solidarity era", labour unions have been the most important stakeholder in all Polish companies, owing both to tradition and to the Polish Labour Code regulations.

As a means of weakening the union, the shareholders of Polmo Łomianki S.A. first focused on its internal leaders. The leaders were bribed by the company authorities with offers of extra money, better jobs, expensive cars, and various excursions in exchange for resigning from the trade union. The company preferred to accept higher short-term costs than to allow the trade union to continue. Moreover, the company authorities decided to plant "reliable" people within the trade union, in order to get information about what was going on at all times. The effects were soon visible: the activity of the trade union operating in Polmo Łomianki S.A. rapidly diminished.

Whenever an employee wanted to join the trade union or to conduct activities that might threaten the management's strategy, the management reacted immediately. The employee was either asked to relinquish further action or quietly and quickly dismissed. As soon as the company had managed to reduce the strength of the trade union and the contracted three-year moratorium on group dismissals came to an end, the door was open for Polmo Łomianki S.A. to execute its strategy of reducing costs by firing staff.

Second stage: Dismissals

The methods for dismissal varied according to the employee's position in the company and influence on corporate activity. Because superfluous or ineffective employee-shareholders could not be dismissed while they possessed shares, they were offered a good price for their shares, an offer they usually accepted. Then Polmo Łomianki S.A. used the following methods of dismissal:
- forcing a group of employees to leave under threat of dismissal on unprofitable conditions or paying very high compensation;
- transferring ineffective or superfluous employees to worse and underpaid jobs, causing them to leave "at their own request";
- changing the employment contract, thus also causing employees to leave "at their own request" – the company gave the employees "a proposal with no refusal", making them take less profitable employment and worse working conditions, for example short-term contracts, which gave the employee no social or medical benefits and made it possible for the company to dismiss employees at short notice;
- making older employees take early retirement;
- depriving employees of their social allowances, e.g. bonuses, which amounted to about 40 per cent of total take-home pay, again causing them to leave "at their own request";

- offering employees the possibility of cooperation based on an out-sourcing model, with a refusal to cooperate meaning automatic dismissal – at first, the company guaranteed the new company regular contracts, but now it commonly invites tenders, and the new company does not get the work.

Evaluating corporate behaviour in the context of the principle of double effect

The Polish case may be helpful in illuminating double effect in the business context because it accentuates two main challenges for the principle: the concept of "legitimate means" in the context of the criterion of "sustainable value creation"; and "proportionality".

Polmo Łomianki S.A. abused the basic rights of its employees, as both a means and a side-effect of sustaining value creation and the survival of the company. The company's owners say they used all legal and morally permissible methods to sustain the business as a value-creating enterprise. The case-study challenges the principle of double effect insofar as the negative side-effect (unemployment) is a means to achieve an intended effect (sustainability). In the context of the sustainability of the company, the dismissals could be defined as a legitimate means. The problem is complex, because the situation affects many enterprises in Poland, and thus the future of the whole economy – not just that of one individual company – is at stake.

The other challenge to the principle of double effect is the concept of "proportionality". The harm done to employees may be treated as justified by the importance of sustaining the company. The choice was, after all, to dismiss some employees or to close the company down and let all the employees go.

There is a grey area related to this situation as well. Although, for example, bribing union leaders certainly constitutes illegitimate means, the illegality of dismissing people left few options. We need to see the principle in the light of this particular context. It is a fact that Polish employees often misuse their union rights and this has negative effects on corporate activity. It is not uncommon for the activities of trade unions to expose companies to huge additional costs. There are many examples of trade unions causing big problems for employers, as demonstrated by the case-studies of the cable factory in Ożarów Mazowiecki (where employees, after striking for a few months, started destroying the factory's equipment) and the clothing factory in Szczecin (where striking trade unionists began physically attacking the managing director).

Once the policy to reduce employment had been carried out, the production costs of Polmo Łomianki S.A. fell year by year. Two years after the company was taken into private hands, the cash-flow problems ceased. Thanks to lower production costs, the company started to earn profits for the first time.

Minimizing side-effect harm

The restructuring process (in terms of dismissals) was certainly damaging to the employees of Polmo Łomianki S.A. who were laid off, as well as to their families and the local community of Łomianki. However, the company did take a few measures to assist the former employees in dealing with the negative side-effects of the dismissals. First, the company accepted the higher costs of granting bigger severance payments than required by the Polish Labour Code. Second, the company organized special courses to help employees retrain for new jobs. Third, where possible the company used early retirement programmes, which was the only option for the older employees, who would have had difficulties adapting to a new market situation and new working conditions.

The results of transformation

Once the second step of the transformation of Polmo Łomianki S.A. – reducing production costs by reducing staff – was completed, the third step was to implement new management procedures based on the Japanese model of Total Quality Management, which involves capital reinvestment. To meet market demand, the company started to replace old equipment and production lines by buying in new technologies. The new components were of higher quality and were much cheaper, resulting in new customers both inside Poland and internationally.

The company also developed a new production profile – plastics processing and engineering. Polmo Łomianki S.A. aims to design and manufacture plastic components for the automotive industry and synthetic materials for the automotive, food, and furniture industries. Plastics processing and engineering are the most vital part of the company's activity, being the most profitable and efficient. The Polish Centre of Research and Certification appreciated these improvements, granting Polmo Łomianki S.A. the title "The Leader" in recognition of the economic and social results achieved through increasing productivity.

The next step was implementation of environment-friendly manufacturing methods. The company now operates according to PN-ISO 9001 Certificate, PN-EN ISO 14001 Standard, QS 9000, and VDA 6.1 Standards granted by the Polish Centre of Research and Certification. As a result, the company was one of the prize-winners in the Polish Quality Prize Contest in the category of small and medium-sized enterprises.

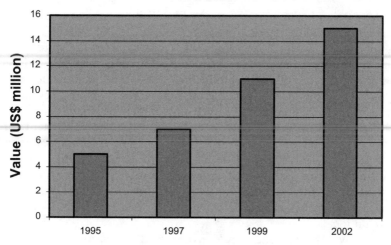

Figure 12.1 Total value of Polmo Łomianki S.A., 1995–2002.
Source: Polmo Łomianki S.A., *Report*, January 2003.

During the period of restructuring, the shareholders decided not to pay themselves any dividends, but to reinvest all the income in order to become more effective and competitive when Poland joined the European Union. The shareholders' equity is now held by 102 people; 75 per cent is held by 8 people and the rest is divided between numerous smaller shareholders. The company is fully controlled by its employees (who number 220), and its net value is about US$15 million (see fig. 12.1).[17]

The new mission of Polmo Łomianki S.A. is "the manufacture and sale of products characterized by the highest-quality standards, the highest technological level, utilizing of environment-friendly materials and which satisfy customers' requirements".[18] The company is gaining a reputation for quality and environment-friendly production not only in Poland but in Eastern Europe in general.

The Polish government's role

In Polish economists' opinion, the state could have played a more active and motivating role in preventing and minimizing the harmful side-effects of restructuring and economic development – expressed in high unemployment rates and social unrest.[19] Both the Polish business environment and Polish analysts and researchers agree that the state should focus on creating attractive investment conditions in order to speed up economic growth in Poland. There is no money in Polish budgets to implement expensive reforms. If they are implemented and failure occurs, it will be dangerous for the whole economy and the situation of the state.

The measures taken by the government to minimize the side-effect harm of dismissals included establishing a relief fund for the unemployed. A drawback of this is that, because unemployment benefits are quite high in Poland, many people would rather stay on benefits than take a job that does not pay much more. This is one reason the unemployment rate in Poland at the end of 2002 was over 18 per cent. Another measure the state used to help minimize side-effect harm caused by the transformation of enterprises was special economic zones. Such zones are limited areas in which, for example, tax rates are lower or there are other inducements to invest in setting up businesses in the area or hiring unemployed locals.

Obviously a labour code should give special protection to employees.[20] Employees need to be protected against dominating employers, but this protection cannot put employees in a superior position. If it did, entrepreneurs would lose the motivation to do business. After all, they are at greater risk than the employees if the economy deteriorates. As long as Polish employees have the upper hand, owing to legal restrictions on dismissal, employers will continue to use unethical methods to get rid of redundant employees. The owners of Polmo Łomianki S.A. say that they are afraid of employing people because they could have serious problems dismissing them later if the economic situation calls for it. This is important because having to keep redundant employees makes a company inflexible and unable to meet market requirements quickly enough to keep ahead of the competition.

As for self-governing bodies within business and industry, they are not well developed. They represent the interests of Polish enterprises in relation to central and local governments as well as the parliament in terms of advising on new legal rules for the economy, but their influence is limited by legal regulations and the strong position of trade unions.

What should be done?

In the following, I consider some measures that could be taken by the Polish government effectively to minimize the harmful side-effects of the transformation process as well as improve the competitiveness of Polish enterprises.

First, the government should make the legislation more flexible. Laws need to be clear to everyone, precise, stable, and univocal.[21] Laws need to fit a changing market situation and offer more attractive investment conditions. It must also become easier to observe the rules. The regulations should function to motivate entrepreneurs and so improve the dynamics of economic growth and at the same time protect employees' rights.

Second, supporting companies' development should be a fundamental task for the Polish government's administrative organs. Development support should be undertaken via advisory and expert services for companies, carrying out analyses and making them accessible, and making it easier for companies to gain access to knowledge, training, and economic information.[22]

Third, one of the main aims of the government's economic strategy should be to lead the Polish economy onto the path of rapid economic growth and job creation. Thus legislative regulations that improve conditions for mainly small and medium entrepreneurs should be implemented.[23] Legal measures should be used to simplify the tax system, facilitate a decrease in labour costs, make relations between employers and employees more flexible, and also remove bureaucratic obstacles. The government has already made some efforts in this area, but thus far only to a limited extent.

The future: EU accession

European Union accession will create a great opportunity for the Polish economy. European Union members can take part in special programmes that provide financial support for small and medium-sized companies to lead to greater competitiveness and higher exports for such companies. As a member, Poland will participate in special programmes, projects, and activities related to scientific research, technological development, computer services, protection of the natural environment, education of youth, social policy and health protection, protection of consumers, small and medium enterprises, tourism, culture, the audiovisual sector, civil rights observance, facilitating trade, energy, transport, and the fight against drug addiction and drug trafficking.[24]

The Poles hope that European Union accession will facilitate completion of the ongoing reforms, and thereby secure solid foundations for the Polish economy. Systemic reforms, responsible policies by the government, and support from the European Union, plus improved competitiveness in the global economy, should enable Poland to return to the path of rapid economic growth.

Conclusion

As this chapter has shown, the issues of side-effect harm and the legitimacy of means cannot be considered independently of context. Assessments of proportionality and the balance of harm against legitimate business purposes sometimes allow companies to employ means that do have negative side-effects – and that might be regarded as illegitimate in other contexts – in light of the greater good of securing a stable economy to the benefit for all. However, it should be clear that this does not justify a lack of preventive and minimizing measures on the part of the company. Responsibility should not be evaded, even for the best of reasons.

Notes

1. See chapter 1 in this volume.
2. Janusz Beksiak (ed.), *Ekonomia* (Warsaw: Wydawnictwo Naukowe PWN, 2000), pp. 247–249.
3. Ibid., p. 246.
4. Marek Bednarski, "Dylematy przekształceń własnościowych w Polsce. Prywatyzacja a komercjalizacja", in Zdzisław Sadowski (ed.), *Polityka gospodarcza państwa w okresie włączania się państwa do układu światowego* (Warsaw: Wydział Nauk Ekonomicznych Uniwersytetu Warszawskiego, 1992), pp. 51–75.
5. Rafał Krawczyk, *Wielka przemiana. Upadek i odrodzenie polskiej gospodarki* (Warsaw: Oficyna Wydawnicza, 1990), pp. 144–149.
6. The official website of Polish Official Statistics is http://www.stat.gov.pl.
7. Polish Official Statistics at http://www.stat.gov.pl.
8. Pawe Wrabec, "Made in (not) Poland", *Polityka* 2, 2003, p. 2383.
9. The official website of the European Secretariat is http://www2.ukie.gov.pl.
10. Ustawa o związkach zawodowych z dn. 23 maja 1991, Dz. U. 2001.79.854 z pó n. zm.
11. Pawe Tarnowski, "Siły na zasiłek", *Polityka* 17, 2000, p. 2242.
12. Bogusław Czarny, Elżbieta Czarny, Ryszard Bartkowiak, and Ryszard Rapacki, *Podstawy ekonomii* (Warsaw: PWE, 1998), p. 171.
13. Dariusz Facoń, "Policja w piaskownicy", *Gazeta Wyborcza*, 29 November 2002.
14. See http://www.rzeczpospolita.pl/.
15. Michał Stankiewicz and Michał Majewski, "Lincz w Szczecinie", *Rzeczpospolita*, 13 August 2002.
16. Bolesław Rok, *Więcej niż zysk, czyli odpowiedzialny biznes. Programy, strategie, standardy* (Warsaw: Forum Odpowiedzialnego Biznesu, 2001), pp. 11–20.
17. Polmo Łomianki S.A., *Report*, January 2003.
18. See the company's website at http://www.polmosa.com.pl.
19. Wrabec, "Made in (not) Poland", p. 2383.
20. Dariusz Stasik, "Żonglerka pracą", *Newsweek*, September 2001.
21. Jerzy Stelmach and Ryszard Sarkowicz, *Filozofia prawa XIX i XX wieku* (Kraków: Wydawnictwo Uniwersytetu Jagiellońskiego, 1999), pp. 158–159.
22. David Begg, Stanley Fischer, and Rudiger Dornbusch, *Ekonomia* (Warsaw: PWE, 1999), pp. 508–509.
23. Grzegorz W. Kołodko, "Transition to a market and entrepreneurship: The systemic factors and policy options", *Communist and Postcommunist Studies* 33, 2000, pp. 275–277.
24. See Urząd Komitetu Integracji Europejskiej at http://www2.ukie.gov.pl.

13

The Orissa case

Heidi von Weltzien Høivik

There is a growing expectation, on the part of a broad range of stakeholder groups, that organisations should perform and behave in a more open, socially caring and responsible way. These principles are even more important in times of intense pressure, for example where there is a real or perceived risk to public health, safety and environment. (Michael Regester, *Ethical Corporation Magazine*, February 2002)

Introduction

The history of Western cultures is marked by processes of economic transformation. Many of these have led to far-reaching, radical changes in societies, such as the foundation of the modern economic welfare systems. But not all changes have occurred without inflicting considerable harm and suffering. Developing countries today face serious challenges resulting from economic change and industrialization, which affect in particular indigenous peoples who live in isolation and are often forgotten. Millions of people in India alone have been thrown out of the socio-cultural networks and eco-systems that have provided them with a meaningful existence for thousands of years. They have been displaced by the construction of dams and canals, mines, industries, defence establishments, and other development projects.[1] They have been forced to take shelter in places alien to them, where they found themselves reduced to the level of "nomads" or "misfits", resembling a cultural ethnocide. "If you are to suffer, you should suffer in the interest of the country," Jawaharlal Nehru once said speaking to villagers who were to be displaced by the Hirakud Dam in 1948.[2]

Thus, although the advent of globalization is by no means a very recent phenomenon, it is only recently that the trends have been identified as being pervasive. What do these changes and trends entail for the poor farmer isolated from the rest of the fast-industrializing world, who is forced to face the harsh realities of this alien world?

Since the liberalization of India's markets in 1990, the incorporation of India into the global economy is pushing ahead fast. The following description of recent events in India involving a Norwegian company and its partners may serve as an illustration of the principle of double effect (PDE), where the responsibility of the firms for side-effect harm is addressed with regard to the rights of indigenous people to determine their own fate.

Further, the case depicts the social unrest caused as a result of years of suppression of the tribal people by the higher castes of the Hindu community in India. The Hindu caste system divides the Hindu population into four different categories: the *brahmins* (the educated class); the *kshatriyas* (warriors); the *vaishnavas* (tradesmen); and the *shudras* (the untouchables). The people on the bottom-most step of the ladder, the Shudras, were the outcasts of society and did the menial jobs of the villages. Many of the tribal communities in India belong to the Shudra caste. Harijan *adivasis*, as they are commonly known,[3] were forced to form their own communities because any interaction with people belonging to the higher castes was forbidden, to the extent that these people could not even drink water from the village wells or worship at the village temples. Over the centuries, these people have been treated like slaves by the higher castes of the Hindu society.

Consequently, the most morally challenging aspects of this case will understandably be related to the sociological and cultural impact on the people staying in and around the project area. Is the firm ethically responsible for the effects such an investment might have on these people, and, if yes, then to what extent? What is the impact that we so emphatically talk about? Where does the responsibility of the firm end and that of the nation or state start – where does one draw the line? How does one weigh the tangibles and the intangibles, and how does one adequately compensate for both? But above all, these questions lead to another baffling one – who is to decide what is beneficial for the people and what is not? Is it those of us who supposedly lead good lives? How does one define a good life: the various forms of stressful living of the industrialized world or the simple, poverty-ridden, yet seemingly happy lifestyle of the indigenous people? Although this chapter cannot answer all of these questions, the reader should bear them in mind while thinking through the case.

In addition to evaluating several moral problems associated with this case, this chapter attempts to provide an overview of the UAIL (Utkal Alumina International Limited) project to mine bauxite and refine it to alumina in Rayagada district, Orissa, India, and of the decisions faced by the management of UAIL, the tribal people, and the local authorities.

Patricia Werhane in chapter 7 in this volume adds another analytical tool, closely linked to the discussion about the PDE, through her definition of the term "moral risk". According to Werhane, "moral risk entails choices where (1) one is uncertain about the outcomes, and (2) achieving what is morally right or good will, in all likelihood, entail doing some evil, engaging in activities that are harmful, that do not respect individuals and their rights, or are otherwise morally questionable. Moreover, ordinarily in these cases, (3) one is uncertain whether the outcome itself will produce a balance of benefit over harm or good over evil, erase the cause of corruption, or improve the occurrence of human rights violations, and (4) not acting itself entails moral risk." Together with the PDE, an analysis of the moral risks involved can be a powerful tool for ethical reflection and decision-making, not least about side-effect harm, and this case is a case in point.

Before introducing the case, I would like to point out that a description of the events based solely on publicly available sources must necessarily fall short of a detailed illustration of how the individuals involved actually reasoned and made decisions. Nevertheless, case-studies can provide the reader with insights into the complexities of dilemma situations and shed light on the context in which managers have to pursue the purpose of their business.

Background

Norsk Hydro's guiding principles

As the case will show, a Norwegian company, Norsk Hydro, in 1993 joined the UAIL project, which was then already established. The original backers were the Indian Aluminium Company (INDAL) – part of the Alcan Group – and Tata Industries, both of which were regarded by Hydro as solid, internationally acknowledged companies. From the onset the project was considered complex, owing to its specific demographic and cultural aspects. Norsk Hydro and its subsidiary Hydro Aluminium could see that industrial development in such a predominantly agrarian area in India would mean major changes for the local community. However, the company believed that the total effect of such economic changes would be beneficial if the project was carried out in a properly planned and considerate manner. This remained the company's position throughout. Early on, the company decided to apply a proactive assessment strategy by hiring a social anthropologist to do some on-site studies for it. In addition, it went public with a set of guiding principles. Hydro's preliminary statement ran as follows (excerpts):

§1 "The values and conduct of UAIL will be in compliance with the standards of international human rights, Indian law and regulation, and the ethics and business practices of each of the UAIL partners."
§2 "We believe that industrialization, when planned and implemented with responsibility and care, is beneficial for the local community and mankind in general in a long-term perspective."
§7 "The projects of UAIL should, as far as possible, benefit different castes, religious groups, men and women to an equal extent."
§8 "UAIL is a religiously neutral organization. UAIL should recognize and respect every religion, world view and cultural tradition equally."

These principles reflect some of the moral problems the company anticipated. In spite of the good intentions, the complexity of the situation – and a series of events that the company could not have either foreseen or imagined, and even less proactively prepared for – constantly altered the scene. The fact that the company was in a partnership with two other main actors complicated the matter. And it is not known whether the principles were drawn up only on paper and were never really fully implemented in the organization by the managers in charge of the project within Norsk Hydro.

The following case-study is first of all meant to present the facts as objectively as possible. I believe in allowing readers to become engaged in a reflection process as if they had to make the decision themselves. At the same time, I am also a disciple of the idea that moral imagination needs to be fostered through the use of case-studies in order to go beyond present-day thinking in business. Therefore, the decision Norsk Hydro made at the end may not necessarily be the best one. In the discussion section of this chapter, I shall attempt to evaluate the case with regard to the PDE and thus test the usefulness of that particular instrument, which is the focal point of this whole book.

Presentation of the joint venture

In 1998, Utkal Alumina International Limited (UAIL) was a consortium of Norsk Hydro, Alcan International, the Tata Group of Industries, and the Indian Aluminium Company (INDAL).[4] UAIL is a US$1 billion, 100 per cent export-oriented project. It boasts of state-of-the-art technology for an integrated bauxite mine and the construction of a township of about 5,000 people and the necessary transportation systems. The mining area is about 1,389 hectares (14 km²). The refined ore will be sold to the parent companies and then transported to the port of Vishakhapatnam for onward transportation. Each of the partner firms has an off-take obligation to buy the extracted and purified ore from UAIL in a pre-defined proportion depending on their respective shareholdings in the company: in 2001, Norsk Hydro held 45 per cent, Alcan 35 per cent, and INDAL 20 per cent (after Alcan in 1999 had acquired the Tata shares, which originally were 20 per cent). The plant will have an initial capacity to produce 100 million tonnes of alumina per year and will have the provision to expand the production capacity to 200 tonnes per year.

The Bhalimali mines are estimated to have reserves of 157 million tonnes of the impure ore. Another 600 million tonnes of reserves are situated within 5 km of the border of Kashipur Tehsil, a sub-district. The core plant is to be located near Doragurha village, which has a relatively flat topography and good soil. Predominantly inhabited by tribal people, the adivasis,[5] with 20–25 families per village, the area remains one of the most poverty-stricken regions in the country, where deaths due to malnutrition, hunger, and diseases such as gastro-enteritis and malaria occur frequently. Education in these parts of the country is negligible; almost as negligible is the presence of basic amenities, which we take for granted. Scantily clad men and women walking bare-foot or squatting in the muddy water of the paddy fields are common sights. The indigenous people, the Paroja-Kondha, have reacted sharply to this invasion of their lives by the industrial conglomerates, especially since they have been kept in the dark about their future prospects. They are set to lose their ancestral land and homes in the "national interest" to make room for large-scale industrial development. Beneath the ground they inhabit is India's largest reserve of bauxite, the ore from which the alumina is produced. UAIL is planning to mine the ore and transport it along a 20 km conveyor belt to a refinery at Doraguda. The processed product, alumina, which is the intermediate material in producing aluminium, will feed the growing demand for light metal for cars and beverage cans. The environmental impact of the venture will be serious, because the region will be transformed into an open-cast mining landscape, which in turn will be more difficult to rehabilitate again. As part of the bauxite process, solid effluents such as "red mud" will need to be sorted in large "ponds". In spite of environmental assessment studies, UIAL has decided to move ahead.

The partners

Firm no. 1: Norsk Hydro (Hydro Aluminium)

Norsk Hydro[6] was founded in 1905 to utilize the abundant hydro-electric power and the excellent infrastructure provided by Norway's fjords for the first industrial production of nitrogen-based fertilizers called "Norges Salpeter". Over the years, Hydro has expanded and its activities have been diversified into various other fields. Today, Hydro is the largest publicly owned industrial corporation in Norway[7] and is a rapidly expanding international firm with total revenues approximating US$10 billion.

Hydro Aluminium, one of the various branches of Norsk Hydro, is today the fifth-largest producer of primary aluminium in the world. Over the past few decades its activities have primarily expanded in Europe and it is only recently that it has turned its attention to expansion in the rest of the world. "Hydro's goal is to increase production of aluminium and sees it as strategically desirable to strengthen its access to alumina and with it its industry in the years ahead."[8] With the aluminium market tightening, Hydro Aluminium has long been searching for bauxite ore, the primary raw material. Hydro Aluminium alone had gross sales amounting to 40 billion Norwegian kroner in 1999 and more than 60 billion in 2002. The number of employees has grown to 27,000 in recent years.

Firm no. 2: Tata Enterprises

Tata Enterprises, comprising more than 85 companies and with an annual turnover exceeding US$9.7 billion, employs more than 270,000 people.[9] It is currently the largest business in India. At the turn of the nineteenth century, Jamshedji Tata (founder of Tata Enterprises) identified steel, hydro-electric power, and higher education as the core areas of strength and development for the country. Since then, the Tatas have explored every field that has a potential for national growth. In terms of capital market performance, as many as 39 listed Tata companies account for nearly 8 per cent of the total market capitalization of all listed companies in India.

The enterprises promoted by the Tatas today encompass businesses in sectors as diverse as metals and associated industries, automobiles, energy, engineering, chemicals and pharmaceuticals, consumer products, finance, exports and overseas operations, information technology and communication, agro industries, and multiple services. In tune with changing global needs, Tata companies have forged a number of global alliances with eminent international partners in several sectors. The endeavour to become India's most trusted business enterprise has been the vision of the Tatas for over a century. The Tata Group represents a century-old tradition of corporate philanthropy in India, with the community not just another stakeholder in business but the very purpose of its existence. In order to be at the forefront of the industry liberalization in India and keeping up with the tradition of Tata Sons Limited, the holding company for the group formed the Tata Council for Community Initiative. The Council focuses on finding solutions to questions such as how companies measure their impact on development in terms of building strong communities as well as providing tangible assistance, how companies take a stand on community development and make their policies. Further, it concerns itself with channelling the core competence of the companies to evolve vocational training programmes for rural and urban youth, providing water for irrigation and drinking water to rural areas, facilitating programmes for women and children on health, education, literacy, and income-generating activities, and working as a network with the government, NGOs, and other development agencies in order to be better informed and mobilize expertise to strengthen programmes.

The Tata Group of companies recently decided to sell off its stake in the Utkal Alumina project, a proposal accepted by the Foreign Investment Promotion Board on 29 June 1999. The Canadian aluminium giant, Alcan, bought out Tata's 20 per cent stake, thus increasing Alcan's equity holding in Utkal Alumina to 35 per cent after the acquisition. The remaining 20 per cent is held by INDAL.

Firm no. 3: Indian Aluminium Company (INDAL)

In India, INDAL is aluminium.[10] Established as the Aluminium Production Company in 1938, it was the first to set up aluminium manufacturing facilities in India. It is a public limited company, professionally managed, with over 7,500 employees and about 30,000 shareholders. Over the years, INDAL has become a fully integrated company, operating through a nationwide network of mines, plants, and marketing offices, all affording access to major ports around the country. Today, the Indian Aluminium Company is a major player in the Indian aluminium industry.

Drawing on the experience and expertise of the world leader, Alcan Aluminium of Canada (the single largest shareholder with 54.6 per cent of INDAL's equity), INDAL has led the way in diverse applications of aluminium in the country. As part of the worldwide Alcan Group, INDAL has access to world-class expertise and technology and has further gained the leading edge in technology and expertise through strategic ventures with world leaders such as Norsk Hydro, Courtaulds, and the Tata Group of industries. INDAL, following in the footsteps of Alcan, is committed to protecting the environment and to community welfare. Its safety record ranks amongst the best in the world aluminium industry.

Firm no. 4: Alcan of Canada

The Alcan Group of companies is an international industrial group engaged in all aspects of the aluminium business.[11] Headquartered in Montreal, it carries out all its activities, which include bauxite mining, alumina refining, power generation, aluminium smelting, manufacturing and recycling, as well as research and technology, through subsidiaries and related companies. Alcan is a publicly owned company with about 20,700 registered holders of its 227 million common shares and 1,200 registered holders of its preference shares; it employs over 30,000 people, and thousands more are employed in its related companies. Since its establishment in 1901, Alcan has developed a unique combination of competitive strengths. With operations and sales offices in over 30 countries, the Alcan Group is one of the most international aluminium companies in the world, and is a global producer and marketer of flat-rolled aluminium products.

The Alcan Group is a multicultural and multilingual company that reflects the different corporate and social characteristics of the many countries in which it operates. Within a universal framework of policies and objectives, the individual subsidiaries and divisions conduct their operations with a large measure of autonomy. Alcan is committed to a process of continual environmental improvement. Community investment has long been a part of Alcan's corporate culture, with the belief that a successful future depends on the right nurturing of the leaders of tomorrow. Matching business principles with environmental and social responsibility is important to Alcan. In 1997 the company released a companion document to its "Alcan, its purpose, objectives and policies" entitled "A code of conduct", which outlines Alcan's expectations on ethical issues, ranging from employee behaviour in the workplace to business practices with suppliers and customers, as well as dealing with human rights, worker health and safety, community needs, and environmental responsibility. It also includes a commitment to conduct business with integrity.

The resistance

One of the major underlying causes of the protests against the Utkal Alumina project has been the lack of concern displayed for the views of the indigenous people by the partners and the state government. The fact that there has been no dialogue between the people and the management of UAIL even after almost eight years[12] – since the papers on the project were originally drawn up – merely adds to the confusion and chaos. The people do not trust big business. The ill effects of similar projects are apparent in other areas of the state, and there is little assurance that the same will not happen again. Other villages have gone through the traumatic experience of displacement and resettlement. What has inflamed the tribes is the manner in which the state government has allowed the preliminary exploration of bauxite without telling them about their possible fate in the future.

Displacement as a process continues long after the people have lost their land and livelihood and is not limited to the narrow concept of their physical ousting from the old habitat.[13] Often when the decision to displace people is taken, there is no definite commitment either to resettle them in an acceptable manner or to let them share in at least a few of the benefits of the project in the form of jobs and contracts. The consequence of such an announcement is a sense of insecurity among those to be displaced by the project or those who are going to lose their land or livelihood. The landless are ignored in cases where the limited rehabilitation of offering compensation money to those who own land is available. Productivity, rather than social investment for the benefit of the people, is seen as the most important criterion in evaluating these projects.

The tribal population has traditionally depended on non-wood forest products for their sustenance. More than 50 per cent of their food came from the forests before the displacement. With displacement, they were deprived of this source and left without any alternative source. Even those who got dry land were unable to get access to non-wood forest products. As a result, several of them left the resettlement camps within a few years of their being resettled there. The situation of those who had to resettle themselves was worse. With limited exposure to a monetary economy, most of the money they received as cash compensation was often appropriated by moneylenders, merchants, etc. While the men took to alcohol to cope with the frustration and disruption caused by the displacement, the women were left to deal with the complete or partial breakdown of their family structures.

Micheal Cernea has explained displacement in the following way.

Displacement implies not only physical eviction from a dwelling, but also the expropriation of productive lands and other assets to make possible an alternative use of the space. This is not just an economic transaction, a simple substitution of property with monetary compensation. Involuntary displacement is a process of unravelling established human collectivities, existing patterns of social organisation, production systems and networks of social services. The concept of displacement also describes situations in which some people are deprived of their productive lands, or of other income-generating assets, without being physically evicted from their houses.[14]

He further points out that displacement consists of two distinct but related processes: (a) displacement of people and dismantling of their patterns of social and economic organization; and (b) resettlement at a different location and the reconstruction of their livelihood and social networks.

Much of the uncertainty in the Utkal Alumina project is caused by the different figures floating around about the project. To give an illustration, UAIL has confirmed that three villages will be displaced. Norsk Hydro estimates that 1,300 families will lose their land, another 250 families will lose more than 50 per cent of their land, and 148 families will be relocated, in all affecting 12 villages. However, a sociocultural impact study states that the promoters of the project claim that 37–40 villages will be affected/displaced, which represents a population of 12,000. The judgment passed by the High Court states that 24 villages would be displaced in the first round.[15] There is, however, no account of how many more will be affected in subsequent rounds. Prakrutiko Sompodo Soroichya Porisodo, which stands for (literally translated into English) "Organisation for the Protection of Gifts of Nature from Harm", a local NGO, says that at least 150 villages will be affected in one way or another. This is indicative of the inadequacy of the documentation and information about the project and the lack of transparency that the indigenous people are faced with.

According to the rehabilitation plan, only one person per family will be employed at the refinery. With almost 97 per cent of the population in the area being illiterate and as such unskilled, the villagers do not have sufficient technical education to get jobs at the refinery. Also, with much of the labour force coming from outside the region, as expected by the villagers, the influx of outsiders poses a threat to the sociocultural structures that have existed within these communities for hundreds of years.

A perfect example of the situation is Jay Kay Pur, close to the headquarters of the Rayagada district. A large percentage of the population of this township comes from the neighbouring state of Andhra Pradesh and other neighbouring regions. A large influx of people into the region is bound to disrupt their community life, their cultural and ethnic identity, existing social structures and mechanisms, and their language. Furthermore, the villagers cultivate their land for three–four months a year and this provides them with sufficient food to last their family for a year. With one earning member in the family, will the wages of that one person be sufficient to feed a family of two, let alone one of four?

One major problem with rehabilitation schemes is that when skills are imparted the focus is invariably on men; the women are often neglected. The few jobs that the women can get are bound to be unskilled and low status because of their high illiteracy and their lower exposure to the external world. As a result, the woman ceases to be an asset to the family. Further, common facilities such as a place for hygiene needs are not replaced. For example, the National Aluminium Company provided houses without toilet facilities. With nowhere for the needs of nature, the displaced persons therefore use a plot that the neighbouring village has set aside for pasture. In planning rehabilitation, it is forgotten that the morning ablutions and collecting water in the evenings also have a social function where the women get together and share confidences. Not being able to attend to these needs further adds to the women's isolation. As a result, women, who are expected by cultural norms to observe greater privacy than men, are unable to attend to their needs of nature.[16]

The consequence of the displacement and the concurrent deprival of resources is out-migration. In some cases men migrate, leaving the women behind in the village. In other cases the whole family has to migrate to the urban slums. In either case, the woman feels the worst consequences. To begin with, most of us assume that the out-migration is purely economic, i.e. that poverty forces the family to leave their village and go in search of jobs elsewhere. In their traditional society, the men were the hunters, the guardians, and the village council leaders. The latter two functions are now taken up by the police and the panchayat, respectively, without providing an alternative, and hunting is all but banned. Men are thus left with no status. They try to compensate for this by migrating to another place in order to improve their economic status and become absorbed into another value system and society. Often the husband returns home with a second wife. Divorce and remarriage were allowed in the traditional tribal societies, but, being deprived of their sustenance, the woman has no choice but to put up with this situation and accept her subordinate status to the second wife. Also, with low exposure to the external world, the tribals have fewer inbuilt coping mechanisms than other social groups. Often the woman is forced to look after the household on her own, and other men, particularly moneylenders and merchants, exploit her powerlessness.

Over the years the unrest has grown to unprecedented levels. Trouble began when the district authorities started acquiring land near Kucheipadar village, 20 km from Kashipur where the bauxite refinery is expected to be located. The people have at times resorted to violence and other forms of force to get their point across to the firms and the state government. A team of surveyors from the Operations Research Group engaged by UAIL were prevented from doing their work and reportedly manhandled at Dimundi and Korolo villages near Kucheipadar. In December 1997, three officials of Hydro Aluminium were kidnapped. The following passage, written by Jo Lawbuary for the NGO Ganesha, is typical of the information published on the Internet:

The government of Orissa, too, has emerged as a force unto itself, in smoothing UAIL's path, and riding roughshod over the adivasis of Kashipur. Not only has the state administration marshalled the special state police force to brutally quash local protest, the government of Orissa has also ignored its own constitution regarding adivasi rights. Indigenous communities in southwest Orissa are legally "Fifth Schedule", which confers on them certain rights. These constitutional rights include consultation of the gram sabha or panchayats (village councils), prior to any acquisition of land for developmental projects in scheduled areas, and before resettling and rehabilitating those affected.

A recent report by the Council for Social Development [CSD], New Delhi, is damning of both the government and UAIL for their neglect in consultation on land acquisition and R and R. CSD found that communication was restricted to merely conveying orders for land to be acquired, and for compensation to be dispensed. The report highlights that the usual requirements of rehabilitation, such as land to land exchange, community resettlement, employment security, protection of livelihood needs or entitlement to common resources have not been taken into account.

CSD reserves singular criticism for the government of Orissa, which "smacks of vendetta and intolerance" in its campaign to silence local non-governmental organisations working with adivasi communities ...

UAIL and the state government, however, do not appear to consider the adivasis' claims as legitimate; when the adivasis reject the concrete shacks constructed as recompense for the loss of their homes, and are not keen, or willing, to become industrial labourers, as an alternative to their lost livelihoods, they are charged as being anti-development, and anti-industrial. Some have been displaced by large-scale industrial development before, and have experienced at first hand, woefully inadequate rehabilitation and resettlement schemes, while few benefit from the offer of new jobs. Loss of self-reliance and the breakdown of communities and families are routinely observed in those that are reduced to "living like refugees in ill-planned rehabilitation colonies", while extra strain on shrinking resources may fuel conflict all round.[17]

Initially, the agitators demanded information on (a) the effect of the alumina projects and the mining on the natural resource base of the area; (b) the terms and conditions agreed upon between the companies and the government; (c) the rights of the native inhabitants of the region to the land, forests, and their homes from which they are being evicted, and the government's position on this; and (d) the benefits, if any, that would accrue to the people of Kashipur from the mining and industrial activity. With the ensuing silence from the companies and the district authorities, the people became impatient and demanded that the project be stopped or the project site be shifted. The people have also appealed to the public both in India and in Norway to take action against the project.

Several petitions have been filed with the High Court of Orissa and letters have been written to the Norwegian government. The petitions talk in depth about the environmental hazards, the inadequacy of the compensation packages, the irregularities of the planned rehabilitation scheme, and the socioeconomic and sociocultural impact on the people. For example, the ash ponds, red mud stacking, and chemical effluents disposed of into the rivers not only contaminate the water, making it unfit for human and animal consumption, but also render the land barren.

The major concern, however, is the inadequacy of the compensation provided to the people and the problems of adapting to the required changes in lifestyle. According to Shankar, a spokesperson for an NGO in Jeypore, the budget allotted for ecological and social rehabilitation (Rs 168 crores, or approximately US$50 million) is not sufficient given the magnitude of the displacement, the ecological destruction, and the obligation on the promoters to establish a justifiable sustainable re-habilitation programme.[18] The NGOs feel that the monetary compensation provided to the people is not adequate in terms of it being rather short lived. The compensation money is deposited in a bank and the people eventually receive only a part of it, the argument being that tribal people know little about operating bank accounts. Another concern is alcoholism, the worry being that monetary compensation will be used to buy alcohol. The local authorities feel that the banking system would counteract this and ensure that the money is spent on worthwhile causes. The people can withdraw only a part of the compensation package and after that they need to get prior permission from the Indian authorities for any further withdrawals.

Several NGOs have been promoting the cause of the tribal people in the region for various reasons. The NGOs in the vicinity of the project area feel that, although the project will bring about development in the area, that development is focused on the area's infrastructure and not on improvement for the people as such.

A small group of people from the villages threatened by the project formed an organization called the Anchayalika Surakshya Parishad (Regional Protection Council) to spearhead the movement against the environmental degradation and displacement of the aborigines. The voluntary organization is widely described by the Rayagada district administration and local politicians as a front to create setbacks to the plans for development. Officials say that the agency has succeeded in throwing a spanner in the developmental work because of its hold over the tribals and a strong network within the area. Moreover, its workers have been spotted on many occasions with the agitating tribals.

(PSSP) Prakrutiko Sompodo Soroichya Porisodo is an organization formed by the Harijan adivasis of Kucheipadar village, about 15 km from the INDAL office in Tikri village. The organization is headed by Krushna Santa (an adviser), who is also a resident of the village. PSSP has put up resistance to the project, saying that "you can take our lives but we will not give up our land". Its struggle has been weakened over time as many of the villagers have accepted the compensation, apparently under the influence of alcohol and threats from the police. The district authorities deny the charge. However, off the record they agree that there have been instances where people have signed the papers under duress but these instances are negligible and if they have occurred the local authorities have not had a hand in it. PSSP has grown hostile towards anyone who represents the firms. It claims that promises have not been met and it sees no reason to believe that things are going to change. According to the "Detailed Rehabilitation Plan" of the alumina project, UAIL has already initiated a number of community-based improvement projects, with active participation from the villagers, and a favourable response has been observed in certain parts of the region. PSSP, however, has consistently refused to have anything to do with UAIL. Any participation by PSSP in any of the programmes started by UAIL would further weaken its stance. Its members seem to be clutching hold of any straw they can to remain afloat and keep their holdings. Another particular reason for the protest is that the valley is surrounded by sacred hills. However, UAIL has agreed not to use explosives on these sacred hills.

Agragamee is another NGO that has its base in the interior of Rayagada, some 20 km from the project site. The NGO is aimed at the creation of a new society, which will ensure decent livelihoods and the space to initiate a critical dialogue among the citizens and with the state. Its activities are also aimed at developing self-sufficiency among the local tribes, especially the tribal women. Agragamee is a politically motivated NGO and has been accused of using the UAIL case as leverage to obstruct the functioning of the district authorities and the companies. Agragamee is also one of the stakeholders affected by this project, not just as an NGO – its office comes under the project operational area. With activities ranging from education, training, and community capacity-building to self-help groups for women, gender disparity workshops, agro service centres, and watershed projects, Agragamee exercises immense control over the people in the area. Agragamee has opposed the project, defining it as destruction behind the facade of development. As such it has opted for an indirect approach. It has been accused of trying to motivate the villagers to protest against the project by emphasizing the negative effects the project might have on the people and at the same time ignoring the positives that could come out of it. As a result, several of the people working for Agragamee have apparently been threatened and some even imprisoned on false charges to stop them from inciting people. With the immense publicity that the project has received abroad, along with the history of animosity between the local authorities and Agragamee, it is not surprising that its members are somewhat cautious about whom they talk to and what they say.

Agragamee questions the right of the firms and the government at large to decide what is good for the people and what is not, without any real dialogue with the ones who are going to be affected by the decisions. Despite all the talk about Agragamee's motives in opposing the project, its question as such certainly holds water. These people have lived in a state of abject poverty and isolation, and mere money is hardly sufficient compensation for the problems and difficulties they will face as a result of the displacement.

With Hydro being the majority shareholder in the UAIL project, the discussion of the case in Norway has centred on Hydro using its shareholding to influence and correct the situation or withdrawing from the project. Several of the NGOs in Norway have been working together to promote the cause of the tribal people of Kucheipadar.[19] This has added extra pressure on Hydro and increased media attention in the home country.

Norsk Hydro's internal learning process

On 23 March 1999, Hydro president and CEO, Egil Myklebust, spoke at a conference in Oslo. He underlined that in his opinion economic growth, social responsibility and environmental responsibility are mutually dependent on each other. He also pointed out that the foundation of Hydro's new corporate directive on social responsibility is the principle of sustainable development, as expressed in the Brundtland Commission's report of the late 1980s. But Hydro's experience in this area is as long as the company is old, Myklebust said. "This isn't new for us," he continued. "Like many other companies, Hydro has been actively involved in the social development of the communities in which it operates – and we have been doing this since our start in 1905. Take Rjukan, for example. When we established operations in the Norwegian town, we did more than build factories. We helped build a society with all the social services."

The principle of sustainable development, according to Myklebust, has put a timely and useful emphasis on something that has been part of industrial and social development for years. He added that three pillars – "economic growth, social responsibility and environmental responsibility – are mutually dependent on each other: If its economic foundation erodes, then a company will also have difficulties solving environmental problems and assuming its social responsibility."

Does that mean that Norsk Hydro has undergone a learning process with regard to the painful experiences the company is confronted with in Orissa? Myklebust pointed out later in the same speech that the ethical challenges are more pronounced when "companies establish operations in other global regions and in particular when engaging in developing countries and in countries with clear cultural differences. UTKAL in India is a good example. Themes like human rights and consideration for the native population, and other questions related to values, have been raised in connection with UTKAL. Coming into India with a background in Norwegian culture and industry is hard. No question." Myklebust further admitted: "There are no easy answers to the questions we are facing with regard to UTKAL. The most important thing for us as a company is to consistently act in accordance with our code of conduct and fundamental values. This is part of what we are trying to accomplish with the new corporate directive." He added his understanding of the situation by saying: "At times, the UTKAL debate in Norway has portrayed the community of Orissa as an untouched idyll. This description is not entirely accurate.... Orissa's native population is growing while its economic base is weakening. And at the same time, the population is being squeezed culturally from external forces. As a result of all this, the community is being asked to choose between continuing the current development or take part in the industrial utilization of its natural resources. One of the most negative effects is related to Orissa's older residents, who will be asked to participate in a faster readjustment process than they are prepared to handle. But who should decide what is right for a community? Who should one listen to? Listening to the local authorities and to the organizations with ties and experience in the area is common sense." Myklebust also acknowledged that industry has a lot to learn with respect to communication outside its own world. In the case of Utkal, he said bluntly that Indian opinion should outweigh Norwegian opinion when it comes to India's development. "I can say a lot of positive things about Norwegians and their sincere desire to help people who are not well off. But I am not convinced that we always know what is best for a developing society. We should remember that India is the second-most populous country in the world, and has the world's largest democracy. Is it right for us, with our green pastures, to tell the Indians in detail what they should do? We should also remember something about opinions; those with the strongest views often get the most attention. I would simply like to see a more rounded debate concerning UTKAL." Myklebust agreed that there are both positive and negative sides to the Utkal project but, when the two sides are added up and compared, he said he believes the result for the local community is favourable.

There will always be opinions and evaluations of industrial development that vary from country to country, according to Myklebust. One argument says that worthy companies should be able to use the openings to establish operations in countries that do not always meet human rights standards, as long as these companies maintain the right principles, for instance with respect to labour rights and the environment. But even if the United Nations does not recommend against entering a country, Myklebust concluded, companies should not necessarily feel that they have the green light to enter. The key is that companies abide by their own sound and fundamental values. "If we, as managers, can defend the decisions we are making for our children in their 20s and 30s, then we have a good starting point."

Five years after its first engagement in UIAL, Norsk Hydro presented new guidelines for its industrial operations in the form of a new corporate directive. The document is in addition to the group's established code of conduct, which includes ethical and environmental principles as well as personnel policies. The directive applies to investments, projects, and business activities, including those in joint ventures where Hydro is operator. In companies in which Hydro's ownership share is between 10 and 50 per cent, the five unconditional principles included in the directive will serve as the basis for conduct:

- Norsk Hydro supports the Universal Declaration of Human Rights and will not engage in activities that impair the enjoyment of human rights.
- Norsk Hydro will engage in open dialogue and consultation with stakeholders in local communities and elsewhere regarding impacts of company operations.
- Norsk Hydro operations will not endanger the physical safety, security or health of members of communities affected by such operations.
- Norsk Hydro will remain neutral in respect of race, religion, gender, age, caste, cultural identity and similar factors.
- Norsk Hydro recognizes the intrinsic value of diverse cultures and traditions in communities where it operates and will act accordingly.

The directive also provides clear instructions for the first time as to how the guidelines will be followed through more specific requirements related to analyses and dialogue. It adds that divisional management, with assistance from Hydro's corporate communications staff, is personally responsible for ensuring that the principles are met. This was not the case when UAIL was established. Did the company learn from its engagement in Orissa?

The final decision

On 17 December 2001, the company released the following press statement:

Hydro Aluminum has informed its partners in UTKAL Alumina International Ltd that they wish to exit from the project. Hydro's decision is based on an assessment of the future market for alumina, as well as the positive development of the company's alumina production facilities in Brazil. The lack of progress for the UTKAL alumina production is also part of the decision. Alumina, also known as aluminium oxide, is an important raw material for production of primary aluminium. Hydro has equity production of alumina in Jamaica and Brazil. The Brazil Alunorte refinery is going through an expansion which will substantially increase Hydro's production capacity for alumina.

A balanced alumina market with a variety of suppliers is envisaged for the coming years. This will allow Hydro to pursue its strategy of alumina supply through a combination of own production, alliances and long term contracts. The shareholders agreement of UTKAL Alumina gives the remaining partners pre emption rights. The legal process required for Hydro to leave the partnership has been initiated.

UTKAL Alumina has not started any construction in the planned project area. Based on partnership policies, some socio economic development work is going on. There is also a continuous dialogue between the company, the government and the local population. The proposed host community of the project in Kashipur, Orissa is in dire need of social and economic development. Mining and industrialization, when implemented in a careful and responsible way, may contribute to a sustainable development in this area and give opportunities for thousands of below the poverty line people to better their livelihood conditions.

On 23 January 2002, an additional press release was published by the company:

Hydro Aluminium has entered into an agreement with Alcan and Indal, a subsidiary of the Aditya Birla Group, to sell its 45 percent share of UTKAL Alumina for a price of approximately USD 6 million. The fullfillment of the agreement is subject to approval from Indian authorities. After Hydro's withdrawal, Indal's stake in UTKAL Alumina will be 55 percent and Alcan's 45 percent.

Discussion

Can company principles as stated on page 224 help prevent or minimize harmful side-effects of otherwise legitimate economic activities? If they can, how is a company to operationalize and live up to these principles? Could a consultation process with the other partners on these principles have led to a common values base? How is one to deal with conflicting interests among the different stakeholders, particularly when there is a clear imbalance of power and recognized legitimacy? How is business to deal with political activism and single-agenda NGOs? Would consultation processes with affected parties prior to entering into a business partnership alter the stakes? Should a company refrain from engaging in a morally risky activity when it sees that its best intentions cannot be fulfilled? And should that be viewed as moral cowardice?

To answer some of these difficult questions, the PDE framework can be applied and if necessary expanded. There is no doubt that the partnership constellation – UAIL – and its intentions are both legal and legitimate in the pursuit of a joint goal: mining bauxite for alumina production. The unintended side-effects can be divided into two sets: known (foreseeable) and unknown (unforeseeable). The most prevalent known negative side-effect was the displacement of people, in this case the lower-caste tribe – the adivasis.

Less foreseeable, maybe, were the sociopolitical norms that still exist owing to the long tradition of the caste system, even though it has been abolished legally. Norsk Hydro did carry out a set of actions to assess the impact of the known side-effects by sending a Norwegian social anthropologist on a site visit to the various villages. He carried out a risk assessment study with regard to the indigenous people who were to be displaced. The findings concluded that the culture, lifestyle, and economic base of the indigenous people would be severely affected. But did the study also assess the role and place of the indigenous people within Indian society? Adivasis have a lower social status than other citizens. To what extent could and should a Norwegian partner take such social imbalances and injustice into consideration?

We must also ask how a Norwegian partner can have consultations with affected parties alone. To what extent is it dependent on the willingness of the other partners to join it? Not all of these questions were evaluated.

The anthropological assessment was done on the advice of the management. However, no assessment was made – as far as is known – to evaluate the partnership with the two Indian companies with regard to their moral position on the anticipated negative side-effects. Nevertheless, there was a general agreement that UAIL would accept responsibility for compensating the displaced people and provide them with new housing, schools, and modern infrastructure. Jointly, UAIL had both the means and the power to do so. The less immediately foreseeable side-effects, dealing with the emotions that the displacement of whole families could arouse, were not assessed and thus not added to the "cost" side. The fact that the partners must have felt that they could disregard or even control the emotions between the "two classes of Indian citizens" aggravated the situation and led to the active involvement of a third party, the NGOs.

What were the moral choices? Remaining an active partner or withdrawing from the entire project? For either decision Norsk Hydro would have to be responsible and would be questioned. There are at least three sets of arguments that business resorts to: the economic argument, the social impact argument, and the moral argument. The economic rationality always looks for the value-creating benefit involved for the business itself, while the social impact assessment is likely to follow the same logic by pointing to the overall economic and social benefits that industrial development will bring to an underdeveloped area and its people. The moral argument, leaning towards either deontological or teleological reasoning, will offer reasoned grounds for voicing concern – using the "do no harm" principle – about industrial development that may benefit a majority of the people but will be very harmful to some. From the reference in chapter 3 of this book to the Sullivan principles, however, we can add that it can be morally justified to stay involved if by doing so one can influence the course of events by exerting pressure to reform existing local attitudes, norms, and laws that are clearly in violation of human rights. This was in fact the position of Norwegian Church Aid, which believed Norsk Hydro could have a positive influence on its Indian partners. For that reason Norwegian Church Aid bought shares in Norsk Hydro in order to have a voice at the General Assembly and a chance to address the UAIL issues in 1998. At the time, this alone resulted in media attention in Norway, particularly since Norwegian Church Aid claimed that UAIL had broken Convention 169 of the International Labour Organization, which requires that companies cannot buy land from indigenous people without providing them with similar adequate land, not money.

On the other side, the economic argument held that remaining involved in such a volatile environment with increasingly "hot" media attention and NGO involvement might have a damaging effect on the company's reputation. In short, the costs of staying in India might be more than the company was willing to pay in the long run. The social impact argument raised, among other things, the problem that, being only one of three partners, Norsk Hydro was too "small" to have control or power over events in order to prevent harm. The moral argument – likely to be linked to the economic argument – was that it is better to withdraw, because this would benefit other stakeholders to whom it has a fiduciary duty as well.

It is tempting to conclude that Norsk Hydro is guilty of faulty moral judgement. In my opinion, this would be a hasty conclusion. There is another dimension of the PDE, not yet fully included in the framework: the importance of power, of having control. Preventing harm from being done requires, in addition to willingness, the power to do so. If a company is in a partnership with others who – let us say – do not view the situation as requiring moral reasoning in order to prevent harm, there is an obvious imbalance of willingness and power to act. Therefore, if a reasonable understanding of moral responsibility cannot be achieved among the partners, the one company, not willing to give up its moral position, will have to withdraw. A company has not only fiduciary duties to create and sustain value for its contractual stakeholders, but also duties towards its other stakeholders – employees, customers, etc. Being the only non-Indian partner in India, Hydro had to accept the local written and unwritten norms and laws even though – as the above case shows – the caste system, and particularly the way it is still acted upon with regard to the indigenous people, is morally speaking in clear violation of human rights. Only if a company has the power to exert reformatory pressure to rectify the moral discrimination against tribal people in India does the company have a moral justification for not withdrawing. I believe the PDE, as a tool for making the kinds of decisions we are talking about here, should be expanded to take the discrepancy between different cultures and social norm settings (often included in the local laws) into account. This is crucial to all business endeavours when expanding globally. Therefore, I would like to expand one of the guidelines suggested by Deon Rossouw in chapter 3 of this volume to read:

When side-effects are caused by social norms or laws that abuse human rights, the actor should exert pressure to reform these. However, if the actor does not have the power to exert such pressure, the negative effects are inescapable. When such inescapable negative side-effects are of an especially grave kind, and the actor actually contributes to them through being involved, the actor should withdraw.

In my opinion, owing to the type of economic partnership Norsk Hydro had entered into with local national partners, and because of the existing laws and norms of India, the Norwegian company had no "power" or leverage on its own to bring about a reform process that would eliminate the negative effects on the indigenous people. Moral convictions are not sufficient when there is no will among the other partners.

Conclusion

The case-study has shown that companies involved with local partners in their country need to be less naive about the extent to which good intentions, including assessment strategies and some form of stakeholder engagement, can prevent or at least reduce negative foreseeable side-effects, unless the company has the power to bring about a clear moral agreement among all the partners to reform existing human rights abuses.

Appendix: Chronology of events

1991	Utkal project officially announced
1993	Norsk Hydro becomes a partner in the Utkal Alumina project
1993	Survey started by the company for the plant area with the help of the local government
11/11/93	Eighteen people's representatives from five villages meet with the Chief Minister of Orissa at Bhubhaneshwar and discuss the issue
27/11/93	Meeting called to discuss the project but none of the farmers who would be losing land are invited, except for four people from three villages
1994	Utkal Alumina International Ltd (UAIL) established. The company initiates infrastructure programmes. Ownership is divided equally between the three companies: INDAL, Tata and Hydro
1995–1997	Licences, permits, and acquisition of land
1995	A representative from the WIDA Centre (Integrated Rural Development of Weaker Sections in India) visits Norway
1995	FIVH (Fremtiden i Våre Hender – The Future in Our Hands) starts the first organization in Norway to campaign for Hydro to respect the rights of the local people and walk out of the Utkal project
1996	Rally organized by the local people attended by nearly 6,000 people. The District Commissioner and a Minister of Labour Affairs visit Kucheipadar to discuss compensation and rehabilitation and receive a memorandum submitted by the people
1996	A demonstration by 10,000 people against the Utkal project. About 5,500 people send a letter to the energy minister in Norway, Jens Stoltenberg: "Take Hydro out of our land."
1996	The company starts paying compensation money by offering liquor and putting pressure on people. Later on, the people block the road to stop company cars from entering the area
1997	Representatives from Strømme Foundation (SF), Bergen College, and NORWATCH visit Kucheipadar. SF criticizes the Utkal project in a report and demands that an adequate compensation and rehabilitation plan be drawn up after speaking to the people
1997	Representatives from Agragamee and another representative from WIDA visit SF
1997	A total of 50 cases have been filed in the court against the project by the people and so far only one has been finalized. Company starts the construction of a model rehabilitation colony at the village of Domkoral, which is destroyed by the people
1998–2000	Changes to the ownership structure: Alcan becomes co-owner, Tata withdraws, and Hindalco (the Birla group) purchases INDAL from Alcan. The protest against the project gets more heated

2002	Hydro sells its 45 per cent share of Utkal Alumina to Alcan and INDAL, a subsidiary of the Aditya Birla Group, for approximately US$6 million. The fulfilment of the agreement is subject to approval by the Indian authorities. After Hydro's withdrawal, Indal's stake in Utkal Alumina is 55 per cent and Alcan's 45 per cent

Notes

1. In the past 50 years, 33 *million* people have been displaced by big dams alone. What about those who have been displaced by the thousands of other development projects? At a private lecture, N. C. Saxena, Secretary to the Planning Commission, said he thought the number was in the region of 50 million (of whom 40 million were displaced by dams); http://www.narmada.org/gcg/gcg.html.
2. As Arundhati Roy wrote in April 1999: "On the one hand, it is seen as a war between modern, rational, progressive forces of 'Development' versus a sort of neo-Luddite impulse – an irrational, emotional 'Anti-Development' resistance, fuelled by an arcadian, pre-industrial dream; on the other, as a Nehru vs Gandhi contest. This lifts the whole sorry business out of the bog of deceit, lies, false promises and increasingly successful propaganda (which is what it's really about) and confers on it a false legitimacy. It makes out that both sides have the Greater Good of the Nation in mind – but merely disagree about the means by which to achieve it" (http://www.narmada.org/gcg/gcg.html).
3. *Harijan* means God's people. The term was coined by Mahatma Gandhi to promote acceptance of a class of people by the larger section of Hindu society. *Adivasi* comes from the Sanskrit word *adi*, and *vasi*, meaning ancient settlers, i.e. the tribal people.
4. Information was collected in 1998.
5. According to a 1981 census, about 6 million indigenous people account for over a quarter of Orissa's total population and 12 per cent of India's total adivasi population; see G. S. Padhi, *Forest resources of Orissa* (Bhubaneswar, India: Physics Institute, 1984), pp. 69–81.
6. See http://www.hydro.com/alu/eng/index2.html.
7. The Norwegian state government owns 51 per cent of Hydro's shares.
8. Statement by Thomas Knutzen (dated 22 May 1998) at a meeting in Oslo.
9. See http://www.tata.com/home.htm.
10. See http://www.indal.com/html/body_.
11. See http://www.alcan.com/About.nsf/Topics-E/Global?OpenDocument.
12. Statement by Krushna Santa, a local spokesperson, interviewed by my research assistant Pooja Kumar, who went on a site visit to Orissa in July 1998.
13. This description is of the displacement that has occurred elsewhere in the state as a result of similar projects.
14. See http://www.labourfile.org/Mining/special_report.htm, and in Sumati Kulkarni and Sulbha Parasuraman, "Future implications of India's population growth", *IASSI Quarterly* 16(3&4), 1997, pp. 23–31.
15. As referred to by the people of Kucheipadar village (PSSP).
16. See also *Development induced displacement in Orissa, 1951 to 1955: A database on its extent and nature*, a report to the Indian Council of Social Science Research (New Delhi: Indian Social Institute, March 1997).
17. See http://www.ganesha.co.uk/articles.htm.

18. As stated to Pooja Kumar, my assistant, who went on a site visit in 1998.
19. Strømme Memorial Foundation, which is now called Strømme Foundation (SF), was established in 1976 to continue the influential work done by Pastor Strømme. The foundation is especially famous for its self-help charity programmes. In India, SF has been involved in supporting local partners (NGOs) in West Bengal, Bihar, and Andhra Pradesh targeting tribals, indigenous people, and marginalized groups. Orissa is one of the four geographical areas given special attention by NORAD (Norwegian Agency for Development), and is the most deprived. NORAD saw the advantage of a joint effort in the state of Orissa and encouraged SF to get involved with the local NGOs in the area. Until 1997, SF cooperated with nine local NGOs in Orissa, mainly in integrated community development efforts related to displacement issues. SF does not have any official partners in the Utkal area.

NORWATCH is a Norwegian NGO founded in the winter of 1995 to monitor the activities of Norwegian multinational enterprises both at home and abroad. It started its work on the Utkal Alumina project in 1995 and has been actively monitoring developments in the project since then. It has also spearheaded the movement to increase public awareness and interest in the project by publishing articles in its quarterly newsletters on Utkal. Together with Norwegian Church Aid (Kirkens Nødhjelp), it has been putting pressure on Norsk Hydro and the Norwegian government (which owns 51 per cent of Norsk Hydro) to take some remedial action to help the people of Kucheipadar.

14

Child labour in the Brazilian citrus sector: The case of Cargill's double effect

Cecilia Arruda

In 2002, Brazil's population was 176 million.[1] In 1995, the United Nations Children's Fund and the Fundação Instituto Brasileiro de Geografia e Estatística (UNICEF/IBGE) Indicators estimated that 3.8 million children were involved in child labour.[2] In 2001, analysis of the same study concluded that 1 million children and adolescents worked and did not go to school, while 4.4 million children and adolescents worked as well as going to school in Brazil.[3] The problem of children working and not being in school seems to be of serious proportions and the multinational companies, as well as large national companies, have always been in the spotlight.

The purpose of this chapter is to present a case where child labour is construed as a side-effect, and to look at how multinational companies can deal with it and what means can be deployed to minimize and eliminate it. The case-study of Cargill Incorporated will be presented as an example of a positive response. The case will then be analysed in light of the framework of the principle of double effect (PDE), evaluating the usefulness of and challenges to the principle.

Background

After the Uruguay and Marrakesh Rounds of the World Trade Organization, nations in Europe and North America raised the social dumping

245

issue in relation to specific markets. Brazil had assumed world leadership in the production of citrus, coal, fibres, shoes, and sugar, and protectionist polices emerged in competitor countries. Coincidently – perhaps for economic reasons – severe denunciations of child labour in these five sectors started appearing in national and international newspapers in 1995.

It is important to explain that Brazilian legislation uses the term "child" for young people under 12 years of age. "Adolescents" are persons aged between 12 and 17 years. Article 227 of the 1988 Federal Constitution states that family, society, and the state should, as a matter of the greatest priority, provide children and adolescents with the rights to life, health, adequate nutrition, education, leisure, professional skills, culture, dignity, respect, freedom, and community and family relationships, and protect them from all forms of negligence, discrimination, violence, cruelty, and oppression. The Article also states that the right to special protection must include respect for the minimum age to be hired for a job (14) and access to school for adolescent workers and others.[4] In 1998, Article 7 (section XXXIII) defined 16 as the minimum age for any kind of work, except for after-school tasks. It further rules out work that can be considered unsanitary, that demands hard effort, or that may be hazardous to the physical, mental, moral, and social development of any person under the age of 18. Nevertheless, the law allows a 14-year-old child to be accepted as an apprentice, as long as the above conditions are respected.[5] This change in the law occurred mostly as a result of the Brazilian government's signing of the International Labour Organization Convention.

Nowadays, business leaders in the citrus sector claim that there has never been child labour in São Paulo State, where the citrus export industry is mainly located. Business leaders felt seriously threatened by international boycotts, mainly from France and the United States, and decided to undertake several measures in order to ensure that they were not using child labour in their operations, and to demonstrate this to the world. At the same time, the unions vehemently denounced the existence of child labour in the citrus, coal, fibres, shoes, and sugar sectors. One of their leaders even stressed that "there are not only children, but an *army* of them".

Although the companies producing for export avoided the use of child labour in their own operations, only two-thirds of the Brazilian citrus farms were providing fruit for the international market. The child labour problem mostly arose on farms managed by agriculturalists interested in the domestic market, and dealing only in the unprocessed raw materials. But the media did not discriminate, and the campaign against child labour seriously affected the whole industry. Cargill Incorporated was then the only multinational company producing juice in Brazil, and it was one of the foremost companies in the citrus sector.

The Cargill corporation

Cargill Incorporated, a North American multinational company, began as a small grain elevator in Conover, Iowa, United States, in 1865. It now provides customer solutions in supply chain management, food applications, and commodities for health and nutrition, as a marketer, processor, and distributor of agricultural, food, financial, and industrial products and services with 97,000 employees in 59 countries.

The organization's "Vision Statement" indicates that Cargill's mission is to create value for its customers, suppliers, employees, shareholders, and neighbours. It also states that the company's performance measures consist of engaged employees, satisfied customers, enrichment of communities, and profitable growth.

Cargill claims to have a strong commitment to sound environmental, health, and safety management and to apply the same high standards of conduct at every Cargill location worldwide. Environmental, health, and safety management is one instance of the company's attitude to public responsibility. The way Cargill says it fulfils this mission is by respecting its neighbours in the communities in which it operates, by protecting and conserving resources such as air and water quality, by participating in land preservation, and by protecting the health and safety of its employees and neighbours. According to Cargill, this public responsibility extends beyond running a safe and environmentally sound plant. It also includes helping to build stronger communities wherever the company is present.

With regard to health and safety, the company's employees are apparently considered to be the most important stakeholders:

Cargill's safety record continues to show strong and sustained improvement around the globe. Cargill's worldwide safety index dropped to a record low of 2.4 in 2001. Cargill's safety index is a device that the company uses to measure the frequency and severity of job-related injuries and illnesses in a company that is rapidly expanding both the number of business units and employees.[6]

Cargill in the Brazilian citrus sector

Cargill Agrícola S.A. was formed in Brazil in 1965, the year of the company's one hundredth anniversary. It began operating in the citrus sector in 1976, attracted by the low costs and consequently high profit margins of the export-oriented juice industry. Cargill entered the Brazilian market with its acquisition of Citrobrasil, a traditional national company that had a plant in the city of Bebedouro in São Paulo State (SP).

Before 1960, the Brazilian citrus sector was oriented towards the national market. Both small and large companies were already processing oranges, and concentrated juice was exported from 1961 to 1962. Suconasa, a subsidiary of North American Toddy, was the first juice plant in the country. José Cutrale, a Brazilian orange trader and exporter, bought it in 1967 and founded what is now one of the largest companies in the sector. Foreign capital had some impact for a few companies, but the sector was mainly in Brazilian hands and control.

In the early 1970s, the military government offered several incentives to both national and transnational investors to provide capital for specific industries, including citriculture. Citrus fruit production in the Brazilian north-eastern states, such as Sergipe, where child labour still is an extremely serious issue, was oriented to supplying the domestic market with unprocessed fruit.

In 1980, Cargill was the only multinational company in the citrus sector in Brazil and, along with 10 local firms, was operating 13 productive plants with 512 extractors. As international trade became favourable for Brazilian products – either *in natura* or in the form of juice – orange production increased by 57 per cent, which required new acquisitions. A pool of 28 large citrus cultivators was created and they began renting machines from the largest companies – mostly from Cargill – for processing the fruit. The French Dreyfus group bought one of the national firms in 1988. By 1990 the citrus sector had 11 companies in operation, with 17 plants and 817 extractors; it was completely dominated by the multinational Cargill and two local companies, Cutrale and Citrosuco, all located in São Paulo State.

Abecitrus – Brazilian Association for Citrus Exporters

In 1985, dissatisfied with excessive governmental interference in the industry, Cargill and three other companies – Citrosuco, Bascitrus, and Citropectina – created the Associação Nacional das Indústrias Cítricas. Concerned with the debate about international trade, tariff and non-tariff barriers, and the processes of regional integration, the Associação Brasileira dos Exportadores de Cítricos (Abecitrus) was founded in 1988 with the purpose of lobbying, influencing specific legislation, and managing the international reputation of Brazilian products.

It was not just business leaders who found these times difficult. Strikes took place at different stages of the production process. Workers' move-

ments indicated a need for better wages, the end of intermediation between planters and processors, and better labour conditions, including
formal contracts for rural workers. Most rural workers were temporarily
hired during the harvest, with no assured social rights. The unions were
not strong, because the market was growing and a dissatisfied worker
could easily and swiftly be replaced by another.[7]

Encouraged by the positive international prospects of the previous
decade, in the early 1990s new companies and plants entered the citrus
business, with the financial support of strong national bankers. In 1993,
Cargill, Citrosuco and Cutrale were the largest companies in the market.
The French Dreyfus group joined them after buying a national firm. In
1994, Cargill employed 3,136 pickers; Coinbra-Frutesp, 6,895; Citrosuco,
12,727; and Cutrale, 13,337. These were the four giants of the citrus sector in the 1990s.[8]

Labour relations in citrus fruit cultivation

As the industry sector was consolidating, informal labour relations in
citrus cultivation were affected by the restructuring of production and
organization in the Brazilian-based companies. In the 1990s, Cargill and
five other citrus giants started to outsource activities such as administration, maintenance, safety, legal consultancy, accounting, and computer
systems. The outsourcing process seriously affected the citrus sector, both
positively and negatively:
- reduction in the cost of services
- better quality of the final product
- flexibility to make quick administrative decisions
- modernization of suppliers' machines and equipment
- less bureaucracy related to administrative and productive processes
- more adaptability as a result of lower fixed costs
- stable economies of scale
- fewer workers directly employed in the productive structure
- reduction in payroll taxes and security costs
- increased tension between unions
- reduction in the number of workers associated with unions.[9]

Besides administrative support, the outsourcing process was also extended to agricultural activities. Before the 1990s, companies were legally
responsible for all phases of citrus production. During the 1990s, the operations of orange picking and transportation were transferred to the
citrus cultivators. The executives of the companies defended this on the
grounds that their business was directed not to development of those activities but to the final product: the orange juice. Thus the farmers and
producers would be completely in charge of citrus cultivation, taking re-

sponsibility for the financial and managerial costs, orange picking, and transportation.[10]

Fundecitrus – research for world-class citrus fruit

In 1992, focused on the quality of the final product, Cargill, Citrosuco, and Cutrale founded the Fundação para o Desenvolvimento da Citricultura no Brasil (Procitrus), which aimed to develop research for the citrus sector. In 1995, Procitrus was absorbed by the Fundo de Defesa da Citricultura (Fundecitrus), a research-oriented scientific institution, which is dedicated to promoting the monitoring of pests and diseases, to conducting inspections of citrus plants, and to engaging in and financing serious scientific and technological research. Founded in 1977, Fundecitrus participated in the growth of the world's largest citrus complex, now located in around 430 municipalities within São Paulo State. Fundecitrus's outstanding achievements have been internationally recognized. Its reputation among producers is also remarkable.[11]

Broadening the market

Since 1997, Cargill has operated two processing plants in São Paulo State (in the cities of Bebedouro and Uchoa). Its competitors are supported by strong Brazilian economic groups. Despite the increasing importance of pasteurized juice in the Brazilian domestic market, the parallel agribusiness was developed by only three companies operating in São Paulo State: Cargill, Citrovita, and CTM-Citrus. They decided to enter the consumer market through joint ventures with companies already consolidated in Brazil: Cargill with Nestlé, Citrovita with Danone, and CTM-Citrus with Santista.

The Brazilian domestic market for ready-to-drink orange juice increased owing to its practicality, an important attribute in the largest urban centres. On the other hand, the price is high for most domestic consumers. In São Paulo, a litre of ready-to-drink orange juice costs around US$1.00, whereas a 5 kg pack of oranges costs US$1.21. The living standard of most Brazilians still does not allow regular consumption of ready-made juice. The way to make brands succeed in the Brazilian market would be to market them adequately through good differentiation. Most of the citrus agribusinesses opted to keep their strategic alliances with companies already consolidated in the ready-to-drink juice consumer market.

In 2002, export-oriented agribusinesses decided to invest in better storage, transportation, and distribution of their products in the importing countries. Cargill, Citrosuco, Coinbra-Frutesp, and other large companies developed their own warehouses in Santos (SP) port, the best one for this purpose in Brazil. They also provided ships and private terminals specifically for export activities. Cargill ended 2002 with four farms for orange production (three in Minas Gerais and one in São Paulo State), one dedicated terminal for exporting frozen concentrated orange juice in Santos (SP), trucks, and a ship of its own for the transportation of orange juice in bulk. Besides this infrastructure in Brazil, Cargill has its own terminals in Amsterdam (The Netherlands), New Jersey (United States), and Kashima (Japan) for its citrus business.[12]

The export agribusinesses also decided to work more closely with consumers in the importing countries. Cargill led this development, buying a Procter & Gamble plant in Frostproof, Florida (United States) in 1993, for processing and blending fruit juices. Other Brazilian companies soon followed Cargill. This strategy helped companies to minimize the effects of the US government's protectionism, which aimed to move Brazilian producers away from this market.[13]

In 2002, Cargill was still one of the largest companies in the citrus industry in Brazil, processing oranges and producing frozen concentrated orange juice, whole orange juice, and citrus pulp pellets for both domestic and foreign markets in Europe, Japan, and the United States. The company also produces the juice brand "Yes", in orange, tangerine, and Swiss lemonade flavours, which is sold through supermarkets and fast-food chains.

Social issues and child labour in the citrus sector

Increasing competition between producers in Brazil put a lot of pressure on agriculturalists, such as the production costs of crops and transportation, management, and phytosanitary treatment. At the same time, international prices have fallen, and protectionism and competition from other countries have increased. Cost reduction thus became vitally important for citrus cultivators. Because increasing investments in inputs and machinery were unavoidable, the cost reduction effort was concentrated on labour.

Farmers and producers opted to make labour conditions precarious: workers were hired with no rights, benefits, or security. Although this reduced costs for the companies, workers experienced an increasing lack of safety and a significant decrease in direct and indirect wages. Because of the weakness of labour relations in the citrus sector, as well as in the whole agriculture sector in Brazil, the second half of the 1990s was characterized by the spread of labour cooperatives.

The cooperatives functioned as intermediaries between farmers and producers, so the workers were not employees legally connected to one particular farm or company. They were paid by the cooperative, according to production, on an autonomous basis. A Brazilian law of 1971 – still in effect in 2002 – established that workers had no legal bonds with the cooperative of which they were members. Thus workers in the citrus sector – as in the whole agriculture sector in Brazil – were not entitled to all the mandatory benefits assured by law to workers hired on legal contracts, such as holidays, bonuses, allowances, insurance, and security.

By 1996, as citriculture faced a global demand crisis, the sector in Brazil depended on about 50,000 workers associated with fewer than 30 cooperatives. Fruit pickers in particular were suffering cuts in wage rates and harsh forms of labour started to appear.[14] In 1997, a Brazilian magazine published a series of articles denouncing child labour in citriculture: 15 per cent of the workers were younger than 14, the minimum age allowed for workers in Brazil.[15] The news shocked international public opinion. Several European countries and the United States put pressure on business and government leaders, and threatened to boycott Brazilian orange juice for this reason.

Defining child labour

The child labour phenomenon is discussed here in terms of the definition of the International Labour Organization (ILO) and the International Programme on the Elimination of Child Labour.[16] Child labour refers to work that is:

- mentally, physically or morally dangerous and harmful to children; and
- interferes in their schooling:
  by depriving them of the opportunity to attend school;
  by obliging them to leave school prematurely; or
  by requiring them to attempt to combine school attendance with excessively long and heavy work.

Two kinds of child labour were found in orange picking. In the first type, the children were paid for the work done. Such cases typically involved tasks that would be difficult even for adults, such as picking oranges at the top of tall trees or gathering fruit dropped by the pickers. Although the child was paid for the work done, often this payment was very small. The second kind of child labour consisted of children helping their parents by picking the most difficult fruits or picking up oranges on the ground, cleaning, or hoeing. In these cases, the children were not paid. Their labour was incorporated in the parents' payment, which meant that the child helped to increase productivity without being compensated.[17]

Eliminating child labour in the São Paulo citrus sector

In June 1996, in Araraquara, São Paulo State, Abecitrus, with the active participation of the ILO, UNICEF, the Abrinq Foundation for Children's Rights, and the Municipal Council for the Rights of Children and Adolescents of Araraquara (Comcriar), sponsored a seminar on "A child's place is in school" as part of its efforts to end the use of child labour. The seminar ended with the Pact of Araraquara,[18] which set out the priorities for this partnership between the private sector and the community:

The Pact of Araraquara

The Public Commitment
ABECITRUS, The Brazilian Association of Citrus Exporters, an entity which congregates processors of frozen concentrate orange juice in the State of São Paulo, considering the purpose of collaborating with the Government of the State of São Paulo and with Abrinq Foundation for Children's Rights, in its campaign for the eradication of children's work in farming activities, as well as to foster school attendance of these children and adolescents under 14 years of age, takes upon itself the engagement:
1. To recommend to its members to demand from their suppliers and other components of the production loop the elimination of any type of children's work.
2. To foster actions which benefit the attendance of children at school.
3. To collaborate in the development of actions which promote the professional qualification of adolescents aiming at their integration in the formal labour market.
4. To recommend to its members to direct the donations foreseen in the Statute of Children and Adolescents and in the Income Tax Legislation, so as to help in the attainment of the objectives of the present engagement.
5. To support the initiatives of the State Government, Municipalities and non-governmental organizations for joint participation in the actions foreseen in this engagement.
6. Finally, to collaborate in the development of campaigns aiming at fostering the awareness of the importance of access and attendance of the Brazilian children at school.[19]

Abecitrus made another pledge: to guarantee funds equivalent to 1 per cent of all income tax contributed by the orange juice industries to be invested in specific programmes for the benefit of children and adolescents between the ages of 7 and 14.

The Pact also established that the organizations and entities directly involved would coordinate their efforts with action taken by the federal, state, and city governments, as well as the citrus sector and the community as a whole, to put an end to the use of children as workers and to guarantee the protection of labour rights for adolescents in their respective cities. Abecitrus pledged to take further action through regular meetings of the Municipal Councils for the Rights of Children and Adolescents of Araraquara.[20] This action would involve promoting formal education on the part of the school community, and urging the local and regional media to publicize all public awareness campaigns aimed at combating the use of children as workers. The Abrinq Foundation created a "Child Friendly Company" programme. Abecitrus created the Child Labour Group, supported seminars to strengthen the councils for rights in citrus-producing regions, and provided facilities for complementary educational activities.[21]

According to Ademerval Garcia, president of Abecitrus:

Child work is a stain that has to be removed from society. Its eradication, although having a strong emotional component, is a rational step, which requires a deep understanding of the problem as well as the political determination to solve it.... These projects are a public and concrete renewal of our determination to eradicate children's work, providing better conditions for the formation and education of our children.[22]

Despite its primary purpose of scientifically supporting citrus growers and the citrus industry, Fundecitrus was one of the first institutions to cooperate in the eradication of child labour in the citrus sector of São Paulo State. The Instituto de Economia Agrícola, part of the Agriculture Department of the São Paulo State government, developed a research project that came up with interesting findings on child labour in the sector. One finding was that children seemed to go to the fields with their parents not for economic reasons but because they had nowhere else to go during the workday. Schools were not flexible enough to allow children to attend classes and also to go to the orchards. Besides, the teaching quality of the schools was so poor that children had no motivation to attend. Being with the family appeared to be more appealing to them. Furthermore, the parents (orange pickers) were concerned about their children being on the streets after class – exposed to violence, drugs, and prostitution.

Supplementary Education Centers

Based on these findings, Fundecitrus became involved in creating two Supplementary Education Centers (SEC-Fundecitrus) in São Paulo State. The first SEC was opened in Araraquara (SP) in 1997. It was based on alternating schedules to make sure that the 200 students were not missing regular school. Following the same concept, another SEC was opened in Itápolis (SP) in 1999. The creation of both SECs resulted from a partnership with the respective city mayor's office and the fruit juice industry. In 2002, the SECs served more than 600 children aged 7–14 years.

The SEC activities are meant to stimulate children's creativity and interest in knowledge, art, and leisure. Providing supplementary education, the SECs prevent school evasion, stress the students' performance, and enrich their regular school subjects with other educational activities. Children attend workshops on drama, music and singing, recreation and games, computers, and schoolwork. The only formal requirement for participating in SEC activities is that the child is enrolled in and attends a public school.

As programme partners in Araraquara, the public authorities assumed responsibility for hiring employees and offering school meals, while businesses such as Cargill (a multinational) and Bascitrus, Citrosuco, Citrovita, Coinbra-Frutesp, and Cutrale (local companies) equipped the rooms for the workshops. In Itápolis, Fundecitrus built the educational centre and Cutrale (a Brazilian firm) was responsible for equipping the workshops. Each SEC's administration relies on a managing council whose members are representatives of Fundecitrus, the City Hall, and the children's parents. This initiative by Fundecitrus was acknowledged by the ILO and UNICEF and won Fundecitrus a "Child Award 1999", along with three other organizations.[23]

Fundecitrus's SEC project encouraged the citrus sector to create several projects, which supported more than 38,000 children and teenagers within São Paulo State in 2002.[24]

The Cargill Foundation

Responding to the Araraquara Pact, the Cargill Foundation launched the "Goes to School" initiative in Brazil, an educational programme that started when Brazilian children went back to school at the beginning of the 1997 school year (February). The basis of the programme was the distribution of a backpack with a basic kit of school materials – notebook, pen, ruler, pencil, and eraser – for children in the first grade in the poorest school areas. More than 14,000 children received the kit, which was distributed with the help of managers of participating units, as well as the municipal authorities. The simplicity of the gift offered by Cargill did not diminish its importance: in many Brazilian cities families are so poor that they cannot send their children to school because they cannot afford to buy even a notebook.

The Cargill Foundation had already achieved good results with a similar scheme a few years earlier. In 1994 it established the "Climb for Literacy" project, which was undertaken by every one of its units round the world, to cooperate in eradicating illiteracy. The project involved raising money from the company's employees for the purchase and distribution of school materials. The results were extremely positive; in Brazil the company distributed 12,000 kits in 1994.[25]

Now Cargill is developing the "Fura Bolo" project, aiming to help 30,000 children in 11 cities. Children enrolled in grades 1–4 receive special assistance to learn Portuguese and mathematics in an entertaining way, through complementary books that take them from reasoning to creativity. The books were created by high-quality Brazilian professionals. In an interesting social approach, the project involved 146 Cargill employees as volunteers. As well as guaranteeing its success, they take part in the teachers' programme with the support and guidance of the authors of the books. The children are encouraged to express their opinion, using stories and legends, puns and rhymes.[26]

The Cargill case and the PDE framework

The PDE, which has been studied in depth in the context of business purposes in previous chapters of this volume, assumes that negative side-effects do occur, even when businesses pursue legitimate objectives by legitimate means.

Cargill started its citrus juice business in Brazil when international demand for the product indicated a profitable opportunity already explored by national companies. The objectives could be considered legitimate and moral: producing a good product, creating jobs, paying taxes. The results seemed legitimate: supporting existing demand for citrus fruit juice with profitable margins, job creation, and economic development. Because child labour was not found at this end of the production chain, the means were apparently legitimate and legal: juice production was highly automated and required trained specialized professionals. Cargill was complying with the laws.

Nevertheless, children were working on the farms where the citrus fruit trees were growing. And although these farms were run mostly by other owners, many of these farmers were Cargill's suppliers and were important links in the citrus fruit juice production chain. A negative side-effect then arose for Cargill from its operating in the country and being involved in the production chain: the low cost of its business was partly a consequence of child labour, mostly in fruit picking. The children's activity raised their parents' productivity, the basis for payment. Although

Cargill itself was deploying legitimate means in its operations, it bene-fited, through lower production costs, from the child labour used as means by its suppliers. Ignoring the indirect or direct child labour in-volvement in the juice business would mean connivance or complicity in the wrongdoing of suppliers. Cargill was therefore under a duty to mini-mize or counteract this negative side-effect.

The negative side-effect of child labour in the production chain cannot be justified as proportionate to the legitimate objective. Even if the chil-dren were only picking up fruit from the ground, they were exposed to circumstances that are not recommended for their age. Perhaps most im-portantly, they were not attending school during the period they were working, and their education was thus jeopardized. Both effects harm the children and are not in compliance with Brazilian laws.

Minimizing side-effect harm

According to Fundecitrus, surveys show that the main reason for children joining the labour force is the lack of a place to go and an occupation to keep them busy while they are not in school. Classes in public schools in Brazil last for no more than four hours a day, and the syllabuses are planned for nine months of the year. Someone has to look after the chil-dren for the rest of the day and during the school holidays. Parents worry more about their children being on the streets than about their salary. Fundecitrus is joining forces with city governments in an effort to reduce the number of children in the labour force and to keep them off the streets. The SECs maintained by Fundecitrus aim to improve the quality of life of children of school age.[27]

Before international non-governmental organizations (NGOs) and journalists raised the issue of child labour in citrus fruit production in the São Paulo region, Cargill had already invested in social action focusing on children living in that area. The national companies, Cargill's com-petitors, apparently had not started any specific social programmes aimed at children and their parents.

Cargill, supporting the Pact of Araraquara, presented a good example of how the stakeholders in the juice production sector could get involved in initiatives to minimize child labour. Once negative side-effects were identified, many institutions were motivated to eliminate them and soon agreed to sign the "Public Commitment". Abecitrus, Abrinq, and the São Paulo State government mobilized society, and both institutional and voluntary work built a solution for the problem.

Together with other large national juice producers and other stake-holders, Cargill took active measures to prevent and minimize the negative side-effects of its indirect involvement in child labour. These initiatives were collaborative in order to transform the means used by suppliers, aiming to make them legitimate, moral, and legal.

Although competition increased in the citrus fruit juice market, the elimination of child labour did not cause another side-effect. On the contrary, the case-study perfectly illustrates how reasoning along PDE lines served perfectly as a tool to overcome the dilemma. Other products were launched and labour payments were increased, as the government established minimum wages for workers. The circumstances were favourable: with lower productivity, children's cooperation was not necessary to cope with the demand.

Even if the large companies producing orange juice are not involved with monitoring the suppliers, their initiatives – individually or in groups – reveal a deep commitment to the cause. Fundecitrus offers technical monitoring of farmers and workers dealing with citriculture. It is not the monitors' responsibility to verify the existence of child labour on the farms, but if they notice such cases they respond by suggesting that the child goes to school or – if older than 14 – becomes an apprentice. As for the government, its attorneys are very active. They keep a close eye on the farms, to make sure that children are not working.

Remaining side-effect harm

The Brazilian legislation allows children aged 14–18 years to work part time as apprentices, as long as they attend regular school. When these adolescents are hired in the citriculture sector, the farmers offer them special professional education as apprentices. Fundecitrus's trainers are aware of their situation and watch over them carefully.

There are no initiatives from either the government or producers to provide adequate schooling and business practice for children in the 14–18 age group as apprentices rather than workers. The lack of schools and teachers is a limitation of the Brazilian public education system for students in this age group. In this case, if working conditions are harmful (the law is very explicit in this sense), child labour is illegal and illegitimate. Considering the criterion of proportionality, young pickers may be more protected working with the family than if they stayed on the streets. Of course their tasks ought to be healthy, avoiding hard work that might be hazardous to their physical, mental, moral, and social development.

Business leaders are aware of the government's incapability of solving educational problems in the short term. In the Brazilian sociocultural context, partnerships between business, government, and society have increased through the joint effort to act constructively. Many NGOs have set up important projects targeting children aged 14–18 years. Activities related to arts in general, sports, information technology, and a broad variety of initiatives have brought together volunteer citizens, government agents, and companies' human and financial resources in an attempt to counteract this specific problem in São Paulo.

When discussing the Brazilian citrus sector, it was mentioned that child labour still occurs in citriculture in the north-east of Brazil. In this case, the negative side-effects might possibly be justified as proportionate to the legitimate objectives of the local producers. Extreme poverty in the area means that children's labour is essential to assure the family's survival – in contrast to the situation in São Paulo State. The large citrus fruit producers have decided not to operate in this particular area, in order to avoid what seems to be persistent and inescapable side-effect harm.

Conclusions

The Cargill case-study posed a challenge to the PDE framework because it required a precise definition of what are illegitimate means to a legitimate objective and what are harmful side-effects of the pursuit. However, the PDE turns out to function very well in terms of addressing the mixed responsibilities involved in the case. Being used as a means by suppliers, the side-effect harm of the producers' involvement in child labour also served as a means for the producers. The companies benefited from child labour by allowing it in the production chain for over 20 years.

It is important to note that responsibility for remedying the situation was first recognized as a result of social pressure. Although Cargill had already invested in children's education, the effort to eradicate child labour started when citrus fruit juice exports were threatened (in 1995). The 20-year period of complicity was not only in the suppliers' activities, but also in terms of benefiting from weak government, because the Brazilian government does not strongly enforce compliance with labour legislation.

Eventually, however, child labour seems to have been eradicated in the citrus sector in São Paulo both as a means (on the part of suppliers) and consequently as a negative side-effect (on the part of producers) through producers' active measures to rectify the negative side-effects and thereby influence the use of illegitimate means. The Brazilian share in the international market is assured and the companies responsible for the products are now widely recognized.

Cargill and other companies in the Brazilian citrus sector associated with Abecitrus and Fundecitrus have received the "Child Friendly Company" seal of approval as confirmation that they do not exploit child labour, that they engage suppliers and clients in their campaign, and that they promote social action that improves school-age children's quality of life. In the course of eliminating a negative side-effect (child labour), Cargill and the other companies produced a positive side-effect: an improvement in children's education and quality of life.

Cargill's mission statement assumes that the long-term goals of creating value to clients, employees, stockholders, and neighbours are the company's responsibility. Insofar as the production of juices totally depends on the suppliers' agricultural activities, it would be correct to include all participants in the productive chain in the group of neighbours.

Notes

1. CIA, *The World Factbook 2002 – Brazil*, http://www.cia.gov/cia/publications/factbook/geos/br.html (accessed 6 April 2003).
2. *Indicadores sobre Crianças e Adolescentes – Brasil: 1990–1999* (Rio de Janeiro: UNICEF-IBGE, 2001).
3. Ibid.
4. *Constituição da República Federativa do Brasil – 1988*. Article 227 defines 14 years of age as the minimum for work.
5. *Emenda Constitucional*, Article 20, 1998.
6. Cargill website: http://www.cargill.com (accessed 18 January 2003).
7. Marcelo Paixão, *Relatório Laranja: uma radiografia da citricultura brasileira por suas firmas e atores* (Rio de Janeiro: FASE – Federação de Órgãos para a Assistência Social e Educacional, 1999), pp. 4–13.
8. Ibid., p. 113.
9. Luiz Paulillo, "O avanço do setor de serviços nos complexos agroindustriais: a terceirizaç o agroindustrial e as cooperativas de mão-de-obra na citricultura", *Informações Econômicas* (SP), 26(9), 1996, pp. 47–48.
10. Ademerval Garcia, "Nova análise da citricultura nos anos noventa", *Laranja* (Cordeirópolis), 14(1), 1993, pp. 1–30.
11. *Fundecitrus Management Report 1995–2002* (Araraquara: Fundecitrus, 2002), pp. 5, 11.
12. Paixão, *Relatório Laranja*, pp. 20–21.
13. Ibid., p. 61.
14. Ibid., p. 60.
15. J. Cedroni and J. Ripper, "Nossas crianças: sucata do progresso", *Atenção!* 1(1), 1995–1996, pp. 15–16.
16. International Labour Organization and International Programme on the Elimination of Child Labour, *Brazil. Child and adolescent domestic work in selected years from 1992 to 1999: A national report* (Geneva: ILO, January 2003).
17. Paixão, *Relatório Laranja*, p. 46.
18. Signed in São Paulo, 28 May 1996, by Ademerval Garcia (president of Abecitrus); Antonio Funari (Regional Labor Delegate); Jair Grava (Unicef's representative); Lucia Vania Abraão Costa (National Secretary for Social Assistance – Ministry of Social Welfare); Mauro Alves da Silva (Secretary General of the Farm Workers' Federation – São Paulo State Department of Agriculture); Oded Grajew (president of Abrinq Foundation for Children's Rights); Osório de Almeida N. Costa (president of the Brazilian

Association of Citrus Growers); Sonia Levi (ILO's representative); Vicente Paulo da Silva (Executive Secretary of the National Forum for the Prevention and Eradication of Child Labour).

19. Abecitrus website: http://www.ABECitrus.com.br (accessed 6 April 2004).

20. Abecitrus website: http://www.ABECitrus.com.br/semius.html.

21. Benedito Rodrigues dos Santos, *Mobilizing corporations to eradicate child labour in Brazil: A study of strategies developed by the Abrinq Foundation for Children's Rights* (São Paulo: UNICEF, 1996), p. 52.

22. Abecitrus website: http://www.ABECitrus.com.br/socialus.html (accessed 6 April 2004).

23. *Fundecitrus Management Report 1995–2002*, pp. 39–41.

24. Ibid., p. 41.

25. Abecitrus website: http://www.ABECitrus.com.br (accessed 6 April 2004).

26. "It is amusing to learn: Cargill creates project that helps 30,000 children", *Revista do Fundecitrus*, 14(100), 2000, p. 5.

27. Fundecitrus website: http://www.fundecitrus.com.br/socialus.html (accessed 6 April 2004).

15

A commentary on the principle of double effect

Chris Marsden

The principle of double effect (PDE) is a pragmatist's charter based on broadly utilitarian principles. From the perspective of a business and those trying to help it address the adverse impacts on society of its operations, it seems to offer a practical, if thought-provoking, decision-making tool. From a human rights perspective, however, it gets dangerously close to providing any individual or institution that violates human rights with a legitimate process for claiming that those violations were necessary to achieve a higher and legitimate goal, in other words, to serve the common good. Nevertheless, decisions in favour of the common good do have to be made and these will often be to the immediate disadvantage of individuals and minority groups. The legitimacy of such decisions depends on the transparency and inclusiveness of the decision-making process and an insistence on the fundamental rights of those affected (based on the Universal Declaration of Human Rights) being upheld and any negative consequences fully negotiated and compensated. This is particularly the case with the "negative side-effects can be justified as proportionate" clause. This could be seen as an invitation to any would-be human rights violators to justify their actions on the grounds that they were acting in their view of the common interest. It needs to be made very clear that, unless an individual or organization makes every effort to understand and mitigate the consequences of their actions in circumstances where those actions will in all likelihood lead to violations, then those actions are not legitimate. This suggests that an additional clause needs to be added to the PDE decision-making process:

Fundamental human rights are upheld at all times and all negative side-effects are fully negotiated on an equal power basis and fully compensated.

Decisions about the common good and its governance are at the heart of politics because they require difficult choices about the relative welfare of different groups within a society or indeed between societies. Traditionally such decisions are the preserve of governments, but increasingly they are being made, whether or not by design or with competence, by multinational companies. How well or badly we determine the processes whereby these choices are made – or by default not made – will be crucial to the future of humankind and its sustainable development. Many now argue that there is an increasing governance deficit in the world. Not only are there many zones of weak governance, for instance in most of Central and Southern Africa, but, even in traditionally well-governed countries, governments are constrained by the demands of global competitiveness to limit the regulation of business externalities and taxation and redistribution policies for the common good. The global economy itself, with its disregard for national borders, is weakly governed by international agencies, often unable to reach consensus, and dominated by the interests of the rich and powerful. This has placed a greater onus on other global actors, especially multinational companies and non-governmental organizations (NGOs), to help mitigate the governance deficit.

Leading multinational companies are increasingly being expected, whether they like it or not, to participate in governance processes. It might be a life sciences company experimenting with new biotechnology; a consumer goods or retail company sourcing from countries with labour practices that abuse human rights; a financial services company determining its ethical investment strategy; a pharmaceutical company being challenged to provide generic drugs at marginal cost to poor countries; a construction company facing local resettlement issues over a dam project; a utilities company concerned with making its services available to the poorest sections of society; a tourism company selling package tours to areas of environmental sensitivity; or an oil or mining company arranging security for its operations in an area of civil conflict. It might be a company policy decision to sign up for a code of practice that it will use to put pressure on rogue host governments, to publish all its revenue and tax payments made to host governments in order to promote transparency, or not to make or take bribes. It might even be a decision by a company operating in a country where known human rights abuses are taking place to close its eyes, keep its head down, and, in effect, tacitly support the status quo.

How do companies go about making decisions of this kind, operating as they do in a market that demands maximum shareholder value? Most companies and business managers require a "business case" to justify taking on what the market will see as extra costs. The business case for any decision that entails externality costs is that these costs can be shown to be compensated for by increased sales, a licence to operate, goodwill, access to capital, or efficiency in production. If this were always clear and positive there would be no problem. As the business case is explored more deeply, however, hard dilemmas will arise and choices between commercial advantage and a less adverse social impact (i.e. non win–win) will have to be made. That is when decisions are needed on the basis of what is right and wrong and what may be best for a wider range of stakeholders than companies are traditionally used to taking into consideration. This is why it is particularly helpful for a company to have a previously agreed set of principles regarding its purpose and behaviour standards and clear guidance for managers on decision-making processes. The decision-making process arising from the principle of double effect (with the suggested additional clause) provides a very clear way of identifying the choices that will have to be made. It also provides the prospect of a common basis on which the outcomes of such decisions can be judged. If this can be achieved, business decision-making in this way could become more the norm and therefore create a "business case" for doing it and a business disadvantage for not doing it. Promoting such a virtuous circle could be the best strategy for government agencies, NGOs, and socially responsible investment firms trying to harness the contribution of multinationals as a positive force in sustainable development.

Take, for example, a company's performance on human rights. To start with, it is vital that the senior management are aware of their company's impact on human rights and understand their company's responsibility under the Universal Declaration of Human Rights to do all it can to secure the observance of the rights contained within it. Types and levels of impact will vary according to company and sector, but in *Human Rights: Is it any of your business?* Amnesty International spells out very clearly its expectations of companies in this respect.[1] First, companies must ensure that their core operations are compliant with all relevant human rights, such as those contained within the seven core conventions of the International Labour Organization and the principles regarding the use of security forces. Secondly, they must do all they can to ensure that their business partners, contractors, and suppliers apply commensurate standards. Thirdly, stakeholders in host communities must be fully engaged in all stages of project impact analysis, planning, and implementation. Fourthly, in countries where there is known, often officially sanctioned, human rights abuse, companies must assert their own human rights standards and do all they can to press the government and its officials to improve their performance.

A company should have a policy on human rights based on upholding the Universal Declaration of Human Rights, but that does not mean that it should immediately try to implement all 29 clauses throughout its operations. Pragmatism dictates that priorities must be set and materiality considered. Some rights, such as the right to life, freedom from torture and inhumane treatment, and freedom of thought, are sacrosanct. Others, such as freedom of association and equal opportunities, may in some locations require longer-term but nevertheless deliberate planning. Others, particularly those associated with national issues such as participation in government, the right to education, and social security, may be left for later discussion with public authorities at an appropriate stage. What is crucial, however, is that managers, particularly those operating in zones of weak governance, understand their company's policy and how to apply it. The principle of double effect applied to the business context is a potentially effective process for doing this.

Ensuring that the proposed business action is legitimate in both means and ends should be axiomatic. What follows is the real test. Many companies now carry out pre-investment risk and impact analyses, including some stakeholder consultation, but these are mainly designed to discover the main problems associated with a project so that the company can work out how best to overcome them. They are rarely comprehensive in terms of social impact and, if the financial prospect is good, the presumption is usually that the project will go ahead. The PDE provides a much more rigorous process requiring thorough and ongoing stakeholder consultation and judgements, which are open to public scrutiny, about negative side-effects being proportionate and kept to a minimum (and respecting human rights). The PDE process does not negate the difficulty of decision-making on the ground, however; it simply helps managers understand better the nature of the decisions they have to make. For example, signature bonuses paid by oil companies to the Angolan government were legitimate but, given their use in fomenting the civil war, were they moral? Was the negative side-effect proportionate? Who should decide? This issue has given impetus to the "publish what you pay" campaign, which calls for more transparency of all company payments to governments, so that more pressure can be applied to ensure proper use of government revenues and to combat corruption. It also highlights the importance of the suggestion by Deon Rossouw for a final PDE clause that negative side-effects caused by operating under regimes that abuse human rights oblige companies to exert pressure on such regimes to improve their human rights performance. Amnesty International would consider a company operating under such conditions to be complicit in the human rights abuses unless it could demonstrate that it was taking active steps to bring pressure to bear on the government and its officers.

An example: BP in Columbia

As an example of how this might work, let us examine the case of BP in Colombia in 1996/97.[2] BP, one of the world's largest and most successful integrated oil companies, had discovered large reserves of oil in the Casanare region of Colombia. This was going to bring significant revenue to the Colombian government, which granted BP the licence to develop these oil fields in a joint venture partnership with the state oil company Ecopetrol (50 per cent), Total, and Triton. Casanare is some 250 miles east of Bogotá, in the foothills of the Andes. Before the oil development, it had been a sparsely populated agricultural area, cut off from government interest and the rapidly developing urban areas of Colombia. Since 1994 this has all changed. Previously small villages such as Yopal and Tauramena rapidly became boom towns, with all the associated problems of rapid development such as inadequate governance, poor infrastructure, and prostitution. Many people in the area benefited from the direct and indirect income flows from the oil-field development and, increasingly, from the region's share of the oil revenues. Many other people, however, lost out or had their overinflated expectations dashed. These people include some of the original peasant farmers as well as incoming fortune seekers. Expectations on BP to provide social support services and act in a quasi-governmental role in the region were very high.

BP employed some 1,000 local people from Casanare directly and nearly 4,000 indirectly as contract workers. The company spent US$10 million a year on social programmes, such as small business development, health education, and local infrastructure, as well as spending a lot of time working to strengthen local citizen groups in managing the oil revenues effectively. A further US$30 million was spent on environmental protection, in addition to its public commitment to comply with not only the Colombian government's environmental legislation but also the company's own global standards.

Colombia had long been plagued by a civil war, and armed opposition groups immediately targeted the oil industry as a military objective, kidnapping and killing people associated with it and regularly blowing up pipelines. Meanwhile, paramilitary organizations with a variety of different affiliations, which were illegal but allegedly often used by the Colombian army to carry out its more brutal counter-terrorist measures, were also murdering local people at will if they were suspected of collaboration with the opposition groups. In order to defend its people and assets, BP's operational and domestic areas for non-local workers were surrounded by barbed wire and guarded by the Colombian military.

Until the latter part of 1996, BP considered that it was doing a good job in very difficult circumstances. First construction and then production were more or less on target. Despite the problems of security and complaints from those in the Casanare community, whose expectations were not being met as fast as they would wish, BP felt that it was doing all it reasonably could to balance the requirement of extracting up to 500,000 barrels of oil a day with local environmental and social considerations. The company was then rocked first by a report to the European Parliament accusing BP of serious human rights and environmental misdemeanours, then by a series of newspaper headlines giving the impression that BP was complicit in killing people in Colombia, and finally by a UK television documentary that implicitly accused BP of collaborating with the army and paramilitary groups to kill people, damaging the environment, and destroying a centuries-old way of life in Casanare.

So what had gone wrong? Remember this was 1996, only one year after the Shell Brent Spar incident, when most companies still considered that, as long as they had the official sanction of legitimate governments and obeyed the law, anything else they did to invest in social infrastructure was voluntary and essentially philanthropic. Any pre-investment risk analysis done at that time did not include social impact and did not engage members of the local community in the process. BP's social investment programmes were good in themselves but, because of the security problems and lack of real understanding and inclusion of community relations in the overall strategy by BP's Bogotá head office, they failed to connect the company with the community it was seeking to serve. The BP staff on site were fresh from the North Sea and the North Slopes of Alaska, where they had faced huge technological and environmental problems but no social ones. They had no experience of managing the expectations of the boom area they had created. It was a condition of the government that the Colombian army should be used to provide the security, and BP did not consider it was responsible for the army's actions beyond its own premises. So what had previously been considered to be a manageable local difficulty became a serious reputation-damaging global issue for the company.

How might a policy that incorporated the use of the PDE process have helped? First, whereas the development of the oil fields in Casanare was clearly a legitimate business end, a more thorough consideration of the means required to achieve it might have led to different approaches. BP should have foreseen the implications of its security arrangements, which were a necessary means to the company's end. The oil field could not be developed without creating a target for the armed opposition groups, without bringing in the army and its links to the paramilitaries, and without endangering the lives of the indigenous local people. It is a moot point whether these should have made BP decide not to go ahead with the project or whether, as the Colombian government would have then simply given the contract to a less scrupulous oil company, BP should have instead insisted on different security arrangements from the outset.

The "honey pot" effect of the proposed development was another major and highly foreseeable side-effect. Yet, although BP was undertaking a good social investment programme and employed an excellent native Colombian community relations team, it was in effect cut off from the main company operations. No prior social impact assessment had been undertaken and community stakeholder engagement was left to the community relations team, rather than involving mainstream management. Not enough was done to understand and minimize the negative side-effects. Nor, until after the crisis, was pressure put on the government to do more for the Casanare region and to address the human rights failings of its security forces. If the BP Colombian management had been operating under a company-wide social impact and stakeholder engagement policy as good as its environmental policy was, and if they had been trained in a thought process such as the PDE, much grief might have been avoided.

BP has learnt much from this experience and now has much better social impact assessment and stakeholder consultation procedures, although these are still inconsistently applied in different parts of the world. The company has also taken an active role in the development of the US/UK Voluntary Principles on security and human rights for extractive companies, which it now uses as part of its contract negotiations with host governments. There is still a problem, however, even for the better companies when it comes to deciding that the negative side-effects of a project are actually too high to go ahead. Companies tend to see pre-investment impact analysis as a process of identifying the side-effects to be negotiated and compensated for (at least possible cost), rather than as a cost–benefit analysis, which, if the foreseen costs prove too high, means that the project will not go ahead. Some NGOs with intimate knowledge of Colombia consider that, given the security situation, the Casanare oilfield development should never have gone ahead in the first place – the foreseeable costs in human life and suffering far outweighing any economic benefits. How that decision could ever have been made in the world of realpolitik is another question. Nevertheless, if ethical decision-making processes such as that of the principle of double effect become more widely used and are made transparent through genuine stakeholder engagement, it will be easier for campaigning NGOs and others concerned to improve the social performance of companies to make more informed judgements on a company's performance, and to react accordingly. That in itself would be progress.

In April 2003, FTSE4GOOD announced its first human rights criteria for companies. These cover prescribed policy items, management systems, and reporting processes. Before long, it is to be hoped, more challenging performance criteria can be introduced. Perhaps PDE can help show the way. In the future, to be eligible for ethical investment status, companies could be required to demonstrate that key investment decisions had rigorously complied with something like the PDE decision-making process. Ethical decision-making would become the expected best practice norm and might finally put to rest the unhelpful distinction between the business case and the moral case for corporate social responsibility.

Notes

1. Amnesty International UK and The Prince of Wales Business Leaders Forum, *Human rights: Is it any of your business?* (London, 2000).
2. The BP case-study is a shortened version of the case I wrote shortly after leaving BP in 1998. It is based on personal experience at the time and conversations with BP staff closely involved. It has subsequently been used in teaching many MBA classes.

Part IV
Conclusion

16

Towards improved business practice: Implementing the principle of double effect

Oddny Wiggen and Lene Bomann-Larsen

We have presented a framework for assessing the side-effect harm of business operations by introducing a revised version of the classic principle of double effect (PDE), known from the just war tradition as well as other ethics discourses. The PDE has been reconstructed to fit the business context without jeopardizing its real meaning – the idea that, as an actor, one is responsible not only for the deliberate outcomes of one's actions but also for unplanned, but foreseeable, results. The revised PDE has then been evaluated in light of concrete cases from the world of business. This evaluation has provided valuable feedback to the framework; it has confirmed the applicability of the PDE, but also drawn attention to some shortcomings.

It is important to keep in mind that the revised PDE is a tool for assessing the *side-effect* harm of corporate activity. As such, it has the advantage of narrowing the scope of corporate responsibility for social and environmental predicaments by tying responsibility closely to what lies within the sphere of the company's own activities. Blaming a company for all sorts of problems that befall a community in which it operates is counterproductive. By limiting the reasonable scope of blame to actual side-effect harm, the PDE helps avoid a moving of the goalposts and may aid decision makers in taking on this responsibility and thereby improve performance.

To repeat, the revised PDE says that:

Preamble: Negative side-effects do occur, even when businesses pursue legitimate objectives by legitimate means. In creating sustainable value for their stakeholders, businesses must ensure in dealing with the negative side-effects of their activities that:

1. consultation with affected parties, as well as risk assessment, is carried out prior to and during the business operation in order to identify negative side-effects;
2. negative side-effects that arise from a business's operations are not made to serve as means to achieving its legitimate objectives;
3. negative side-effects can be justified as proportionate to the legitimate objectives;
4. active measures are taken to prevent or minimize negative side-effects;
5. the negative side-effects are inescapable – it is not possible to achieve the legitimate objectives with fewer or no side-effects.

Possible weaknesses of the PDE framework

Several concerns have been raised about the PDE by authors in this book. One is the doubt expressed by Upendra Baxi with regard to the Bhopal case. Baxi's apprehension relates partly to the *scale* of the Bhopal catastrophe. Can such large-scale human disasters, resulting from a pursuit of profits, be justified at all – by the PDE or any other measure? Can we even properly speak of *side-effects* when referring to this kind of event? The Bhopal case appears to shatter the normative force of the PDE.

Most of us feel uneasy discussing human disasters in dispassionate terms such as those of side-effect harm, and it is important to keep in mind that not all undesirable events can be dismissed as mere side-effects. The Bhopal case seems to entail a violation of two criteria: choosing legitimate means; and proportionality. It was foreseeable that a disaster could follow from the low security standards implemented at the plant, and no one would say that the Bhopal catastrophe was a permissible side-effect. Yet the Bhopal case confirms the need to integrate a way of thinking guided by the PDE into the planning of a business project. If the decision makers had applied a line of reasoning in accordance with the PDE from the beginning, the conditions that led to the disaster might not have been present and it could have been prevented. The Bhopal case serves to demonstrate how important it is that thinking about the possible consequences of one's engagement beforehand and actively working to prevent or minimize harm must permeate corporate decision-making.

Another concern is expressed by Deon Rossouw in chapter 3 in the theoretical part, and is supported by Amnesty International's Chris Marsden in his commentary in chapter 15 in the case-study part. Rossouw argues that the PDE cannot sufficiently capture the moral challenge of operating in a regime that severely abuses human rights, such as South Africa under apartheid. He therefore suggests adding another criterion to the PDE:

When negative side-effects are caused by jurisdictions that abuse human rights, companies doing business there must exert pressure on such jurisdictions to improve their human rights record.

A jurisdiction that abuses human rights will have laws that are themselves unacceptable from a human rights perspective; in other cases, it is not the *laws* that represent the problem, but the way they are enforced.

If the suggested criterion is intended to cover cases where companies substantially contribute to (or benefit from) a jurisdiction that abuses human rights, then it seems to be covered by the PDE in its more general wording. The contribution may merely be passive moral support. If such support significantly helps to maintain or prolong the abusive regime, it may be regarded as a harmful side-effect that the company is under an obligation to counteract. As stated earlier, any measures taken to prevent or minimize side-effect harm must actually serve to rectify the situation. They should not be token gestures. If a company pollutes a community's drinking water, it does not help if the CEO plants flowers in the local park. Therefore, exerting pressure on the regime may be the correct response with regard to jurisdictions that abuse human rights.

Still, a general duty to intervene when human rights are abused by a third party is not as such promulgated by the PDE. It must be demonstrated that the company itself is linked to the human rights abuses by virtue of its own activity. PDE does not cover "silent complicity" unless a legal or indisputable moral duty to intervene were to be established; in which case we could speak of omission and of responsibility for the side-effects of wrongful inaction. As yet, no such duty is established.

Heidi Høivik supports Deon Rossouw's suggested additional criterion, but recommends that it is expanded to read as follows:

When side-effects are caused by social norms or laws that abuse human rights, the actor should exert pressure to reform these. However, if the actor does not have the power to exert such pressure, the negative effects are inescapable. When such inescapable negative side-effects are of an especially grave kind, and the actor actually contributes to them through being involved, the actor should withdraw.

In her expansion of Rossouw's additional criterion, Høivik reintroduces the term "inescapability" and suggests that, if the harm is both grave and truly inescapable, withdrawal is the responsible thing to do. This conclusion is in accordance with the requirement of proportionality, namely that a balance of good over harm must be maintained; if that is not possible, one must abstain from the activity. However, it should be noted that the side-effects of the withdrawal must also be taken into account, insofar as withdrawal is a deliberate and potentially harmful act.

Another substantial observation regarding "inescapability" is made by Robert Allinson and Pat Werhane in their case-study chapters. They both show that the PDE has its primary function when the side-effect harm is in fact inescapable. If an alternative option is available that produces less side-effect harm or none at all, the company in question should choose that option instead. The company is urged to use its *moral imagination* in the search for alternative courses of action. This is an important point: if side-effect harm can be avoided altogether or reduced by choosing another course of action, then one ought to do this. Werhane reminds us that there is always the option of abstaining from engagement, and Allinson's case even shows that searching for another option at the outset of the project would have saved the company huge amounts of money.

One final point that is implied in several of the cases and made explicit by Ogbonna Ike is the problem of shared responsibility. Ike points out that the PDE does not clearly delineate responsibility when it is spread across several actors. In cases of complicity, the company is not the sole perpetrator, or even the primary perpetrator. The problem of shared responsibility is perhaps most pressing in joint ventures between several companies and a government. According to the PDE, responsibility is qualified not by the number of actors involved but by the degree of each actor's intent. Each party is equally responsible for the results of the project insofar as these results are deliberately chosen by the actor, either as means or as ends, and this responsibility is not lessened by the fact that the intent is shared by many. However, the PDE does distinguish between the responsibility one bears for one's chosen ends and means and the side-effects of these choices. Negative social consequences of joint ventures are rarely part of the company's deliberate strategy, but becoming implicated in such consequences may be a side-effect of the joint venture with governments. In such cases, the company does bear responsibility, albeit not to the same degree as the government. Nevertheless, this co-responsibility obliges the company to take action to rectify the social consequences, action that may be most effective if it takes the form of pressure on partners (e.g. partnerships for development) as well as financial contributions to projects that serve society.

Operationalizing the PDE

The PDE is not exhaustive in terms of evaluations of corporate social responsibility (CSR), although it does suggest a way of thinking about side-effect harm specifically. It is therefore not always relevant to decision-making. It does not fit all ethical challenges in business; and some of its various aspects may fit one particular situation and some may fit others.

What is important is that decision makers incorporate the PDE in their way of thinking, that they sincerely address the issue of side-effect harm throughout the whole process, thus assuming responsibility for their own actions. CSR in general, and thinking about side-effect harm in particular, should not be left to one employee or a group of employees in charge of ethics or social issues, or merely put in a mission statement to be held up to the public. It should permeate all levels of the organization at all stages of the process, as an integral part of the company identity; *"this is what we do because this is who we are"*. The decisions and actions of a company reflect its self-understanding. An integrated way of thinking guided by the PDE will ensure more responsible operations, improving both performance and stakeholder relations for the company.

Guidelines for implementing the PDE in decision-making procedures

- **Ensure that the company's operations are legitimate, as regards both ends and means**. The company should operate in such a manner that it creates sustainable value for its stakeholders. The operations should be conducted in a legally and ethically sound manner.

- **Take steps to foresee the foreseeable**
  Conduct research on the specific country in order to understand its culture and its political and financial situation and what effects the company's operations will have.
  Identify potential stakeholders.
  Identify possible side-effect harm on stakeholders by conducting stakeholder-inclusive risk analysis.
  Gain knowledge of possible side-effect harm by engaging stakeholders in dialogue.

- **Consider who you are associating with**. Complicity can be a side-effect on many levels. Look at who is supported materially, politically, or morally by the company's engagement, by a joint venture, or by employed security staff.

- **Minimize side-effect harm**

  If the company is operating within a jurisdiction or regime that abuses human rights, make sure the company does not contribute to or benefit from the human rights abuses. If it does, take steps to exert pressure on the authorities.

  If the company must rely on others for the security of staff and assets, remember that the company is responsible for their actions as well. Lay down clear guidelines for how security personnel should act when representing the company.

  Consider the recipients of revenues and signatory fees – counteract corruption by working for transparency.

  Weak or absent domestic laws on labour and the environment should not be exploited for profit. Set higher standards for the company and follow international standards.

- **Use moral imagination – good over harm is not a matter of mathematics**

  Are the side-effects really inescapable, or is it possible to find an alternative course of action with fewer or no side-effects?

  If the side-effects are inescapable, are they so severe that the operation cannot reasonably be justified to those affected by it?

  Would it be more responsible to abstain or withdraw from investment?

Being a responsible company entails assuming responsibility for the consequences of the company's own activities. Because a responsible company has higher credibility among consumers, incorporating this type of responsibility policy at all levels of the organization may in turn result in improved performance and stakeholder relations for the corporation.

Index